COMPANION STUDIES

Racine, or, The Triumph of Relevance, by Odette de Mourques

Goethe, a critical Introduction, by Ronald Gray

A Generation of Spanish Poets 1920–36, by C. B. Morris

Other volumes in preparation

TOLSTOY

A CRITICAL INTRODUCTION

TOLSTOY

A CRITICAL INTRODUCTION

R. F. CHRISTIAN

Professor of Russian
University of St Andrews

CAMBRIDGE
AT THE UNIVERSITY PRESS
1969

69- 645

Published by the Syndics of the Cambridge University Press
Bentley House, 200 Euston Road, London N.W.1
American Branch: 32 East 57th Street, New York, N.Y.10022

© Cambridge University Press 1969

Library of Congress Catalogue Card Number: 69–19373

Standard Book Numbers:
521 07493 2 clothbound
521 09585 9 paperback

Printed in Great Britain
at the University Printing House, Cambridge
(Brooke Crutchley, University Printer)

CONTENTS

PREFACE

This book, written at the invitation of the Syndics of the Cambridge University Press, is one of a series of volumes introducing the works of major European writers to students and the general public. The terms of reference require it to be both introductory and central, and to assume little or no knowledge on the reader's part. I have tried to comply with these terms, and also to keep biographical and background information to a minimum in order to concentrate on the works themselves. Much space has inevitably and rightly been devoted to Tolstoy's two major novels, but I have also touched on most of his narrative and dramatic writings, the bad as well as the good. I have ignored his polemical articles and his religious treatises—for all their intrinsic interest and importance for an understanding of Tolstoy—as falling outside the scope of this series, which is literary, rather than biographical or historical. I would like to express my gratitude to the Secretary of the Clarendon Press for allowing me to abridge parts of my book, Tolstoy's 'War and Peace': A Study, and to reproduce them in substantially the same form in Chapter 5. I would also like to thank Dr Inna Baykov for reading through the typescript and offering many valuable criticisms and suggestions.

R.F.C.

St Andrews
July 1968

I

FIRST BEGINNINGS

Lev Nikolaevich Tolstoy began his career as a writer at the age of twenty-four, when the September issue of *The Contemporary* for 1852 published his *Childhood* under the cryptic initials L.N. It was a promising, if somewhat apprehensive, beginning by a young man whose early life had been relatively undistinguished. His many biographers have told in detail the story of his aristocratic family background, his happy childhood years at Yasnaya Polyana, the early loss of his mother, the move to Moscow when Tolstoy was eight, the death of his father, and the new move to Kazan. They have recorded his unspectacular years as a student first of oriental languages and then of law at Kazan University, his withdrawal from the university on inheriting the estate of Yasnaya Polyana in 1847, his dissipated life in Petersburg and Moscow relieved by sober periods as a country landlord, his growing gambling debts, and his eventual escape to the Caucasus where, after seeing action as a volunteer, he enlisted in the regular army in 1852.

Tolstoy was not an exceptionally avid reader from an early age, nor a precocious literary prodigy with a facile pen. Reading and writing were not an obsession with him, for he was the product of a class which valued physical and social accomplishments as highly as literary and intellectual distinction. In one of his earliest recorded diary entries he wrote: 'One-sidedness is the main cause of man's unhappiness';[1] and Tolstoy was nothing if not versatile. Hunting, shooting, music, gymnastics, cards, women and the cultivation of social *savoir faire* occupied much of his time as a young man, and perhaps many an industrious and book-loving schoolboy or student today would read more widely and write more fluently than he did at a comparable age. Although he had travelled to the Caucasus and taken part in fighting, there have been many young men, especially in the twentieth century, with more

[1] J.E. XLVI, 7.

experience of travel and warfare and a wider acquaintance
with the different classes of society than he had. His literary
education and his knowledge of life, then, need to be kept in
their proper perspective, and not only when viewed against
writers of today but even in comparison with some of his
own contemporaries.

How wide was Tolstoy's early reading and what were the
most important books he read? This question is often answered
by referring to the list he compiled in 1891 for a Petersburg
bookseller, who had asked him to write down the books
which had made the deepest impression on him at different
periods of his life. Obviously this list is neither exhaustive nor
accurate, drawn up as it was when Tolstoy was sixty-three,
and inevitably subject to later prejudices and the quirks of
memory. But it remains a valuable and interesting document.[1]
For the first period of his life, to the age of fourteen, Tolstoy
singled out above all the folktales of Russia, the better-known
Russian *byliny*—popular narrative poems of ancient Russian
heroes—and the story of Joseph from the Bible as having
made an 'enormous' impression on him in his most impressionable years. Under the heading 'very great' impression, the
only entry is *The Little Black Hen*, a fairy-tale written in 1829
by Pogorelsky, illustrating the moral, dear to Tolstoy's heart,
that once your sins get the upper hand there is no escaping
from them. Finally, the word 'great' describes the impression
left by the *Arabian Nights*, and one poem in particular by
Pushkin—*Napoleon*. Pushkin wrote this poem in 1821 on
hearing the news of the Emperor's death on St Helena. In
essence it is a conventional tribute to a great man, an autocrat,
a proud tyrant, contemptuous of the people and overtaken in
the end by Nemesis, but a man whose fate was inextricably
bound up with the fate of Russia and who alone made possible
her finest hour. 'Praise him!' the peroration reads. 'He
showed the Russian people the way to their lofty destiny, and
from the darkness of banishment bequeathed to the world
eternal freedom.' There is no hint here, of course, of that

[1] J.E. LXVI, 67.

iconoclastic attitude to the Emperor or the disparaging assessment of his achievements which were to be Tolstoy's distinctive contribution to the Russian literary treatment of the Napoleonic legend.

For the second period of his life, from the age of fourteen to twenty, Tolstoy's list is longer and branches out to include French and English literature. The works which created an 'enormous' impression at this age are headed by the Sermon on the Mount. Somewhat surprisingly, Gogol's *Vii*—a highly romantic, blood-curdling Ukrainian fantasy of witches and gnomes, coffins, churches and devils, which belongs unmistakably to the literature of the uncanny—is the only work of Russian fiction to be put in the same category, while French literature provides Rousseau's *Confessions* and *Émile*, and English literature *David Copperfield* (although in fact this was probably read a few years later, in a Russian translation). In his next category in descending order of importance, Russian literature figures prominently with Pushkin's *Evgenii Onegin*, Gogol's *Dead Souls*, Turgenev's *A Sportsman's Sketches*, Lermontov's *A Hero of our Time* and two lesser-known works, Grigorovich's *Anton the Hapless* and Druzhinin's *Polinka Sachs*. All were completed in Tolstoy's own lifetime, and all except the last two are established Russian classics. Grigorovich, who once shared a flat with Dostoevsky and did much to launch him on his literary career, was the pioneer of the humanitarian story of social protest with its grim but sentimental depiction of peasant life, the misery and oppression of the defenceless serf. Druzhinin's novel, following George Sand, was concerned with marriage and women's rights. Both Grigorovich and Druzhinin became close friends of Tolstoy, and while his opinions of their literary merits fluctuated, his attraction to the subject matter of their early stories is significant. With the exception of *Evgenii Onegin*, itself a *novel* in verse, all the works of Russian literature which made a 'very great' impression on Tolstoy in his late teens were prose works. They were nearly all written in the 1840s, and for their content they drew heavily on contemporary Russian life. At this stage the lyric poetry of

Pushkin and Lermontov and the early stories of Dostoevsky did not apparently leave the same indelible mark on him, nor is any mention made of Griboedov's comedy, *The Misfortune of Being Clever*, before 1855. To the same order of importance Tolstoy ascribes Rousseau's *Nouvelle Héloïse*, Sterne's *A Sentimental Journey* and Schiller's *Die Räuber*, a play of exceptional interest for Dostoevsky also, and one which his brother translated into Russian. Shakespeare, French classical comedy, Greek tragedy and Hoffmann and the German romantics stand out conspicuously by their absence from the works of European literature cited; but at a lower level, Tolstoy selected Gogol's *Government Inspector*, *The Tale of the Two Ivans* and *Nevsky Prospect*, and, from foreign literature, Prescott's *Conquest of Mexico*, as books which had made a 'great' impression on him before he was twenty.

In the first draft of his list Tolstoy originally included *Le Comte de Monte Cristo* and *Les Trois Mousquetaires*, which we know that he read avidly at an early age, although the enthusiasm soon wore off. Also included at first in the final draft, but later deleted, were the novels of the now almost forgotten Russian writers Marlinsky and Begichev. Marlinsky (the pseudonym of Bestuzhev who was involved in the Decembrist uprising of 1825) enjoyed a tremendous vogue in the 1830s and occupied in prose a position comparable to that held by Pushkin in poetry. He was a major figure in the short-lived Russian romantic movement, with his extravagant rhetorical novels on exotic themes, passionate heroes and stirring battles, and his no less popular *haut monde* love stories: epistolary, epigrammatic, and abounding in balls and banquets. The English reader may catch the flavour of the latter from Dostoevsky's clever parody of Marlinsky (disguised as the author of *Italian Passions*) in his first novel *Poor Folk*. Begichev is remembered today, if at all, for *The Kholmsky Family*, a sentimental, moralising novel of the domestic life of the Russian gentry in the 1830s.

Tolstoy's second list spans the years 1848–63 and is very brief, being confined to Goethe's *Hermann und Dorothea*, Hugo's *Notre Dame de Paris*, the poetry of the Russians Fet, Koltsov and

Tyutchev, and translations of the *Iliad*, the *Odyssey*, and Plato's *Phaedo* and the *Symposium*. Most of these works were read after *Childhood* had been published, and have little or no bearing on Tolstoy's first formative years. In order to fill out the picture of his early reading we may turn to his diaries and letters, which at least have the authentic ring of contemporaneity, but are of limited value in the sense that the diaries contain large gaps, while relatively few letters written before 1852 have survived. Scattered references and fragmentary diary entries testify to his wide reading of contemporary fiction, especially the novels of George Sand, Dumas and Eugène Sue, and of major works of Russian, French and English history: Mikhailovsky-Danilevsky, so important a source for the military campaigns in *War and Peace*, Hume's *History of England* and Dumas' *Louis XIV et son siècle*. It is clear that Tolstoy was well read in the literature of the eighteenth century, and his general education was inevitably grounded on Rousseau, Voltaire, Montesquieu and Goethe (*Die Leiden des jungen Werthers* is singled out in particular) as well as on the histories and sentimental stories of Karamzin. It would be a mistake, however, to give too much stress to the antiquated nature of his literary interests, for all his addiction to Rousseau, or to label him 'a militant archaist, upholding in the middle of the nineteenth century the principles and traditions of the vanishing and partly vanished culture of the eighteenth century'.[1] It is more true to say that he is 'one of those rare figures who represent a cultural span far greater than that of their age. Like Goethe, whom Friedrich Schlegel defined as both the Shakespeare and the Voltaire of his own nation and time, Tolstoy was a child of both the Enlightenment and the nineteenth century.'[2] Tolstoy was a regular reader of the major contemporary journals which published every month much of the best new writing in Russian and European literature—*The Contemporary* and *The Notes of the Fatherland*.

[1] B. M. Eykhenbaum, *Lev Tolstoi, kniga pervaya, 50-e gody* (Leningrad 1928), p. 11.
[2] R. Poggioli, *The Phoenix and the Spider* (Cambridge, Mass. 1957), p. 95.

The former was probably the best literary periodical in Russia in Tolstoy's youth. Founded by Pushkin in 1836, it had been transformed by its new editors, Nekrasov and Panaev, in 1846, and a decade or more later was to become the centre for radical literary criticism of a markedly sociological flavour. In the 1840s and early 1850s Turgenev, Herzen, Goncharov, Druzhinin and Grigorovich were all publishing their early writings there. It printed translations of Goethe and Schiller, George Sand and de Musset, Shakespeare, Fielding (*Tom Jones*), and Dickens (including *David Copperfield*), as well as numerous reviews, articles on English and French life and surveys of foreign literature, science and the arts. It was to *The Contemporary*, naturally enough, that Tolstoy sent his own first literary contributions.

Although *Childhood* was Tolstoy's first published work, a study of his archives has brought to light some juvenilia and several essays and trials of the pen. The few surviving schoolboy essays and recapitulations of stories and fables written when Tolstoy was ten or eleven tell us only that he was adept at the art of simple and lucid résumé and that his spelling and punctuation left much to be desired. Of the few unfinished articles and essays dating from his late teens and early twenties, *Some Philosophical Observations on a Discourse of J. J. Rousseau* is a critical rejoinder to Rousseau's essay on the theme 'Has the restoration of the arts and sciences had a purifying effect upon morals?', which won the prize of the Academy of Dijon in 1750. Rousseau started from the thesis that 'the mind, as well as the body, has its needs: those of the body are the basis of society, those of the mind its ornaments'. The arts, literature and the sciences, he argues, stifle in men their sense of liberty, cause them to love their slavery and make of them what is called a civilised people. History has shown by the example of Egypt, Athens and Rome, that the progress of science leads to dissoluteness, effeteness and degeneration, to conquest and slavery. By contrast, the Persians, the Germans and the Scythians—simple, innocent and virtuous—were victorious in battle. Sparta is praised at the expense of Athens. Socrates is quoted for his adverse criticism of poets, sophists, orators and artists. The arts and sciences, Rousseau continues, were born of vices. They are cherished by luxury. Contrast their state with the pristine innocence of primitive men. Contrast the enervating nature of sedentary occupations with the rigour of warfare and the cultivation of military virtues. But, he goes on, 'if the cultivation of the sciences is prejudicial to military qualities, it is still more prejudicial to moral ones... On every side we see huge institutions where our youth are educated at great expense, and instructed in everything but their duty... The question is no longer whether a man is honest, but whether he is clever. We do not ask whether a book is useful, but whether it is well written.' Inveighing against education, Rousseau directs his invective equally against philosophy and its practitioners, and what he regards as their contradictory teachings. To crown it all, there is the art of printing, thanks to which 'the pernicious reflections of Hobbes and Spinoza will last for ever'.

These dogmatic and juvenile assertions were the target for one of Tolstoy's earliest literary assaults, confined to the pages of his exercise books. His main contention was that the more free a man is, the more he is able to do good or evil, and that people who have burst the bonds of ignorance are able to do more good (or more evil) than those whose ignorance fetters their freedom of action. Tolstoy's objections to Rousseau's belief that lack of knowledge is not a fetter and that the ignorant cannot be enslaved and must therefore be free are not entirely to the point and, not surprisingly, lack the intellectual power of the mature thinker. Nevertheless the unfinished essay in which they are advanced contains some interesting observations when viewed in the light of his later thought—not least his proposition that the shortcoming of philosophers is that they try to solve philosophical problems historically (i.e. by reference to the so-called facts of history), while for him 'history is one of the most backward sciences—it is studied for itself, and not for the sake of a philosophy, which is the only reason why it should be studied'. 'History', he writes, 'will not reveal to us what the relation was at different times between the arts and sciences and good manners, between good and evil, between religion and the civilised state, but it will tell us —and that incorrectly—where the Huns came from, where they lived and who founded their empire etc.'[1] In his polemic against Rousseau, Tolstoy argues that history should be studied for the philosophy of living it can provide and not for the facts, dubious and irrelevant as they can be in the historian's hands. And yet Rousseau himself was trying to do precisely that—to use historical example to provide himself with a way of life—if only to the extent of selling his watch on the ground that in the simple life he aspired to lead, he would not need to know the time.

Philosophy as a guide to regulating one's life is the subject of another of Tolstoy's youthful fragments—*On the Purpose of Philosophy*. Philosophy, he contends, is the science of life. Life is the striving for happiness and well-being. To satisfy this striving, man must not seek happiness in the world outside him, but in the education of himself. The purpose of philosophy is to show *how* man should educate himself and— since he lives in society—what his relations with other people should be:

If everyone were to strive after his own good, seeking to find it outside himself, the interests of private individuals would clash and the result would be confusion. But if everyone would strive for his own self-improvement, there could be no breach of order. For everybody would do for everybody else what he would wish them to do for him.[2]

But how is one to practise philosophy? The answer is to train the will, study psychology and the laws of nature, develop the mental faculties, analyse all the problems which crop up in one's private life, strictly observe the rules of morality and obey the laws of nature. Psychology, mathematics, physics, self-discipline and moral conduct will produce the good life. But in effect enlightened self-interest is the ultimate ethical sanction.

[1] J.E. I, 222.   [2] J.E. I, 229.

8

The pursuit of happiness and virtue and a utilitarian morality dominate another brief speculative fragment of the same period, short enough to quote two of its three paragraphs in full, since it has not to my knowledge been previously translated into English:

Why do people write? Some to acquire money, some fame, and some both. But there are people who say in order to teach virtue. Why do people read, why do they bestow money and fame on books? People want to be happy; that is the common cause of all actions. The only path to happiness is virtue, consequently it makes sense to read only those books which teach virtue. What are these books? Dogmatic books, based on the principles of reason, and theoretical books—common sense admits of no others.

But surely those books are beneficial which, by portraying virtue in a refined manner, exert an influence by example? Almost everybody agrees that virtue means the subordination of the passions to reason. But instead of inclining people to reasonable behaviour by developing their reason, poets and novelists, historians and natural scientists incline them to unreasonable actions by developing their passions. People will say that the natural sciences are necessary for the comforts of private life. But do the comforts of private life further the development of virtue? Far from it. On the contrary, they subordinate us still more to the passions.[1]

How to subordinate the passions and harness them to useful activity is the problem which is central to Tolstoy's search for a philosophy of life and ultimately a system of aesthetics. That the solution to the problem is related to some form of religious belief, or at least that the consequences of unbelief are morally injurious and degrading, is hinted at in another fragmentary essay, *On Prayer*, which may originally have been intended as a chapter in *Childhood*. Here Tolstoy, with his characteristic love of classification and categorisation, divides unbelievers into three groups—those who think too much, those who are vain and those who are weak. 'To the second category', he writes, 'belong those who, infatuated by philosophical theories (*which novels have made accessible to all*[2]), have exchanged

---

[1] J.E. I, 246.   [2] My italics.

their Christian beliefs imbibed in childhood for pantheistic ideas or the complicated hypotheses of witty writers or of their own invention. Each of them makes up his own religion, lacking in foundation or consistency, but adapted to his particular passions and weaknesses. They believe what pleases them and reject what is burdensome; they sacrifice their previous beliefs in order to gratify their petty vanity.'[1] Tolstoy is critical of the thinkers and of the weak-willed too, but it is the egoists who bear the brunt of his irony.

In all these discarded juvenilia the hand of Tolstoy is un-mistakable, spelling out the harmful potential of literature, the blinkered vision of the professional historian, the emptiness of philosophy divorced from life, the interdependence of moral behaviour and religious belief. Unmistakable, too, are the blunt and brusque asseverations, the neat groupings, the confident generalisations and the rather graceless and ponderous style which nearly always characterised Tolstoy the thinker, and which was a source of considerable worry to him as a young man. It was partly this concern to improve his style, and partly an enthusiastic admiration for the unorthodox and humorous Sterne, which led Tolstoy to translate *A Sentimental Journey* into Russian. It is interesting that both Tolstoy and Dostoevsky chose translation as a literary exercise in style and expression before committing themselves to original writing—although Dostoevsky's choice of *Eugénie Grandet* presented fewer problems than those posed by the erudite and eccentric Englishman. Tolstoy completed about a third of the novel, working in all probability from a French translation as well as the English original. Some of his renderings show a very imperfect knowledge and understanding of the text. It is not an accurate translation, nor does it read well. But its very choice illustrates its author's youthful addiction to the literature of sentimentalism, in his own country to Karamzin, and further afield not only to *A Sentimental Journey*, but also to *Paul et Virginie* and *Die Leiden des jungen Werthers*, all of which he read in the space of a few months in 1851. What attracted Tolstoy,

---

[1] J.E. I, 248.

no doubt, in Sterne's novel was the combination of a warm heart, tears and *la sensibilité*, with a broad humour, wit and a touch of impropriety. No less attractive to him was the way in which the story was told. Much later his wife described his initial reaction to reading the novel (as recounted, of course, by her husband, who did not know her at the time) in the following words:

One day, after reading Sterne's *Voyage Sentimental*, and being excited and absorbed by his reading, he was sitting by the window deep in thought and watching everything going on outside. There goes a policeman. Who is he? What sort of life does he live? And there goes a carriage. Who is inside? Where is he going and what is he thinking about? And who lives in that house? What is their inner life like? How interesting it would be to describe it all; what an interesting book one could make of it.[1]

The first-person narrative, the self-centredness, the frequent asides and comments on human foibles, the fondness for classification and the short interconnecting chapters of *A Sentimental Journey* must all have been endearing features to Tolstoy, if we are to judge by his own earliest essays at creative writing. Not that he was without his criticisms of Sterne, and in particular his discursiveness, as he wrote in his diary in 1851:

In spite of my favourite writer Sterne's enormous talent for story telling and for clever talk, even his digressions can be wearisome.[2]

But as a model of good style and a source of memorable observations and reflections, Sterne had few equals for the infatuated Tolstoy. In his diary for 1851 we find, side by side with an epigram from Seneca, the following quotation from his 'favourite' writer, culled indirectly from the French *Mémoires de L. Sterne*:

La conversation est un trafic; et si l'on l'entreprend sans fonds, la balance penche et le commerce tombe.[3]

[1] Quoted by N. N. Gusev, *Lev Nikolaevich Tolstoi, Materialy k biografii 1828–1855* (Moscow 1954), p. 275.
[2] J.E. XLVI, 82.　　　　　　　　　　[3] J.E. XLVI, 78.

Next year he wrote:

Read Sterne. Marvellous.

'If nature has so wove [i.e. woven] his [i.e. her] web of kindeness, that some threads of love and desire are entangled in [i.e. with] the piece—must the whole piece be rent in drawing them out'.[1]

This quotation from *A Sentimental Journey*, characteristically rather inaccurately reproduced, left a remarkable impression on Tolstoy. We meet it again as an epigraph (later deleted) to a version of Chapter 18, 'The Maid's Room', in *Boyhood*. The image of the web of love recurs in a diary entry for 1856: 'Yes, the best way to true happiness in life is to spin on all sides like a spider a stout web of love and to try to catch everything you meet in it';[2] while in *The Cossacks* the hero Olenin writes down in *his* diary: 'The one thing needed to be happy is to love, to love unselfishly, to love everyone and everything, to spread out a web of love on all sides and catch all who come into it.'[3]

These are indirect echoes only. The direct influence of Sterne on Tolstoy's early writing to which he alluded towards the end of his life in his *Recollections*, is most clearly felt in the unfinished tale *A History of Yesterday*, which was written in the spring of 1851. As this is unlikely to be known to readers outside Russia, and as it is in many ways untypical of Tolstoy, I shall summarise it at some length. He begins:[4]

I am writing the history of yesterday not because yesterday was in any way remarkable or could be called remarkable, but because I have wanted for a long time to tell the story of the intimate side of the life of a single day. God alone knows how many varied and interesting impressions, and thoughts aroused by these impressions, occur in a single day—obscure, imprecise but none the less intelligible to our souls. If it were possible to recount them in such a way that I could easily read myself and others could read me as I am, the result would be a very interesting and edifying book—such indeed, that

---

[1] J.E. XLVI, 110.   [2] J.E. XLVII, 71.
[3] *The Cossacks*, Ch. 28.   [4] J.E. I, 279 ff.

there would not be enough ink in the world to write it or enough printers to publish it. But to business.

I got up late yesterday, because I went to bed late the night before.

Whereupon the narrator craves forgiveness for speaking about the day *before* yesterday, 'for novelists, you know, write whole stories about their heroes' immediate forebears'.

'I was playing cards...,' he goes on, providing himself with the first cue for a digression on the game of cards; on what Rousseau said about the desirability of having something to do with one's hands in society; on the fact that cards, similarly, give the mind something to do; on the complaint that there is no conversation nowadays; on conversation in general; on the fact that women also play cards. 'And so I was playing cards...' at which point the narrator indulges in the sort of pun which cannot be paralleled elsewhere in Tolstoy, and which, because of the freer Russian word order, cannot be reproduced in English. Literally it goes: 'Why does this woman love me (how I wish I could put a full stop here) to embarrass?'—a cue for another long digression on 'this woman', only occasionally interrupted by brief factual statements which jerk the narrative forward—'I looked at my watch and got up'..."Stay to supper," said her husband.' The general pattern is to ring the changes on snatches of conversation, introspective musing, random thoughts and observations, and bald narrative. A paragraph or two will illustrate how Tolstoy constructs an untypically Tolstoyan dialogue between the narrator and the woman he is conversing with:

Whether she wanted to put an end to this conversation which I found so pleasant, or to watch me refuse, or to know whether I would refuse, or simply to go on playing—the fact was that she looked at the numbers on the table, ran the chalk over it, drew a figure undefined in mathematics or painting, looked at her husband and then from him to me. 'Let's play three more rubbers.' I was so absorbed in watching—not these movements but that thing called *charme* which it is impossible to describe—that my thoughts were far away and could not clothe my words in an apt form; I simply said: 'No, I can't.' No sooner had I said this than I began to regret it—

that is, not all of me, but one little part of me. There is no action which some little part of the soul does not condemn; on the other hand there is always some part to be found which will say on your behalf: what does it matter if you go to bed after twelve; you don't know that you'll ever have such a good evening again. Evidently this part spoke very eloquently and convincingly (although I'm not able to convey it), because I grew alarmed and started looking for excuses. In the first place, I said to myself, there won't be much fun: you don't like her at all and you're in an awkward position. Then again, you've said that you can't, and you've lost face...

'Comme il est aimable, ce jeune homme.'

This phrase, which followed straight after mine, interrupted my thoughts. I began to apologise for not being able to stay, but since this required no thought I continued to deliberate with myself: how I love her talking about me in the third person. In German it's rude, but I would love it even in German. Why can't she find a decent way of address? It's obvious that she finds it awkward to call me by my Christian name, or by my surname and title. Can it be because I?...'Stay to supper,' said her husband. Since I was busy pondering over third-person formulas, I didn't notice that my body, having made polite excuses for not being able to stay, put my hat down again and sank imperturbably into an easy chair. It was apparent that the intellectual side of me took no part in this folly...

Left alone with his friend's wife, the narrator continues to think aloud, to undam his stream of consciousness and to fabricate a silent dialogue between 'him' and 'her', going on beneath the surface exchange of commonplaces and reproduced as a stylistic variation, in direct speech, under the alternate headings 'she' and 'he'. The whole first section is rounded off by another characteristically bald narrative statement: 'Her husband came back. We sat, ate and talked for a bit, and I went home at half-past twelve. (Muzh prishel. My posideli, pouzhinali, pogovorili i ya poekhal domoi v polovine pervogo'.) Only the Russian version, of course, can bring out the conscious striving after effect, the deliberate alliteration, the frequent change of sentence length and the careful construction of the coda.

In the Sledge, the second section of the story, begins briskly and abruptly:

It is now spring, the 25th of March. The night is still and clear: a new moon is visible behind the red roof of a big white house opposite; there is not much snow left. 'Let's go, driver.'

No doubt if an earlier version existed we could by comparison show how Tolstoy worked up his material to create yet again the series of double alliterative effects which strike one in this passage also: Noch' tikhaya, yasnaya; molodoi mesyats vidnelsya naprotiv iz za krasnoi kryshi bol'shogo belogo doma... The visit is over, and it is time to say goodbye. The host's innocent question—'When shall we see each other again?'—prompts some speculation on the meaning of each word in this hackneyed formula, after which follows the journey home, which takes the form of a series of thoughts about the narrator's driver in particular and about drivers in general and their relation with one another and with their masters, interrupted by an encounter with a policeman, and ending with a short disquisition on words of abuse. The third section is entitled *At Home*, and begins in a businesslike way:

I arrived home...For a long time I could get no reply...While I was ringing, this is what I was thinking about...

Prominent among his thoughts is the need to have an aim in life—in his case 'an all-round education and the development of all one's faculties'; and an important means to this end—'a diary and a Franklin journal':

In the diary I confess all the wrongs I have done every day. In the journal my weaknesses are listed in columns—laziness, deceit, gluttony, irresolution, love of showing off, sensuality, insufficient *fierté* and suchlike petty passions: then I transfer all my misdeeds from the diary to the journal and tick them off in various columns.

The strictly autobiographical nature of this passage is amply borne out by a reading of Tolstoy's own diaries and his own 'Franklin journal'. Autobiographical, too, is the narrator's doubt whether such methods have any value and whether one can achieve anything positive by such a negative approach. The interlude on the subject of diaries concludes with the words

'I said my prayers and went to bed', which in turn lead naturally into the longest and last of the digressions—sleep. Here the flippant and the jocular predominate at first, and the result is such passages as:

'Morpheus, take me into your arms.' This is a god whose priest I would gladly be. Do you remember the young lady who was so offended when somebody said to her: 'Quand je suis passé chez vous, vous étiez encore dans les bras de Morphée.' She thought that Morpheus was Andrew Malapheus. What a funny name! But what a wonderful expression *dans les bras*: I can imagine the position *dans les bras* so vividly and gracefully—particularly vividly the *bras* themselves—arms bare to the shoulders with little dimples and folds and a white nightdress open and innocent...

Tolstoy, it is true, had second thoughts about this self-conscious offering to the literature of sentimentalism, and after striking his pen through it, steered the story away in a different direction, theorising on the nature of sleep and dreams in a tortuous and clumsy language whose content, however, is more interesting than its style.

At the moment of waking up, we bring all those impressions which we had while going to sleep and while asleep (a man is hardly ever completely asleep) to a unity under the influence of that impression which contributed to our waking up...In what way are you to explain the fact that you have a long dream which ends with that circumstance which woke you up: you dream that you go out hunting, load your rifle, spring the game, take aim, fire—and the noise which you took for the shot was a water jug which you knocked on to the floor while you were asleep?

This is a fact which fascinated Tolstoy, and one which he made frequent use of as a literary device when composing dream sequences in his own novels and stories in later years.

Tolstoy's *A History of Yesterday* never in fact got as far as yesterday—which would no doubt have pleased Sterne. For the Sterne flavour is unmistakable in the digressions, and the digressions within digressions, the pedantry, the self-conscious whimsy, the play on words, the snatches of conversation interrupted by reflection and commentary and rounded off by short factual statements, even the frequent dashes and parentheses. The occasional diary-like entries and the passage on the subject of diaries are evidence also that Tolstoy's own writing habits no less than his reading tastes are reflected in this early story which, like much of his juvenilia, is related less to contemporary life than to literature.

The first diary that has come down to us dates from March 1847. After three months there is a long gap until June 1850, and a further gap until the end of that year. The diary for 1851 continues until September. That for 1852, the year when *Childhood* was published, is kept fairly fully throughout the year. As a private prelude to Tolstoy's public literary début the fragmentary diaries for this five-year period are necessary reading. In April 1847 he wrote:

I have never kept a diary before because I saw no use in it. But now that I am concerned with the development of my own faculties, a diary will enable me to judge the course of this development. The diary must contain a table of rules, and my future acts must be defined in it.[1]

As one would expect from this, the diary is as much a projection of what he plans to do as a record of what he has actually done. It abounds in resolutions, programmes, plans of work, rules of behaviour. One day he will formulate six rules of conduct. Another day he will draw up an eleven-point plan of action for the next two years. On one and the same day he will plan to go to Mass in the morning and a brothel in the evening. He frankly records his venereal disease and sexual promiscuity, while continually making rules 'not to have a woman' and not to play cards—'except in the last resort'. Equally typical is his decision 'not to read novels'. But his *video meliora proboque, deteriora sequor*, his constant preoccupation with his own improvement, his puritanical obsession with self-perfection and his frank, intimate, and no doubt grossly exaggerated

[1] J.E. XLVI, 29.

account of his failure to live up to his resolutions by no means exhaust the contents of his diaries. On the literary side there are thoughts prompted by his reading—mostly rather cursory except for a detailed commentary on Catherine the Great's *Nakaz*, the elaborate instructions she drew up for a national committee entrusted with the formulation of a new code of law. There are excerpts from various books which have particularly interested him—quotations from Sterne, George Sand, Seneca, Lamartine, Bernardin de Saint-Pierre. There are progress reports on his own writing and projected writing, with some criticism of it. His *obiter dicta* include the sentence: 'It seems to me that it is impossible to *describe* a man; but it is possible to describe the effect he has on me'[1]—a sentiment which throws light on Tolstoy's own methods of character creation. Apropos of a poor number of *The Contemporary* he says: 'It is strange that bad books indicate to me my short-comings better than good ones; good books make me lose hope.'[2] Finally there are some acute observations on abstract themes, on the moral and physical varieties of bravery, on prayer, and on the inevitability of spiritual isolation in man, some of which reappear in very similar words in Tolstoy's own stories and bear out the frequently expressed opinion that there is a close connection between them and his diaries.

From Tolstoy's diaries and letters we can get a general picture of the way in which his beliefs on the fundamental questions of life were taking shape by 1852. As a young man he had experienced the loss of religious faith and indifference to organised religion common to the majority of thinking people of his age. For a time he had been attracted to the philosophy of enlightened self-interest. But self-interest, he believed, easily degenerates into self-indulgence and selfishness. The aim of life is happiness, and the happiness of a virtuous man, he wrote, is the highest and most secure form of happiness because it comes from within and is not at the mercy of fate and the outside world. But how to be virtuous when the tyranny of the self impels one to vice? Tolstoy sought the

[1] J.E. XLVI, 67.   [2] J.E. XLVI, 105.

answer increasingly in the moral sanctions imposed by a religion which provides a satisfying ethical programme and indicates a method of achieving it. Perhaps the most concise statement of what he believed at the outset of his literary career is his *profession de foi* recorded in his diary towards the end of 1852:

I believe in one, incomprehensible, good God, the immortality of the soul and eternal retribution for our acts; I do not understand the secret of the Trinity and the birth of the son of God, but I respect and do not reject the faith of my fathers.[1]

It would, of course, be wrong to think of Tolstoy as a practising Christian. Church dogma and ritual had little or no appeal for him, and his powerful mind was constantly exercised by the seemingly incomprehensible problems of faith. Perhaps it would be fairest to say at this stage in his life that he could see no higher ideal than that professed by the Christian religion, and that for the time being, at any rate, he was content to leave the door open.

1 J.E. XLVI, 149.

2

'CHILDHOOD'

When Tolstoy sent the manuscript of *Childhood* to Nekrasov, the editor of *The Contemporary*, in the summer of 1852, he wrote in the accompanying letter: 'This manuscript is really the first part of a novel—*Four Periods of Growth*; the appearance of the subsequent parts will depend on the success of the first.'[1] Four versions exist of the first part of the projected novel; they were written over a period of eighteen months in 1851 and 1852, and the first differs considerably from the other three. In addition, two 'addresses' have survived, one *To my Readers*, the other *To the Critics*—both written at the same time as the second version and perhaps intended to be additional chapters of this version.

When *Childhood* was first published in September 1852, Nekrasov took the liberty of calling it *A History of my Childhood*. Tolstoy's reaction was prompt and angry:

I was extremely displeased to read in *The Contemporary*, No. 9, a story entitled *A History of my Childhood* and to recognise it as the novel *Childhood*, which I sent to you...The title *Childhood* and the few words of the introduction explained the idea of the work; but the title *A History of my Childhood* contradicts the idea of the work. Who is interested in the history of *my* childhood?...[2]

This letter to Nekrasov was never posted, and there is no doubt that what Tolstoy himself said about the idea and genre of his first work is not altogether unambiguous. Speaking about it in old age he wrote: 'My idea (in writing *Childhood*) was not to tell my own story, but the story of my childhood friends'[3]— that is to say, the illegitimate children of the amorous gambler A. M. Islenev (Tolstoy's wife's grandfather) and Princess Kozlovskaya, the Islenev who was the prototype of the father of the little boy Nicholas Irtenev, the hero of *Childhood*. There were six children in all, who took the surname Islavin,

[1] J.E. LIX, 193.   [2] J.E. I, 331.   [3] J.E. XXXIV, 348.

and Tolstoy was especially friendly with the youngest boy—
'externally very attractive but profoundly immoral', as he
later described him—and about whom he wrote in his diary for
1851, 'My love for Islavin ruined the whole eight months of my
life in Petersburg. Albeit unconsciously, I thought of nothing
else but how to please him.'[1] But the story of the Islavins
became interwoven with the events of his own childhood to
such an extent that Tolstoy found it perfectly natural to cast his
narrative into what he called an 'autobiographical form', and
these words occur quite frequently in his letters and drafts,
together with such blunt statements as 'I am writing an
autobiography'. It is therefore not surprising that Nekrasov
should have been misled.

Childhood as we know it in its published form is a collection
of scenes and portraits from the reminiscences of Nicholas
Irtenev, told in the first person and bound together by commentary and generalisation. Aged twenty-four, he looks back
to his life as a precocious, imaginative, vain and gauche young
boy of ten. The story's twenty-eight short chapters are largely
concerned with the events of two single days in the narrator's
childhood—a day in the country and a day in town. Chapters
1–13 represent a day in the country, with descriptions of
lessons, visits, hunting, games, and 'something in the nature of
first love', and portrait sketches of the boy's tutor, mother,
father and nurse. A short interlude of two chapters describes the
move from country to town and is the occasion for a generalised
encomium to childhood as the happiest time of life. Chapters
16–24 are devoted to grandmother's name-day a month later,
while a final coda moves the action on a further six months to
the illness and death of the boy's mother and the death of his
old nurse.

The final version of *Childhood*, while very similar to the
second and third versions, is substantially different from the
first draft, which is not available in English translation. The
latter purports to be a series of notes sent by the writer to a
friend, with a brief introduction explaining why they were

[1] J.E. XLVI, 237.

written and why they are being sent. 'Why did I write them?', he asks. 'It was interesting for me to observe my own development, but the main thing I wanted to do was to find in the imprint of my life some principle or purpose to guide me...'[1] He fears that he may have been too frank about his weaknesses, but asks his friend to be his judge and confessor. Thereupon he launches into the history of his mother and father with some digressions and classifications of people into groups; moves on to the story of a single day—his German tutor, the conversations between his father and mother, the hunt, the departure for Moscow; continues with his schooldays in Moscow and their unpleasant associations of laziness, lack of progress and lack of affection; expatiates on sensibility and the need to write from the heart; returns to the theme of his father, his father's letter from his wife, the children's letter from their mother, in which they learn that they are illegitimate; relates their return home and their mother's death, and finally takes the story far beyond the scope of childhood into boyhood and youth.

It has been observed that Tolstoy, whose response to literary tradition had already been felt in his experiments with sentimentalism and his addiction to a Rousseauesque strain of confession, started his first draft of *Four Periods of Growth* in the form of an epistolary novel, and may have had in mind the fact that several literary heroes left home at an early age and were not infrequently illegitimate children (Tom Jones, Oliver Twist, Candide). But this idea, if it was originally there, was not carried forward into the second version, where the theme of illegitimacy disappears. The second and subsequent versions dispense with the original opening gambit—'notes to a friend'. The book begins, as the boy's daily life would begin, with an early morning call from his tutor. New material, notably the story of the nurse and governess, Natalya Savishna, and her death, and the name-day party in Moscow which makes up the second day of *Childhood*, is included, and the whole divided up into chapters with title headings. Originally conceived as the story of another family, *Childhood* becomes

[1] J.E. I, 103.

increasingly autobiographical, while at the same time retaining in the characters of the boy's father and mother the elements of fiction (Tolstoy's own mother having died when he was only two).

Among Tolstoy's papers dating from the period of the second version of *Childhood* there is a solitary chapter entitled *To my Readers*, in which he pays his due to a much-used literary convention. In the course of the chapter he says:

I require very little of you for you to be accepted as one of my chosen readers. You should be sensitive—that is, you should some-times be able to experience heartfelt pity and even shed a few tears over a fictitious person you have loved, or rejoice for him with all your heart and not be ashamed of it; you should love your memories of the past; you should be a religious person; you should, as you read my story, look for the places which will touch your heart and not the places which will make you laugh; you should not envy and despise good society if you do not belong to it, but observe it calmly and dispassionately. But above all you should be an *under-standing* person, one of those for whom I see on acquaintance that there is no need to interpret my feelings and my general tenor but who, I see, understands me and whose soul finds a response to every sound in my own soul...

The chapter concludes as follows:

It is possible to write from the head and from the heart. When you write from the head, the words fall into place on the paper in an obedient and well ordered manner. But when you write from the heart, there are so many thoughts in your head, so many images in your imagination, so many memories in your heart, that their expression is incomplete, inadequate, halting and crude.

Perhaps I was mistaken, but I always used to stop when I began writing from the head and tried to write only from the heart.

I must admit to another strange prejudice too. In my opinion the personality of an author or composer is an anti-poetic personality, and since I was writing in the form of an autobiography and wished to interest you as much as possible in my hero, I did not want him to bear the author's imprint and so sought to avoid all authors' devices—learned expressions and long periods.[1]

[1] J.E. 1, 208.

This chapter, or rather these excerpts from it, emphasise Tolstoy's youthful addiction to the literature of the heart, and imply clearly enough that although he has chosen the auto-biographical form, it is the autobiography of somebody else that he is allegedly recreating. The *final* version of *Childhood*, however, would seem from external evidence to be as much a record of the life and thoughts of Tolstoy himself as of his friend. Subjective elements, perhaps inevitably, loomed larger than he had foreseen. At the same time there are fewer overt author's intrusions and less contrived sentimentalism. A few faintly erotic and mildly improper phrases and passages have been omitted, together with some digressions which might with advantage have been retained. One such deletion is a long and interesting passage on music and art which contrasts the young boy's feelings as he listens to his mother playing Beethoven with the affectation of a well-known French author in describing the suggestive powers of music:

In a certain French novel, the author (whose name is very well known) describes the impression made on him by a Beethoven sonata [in fact Balzac in *César Birotteau* is talking about the fifth symphony] and says that he can see angels with azure wings, palaces with golden columns, marble fountains, glitter and light—in short, strains every fibre of his French imagination in order to draw a fantastic picture of something beautiful. I don't know about other people, but when I read this very long description by this Frenchman, I could only envisage the effort he put into it to think up and describe all these charming things... [1]

Tolstoy continues, with rather ponderous common sense, by observing that since he has never *seen* any angels with azure wings or palaces with golden columns, any comparisons involving them are pointless. In this respect he is critical of French literature in general, and censures the French for comparing the beautiful with its imitations—with pictorial or plastic representations of the living reality:

[1] J.E. I, 177 ff.

The French have a strange propensity for communicating their impressions in pictures. In order to describe a beautiful face they write: it resembled such and such a statue; or nature: it reminded me of such and such a picture; or a group: it reminded me of a scene from a ballet or opera. They even try to communicate feelings pictorially. A beautiful face, nature or a live group are always better than any statues, panoramas, pictures or stage sets.

Tolstoy takes another example, this time from Lamartine, to ridicule the hackneyed comparison of the beautiful with precious stones. Speaking of Lamartine's description during a perilous boat journey of drops of water falling off a pair of oars into the sea 'comme des perles tombant dans un bassin d'argent', he says:

As I read this phrase, my imagination was immediately transported to the maid's room, and I pictured to myself a maid with her sleeves rolled up washing her mistress' pearl necklace over a silver wash-basin and accidentally dropping a few of the pearls in; and by this time I had forgotten about the sea and the picture which my imagination had been painting for me a moment ago with the poet's help. If Lamartine, the brilliant Lamartine, had told me what colour the drops were, or how they fell and trickled down the wet blade of the oar, or what little circles they made as they fell into the water, my imagination would have trusted him, but the reference to a silver basin made my mind fly far away.

Tolstoy goes on to condemn with a typically heavy irony and a partiality for generalisations based on inadequate premises the tendency which he sees above all in the French, to a lesser extent in the Germans and the Russians, and least of all in the English, to abuse the simile and metaphor and especially comparisons involving precious objects—'eyes like turquoises and diamonds, gold and silver hair, coral lips, golden sun, silver moon, sapphire sea...'. Tolstoy himself rarely offends against these anti-romantic principles or lays himself open to the sort of criticism which he is here levelling against Lamartine and which is so reminiscent of Chekhov's strictures on the early Gorky's over-exuberant style. When he describes, in another version of this same discarded chapter, the effect which music has upon him, he does so not by likening that effect to something else, but by trying to discover the origin of it:

Music does not affect the mind or the imagination. While I am listening to music, I don't think about anything and don't imagine anything, but a strange, delightful feeling so fills my soul that I lose all awareness of my existence; and this feeling is—recollection. But recollection of what? Although the sensation is acute, the recollection is obscure. It seems as if you are recollecting something which never happened. [—the only phrase which Tolstoy retained from this passage].

Is not recollection the basis of the feeling which any art arouses in you? Does not the delight afforded by painting and sculpture come from the recollection of images? Does not the feeling inspired by music come from the recollection of feelings and the transitions from one feeling to another? Is not the feeling inspired by poetry the recollection of images, feelings and thoughts?

If recollection is for Tolstoy the source of aesthetic pleasure, it is also very near the source of his own early inspiration as an artist, and it had a vital influence both on his choice of subject matter and his manner of composition. Recollection rather than invention is the basis of his first literary work, which is neither a novel nor an autobiography, but an autobiographical novel of childhood.

It has been claimed that 'the essential autobiographical novel is one that centres in experiences which transform and mould a character, not one which merely revolves around a single, outstanding, real experience'.[1] This is essentially true of Tolstoy's work. For the most part it moves from specific description to generalisation and back to the concrete occurrence. In the process of doing so it contrives to give the impression that the central experiences recounted are typical and representative. Tolstoy could have kept closer to 'the truth', but ironically enough he would not have told us so much about his real self if he had merely retailed exactly what happened to him. One of the advantages of choosing the fictional, instead of the strictly autobiographical form is connected with

[1] R. Pascal, 'The Autobiographical Novel and the Autobiography', *Essays in Criticism* (April 1959).

the fact that the essential nature of a man is not always expressed in what he actually does. His potential may not be realised. The circumstances of his life may deny him the necessary outlets for self-expression. They may prevent him from doing what he knows he could have done, or from showing himself as only he knows himself to be. In writing an autobiographical novel he can modify what actually happened in order to find out the truth about himself, to learn from it, and perhaps to shape his subsequent life accordingly. For this reason it is more appropriate for a young man to choose the fictional form, and for an old man to write an autobiography.[1]

Towards the end of his life Tolstoy wrote that his *Childhood* was badly and insincerely written, that it was an incoherent jumble of events from his own and his friends' childhoods and that 'at the time of writing I was far from independent in my forms of expression, but was under the influence of two writers—Sterne (*A Sentimental Journey*) and Töpffer (*La Bibliothèque de mon oncle*)—who had a great effect on me just then'.[2] In fact there is little in *Childhood* to suggest the influence of Sterne (although, as we have seen, there is ample evidence of it in *A History of Yesterday*) and considerably less in the first draft of *Four Periods of Growth*. As for Töpffer, too much may have been made of the rôle played by the description of two days in a boy's life which occurs in a very different setting in both Töpffer's and Tolstoy's stories. *La Bibliothèque de mon oncle* is devoted much more to boyhood and youth than to childhood; its three parts do not correspond to stages of growth and development, but rather to the different romances of its hero Jules. It has no recognisable shape or form; Jules is not seen against his social background, nor is his author concerned with his moral and intellectual development. For comparative purposes, the early chapters of *David Copperfield* have more affinity with *Childhood* than either *A Sentimental Journey* or *La Bibliothèque de mon oncle*. Tolstoy, as a regular reader of *The Contemporary*, must have read many of the numerous works of an autobiographical nature which appeared in the

[1] R. Pascal, 'The Autobiographical Novel'.   [2] J.E. XXXIV, 348.

2-2

original or in translation in that journal during the late 1840s and early 1850s. Translations from West European literature included Goethe's *Wilhelm Meister*, Lamartine's *Confessions*, Charlotte Brontë's *Jane Eyre*, Andersen's *Story of my Life*, Chateaubriand's *Mémoires d'outre-tombe* and Dickens's *David Copperfield*. Of the two best accounts of childhood in nineteenth-century English fiction, *Jane Eyre* and *David Copperfield*, Tolstoy certainly read the latter before his own *Childhood* was published. Indeed his dog Dora is said to have been named after David Copperfield's first wife! In both books the events are mainly described as seen through the eyes of a young boy; both boys have an affectionate nurse, an idealised, sentimental woman with a heart of gold; both boys lose their mothers at an early age; both experience the pangs of first love; both suffer from their early education (although it is only in the *first* draft of *Childhood* that the horrors of Nicholas' first experience of school are recorded). Both books share a common sentimentality, a fondness for the repetition of characteristic details in speech habits or physical descriptions and an occasional rhetorical flourish in digressive or reflective passages. One or two passages are particularly striking for their similarity of approach. An obvious example is the description of the impression made on a young boy by the death of his mother, and the self-conscious cultivation of his grief:

Before and after the funeral I wept continually and was miserable, but I am ashamed to recall my misery because it was always tinged with a certain feeling of egoism: now a desire to show that I was more grief-stricken than anyone else, now concern about the impression I was making on others, now an idle curiosity which made me observe Mimi's bonnet or the faces of those around me. I despised myself for not experiencing sorrow to the exclusion of all else, and I tried to conceal all other feelings; because of this my grief was insincere and unnatural. Moreover, I experienced a certain pleasure in knowing that I was unhappy and I tried to stimulate my sense of unhappiness, and this egoistic feeling did more than anything else to stifle my real grief.[1]

[1] *Childhood*, Ch. 17.

Compare Nicholas' alleged feelings with those attributed to David Copperfield in the same situation:

I stood upon a chair when I was left alone, and looked into the glass to see how red my eyes were, and how sorrowful my face. I considered, after some hours were gone, if my tears were really hard to flow now, as they seemed to be, what, in connection with my loss, it would affect me most to think of when I drew near home—for I was going home to the funeral. I am sensible of having felt that a dignity attached to me among the rest of the boys, and that I was important in my affliction.

If ever child were stricken with sincere grief, I was. But I remember that this importance was a kind of satisfaction to me, when I walked in the playground that afternoon while the boys were in school. When I saw them glancing at me out of the windows, as they went up to their classes, I felt distinguished, and looked more melancholy, and walked slower...[1]

Now and again one is struck, when re-reading *Childhood* and *David Copperfield*, by a fairly close correspondence in the imagery or narrative detail—whether it is the image of the two mothers as angels, watching over their boy from above or flying down from heaven on wings of love, or the description of two women absorbed in their own thoughts and not noticing the water which is overflowing:

Mother was sitting in the drawing-room pouring out tea; in one hand she was holding the teapot and with the other the tap of the samovar, from which the water poured over the top of the teapot on to the tray. But although she was staring intently at it, she did not notice this, nor did she notice the fact that we had come in. (TOLSTOY)[2]

On going down in the morning, I found my aunt musing so profoundly over the breakfast table, with her elbow on the tray, that the contents of the urn had overflowed the teapot and were laying the whole tablecloth under water. (DICKENS)[3]

It would be otiose to point to the many differences in purpose and approach between the two novelists, to Dickens' overt

[1] *David Copperfield*, Ch. 9.   [2] *Childhood*, Ch. 2.
[3] *David Copperfield*, Ch. 14.

social criticism, his relative lack of interest in David's inner spiritual development, the greater superficiality of his characters, his broader comic vein. What is important is that Dickens' novel forms part of the climate in which *Childhood* was written. The same may perhaps be said, too, of Karamzin's *A Knight of our Time*, in which Russia's best-known exponent of sentimentalism made it his objective 'to tell in novel form the story of a friend of mine', in other words, to write an autobiographical novel about someone else's childhood. Points of similarity between Karamzin's and Tolstoy's stories include their emphasis on childhood as a unique time of happiness, and love as an over-riding emotion in a young boy's life; more tangibly, they share certain episodes in common—the death of the boy's mother at an early age and the feelings flowing from it, his early education at home at the hands of a tutor, and his first experience of a frightening storm (in Tolstoy's case this is described in *Childhood*'s sequel, *Boyhood*).

In the very first few pages of *A Knight of our Time* we meet the name of Rousseau, and it is not surprising that there is a considerable volume of literature devoted to the subject of Rousseau and Tolstoy. Tolstoy himself was partly responsible for this. 'Rousseau was my teacher from the age of fifteen,' he wrote in 1905. 'Rousseau and the Gospels have been the two great and fruitful influences in my life.' On another occasion he said 'Many [of Rousseau's] pages are so near to me that it seems as if I wrote them myself.' The parallels between the two men have often been drawn; nowhere, perhaps, as neatly and precisely as in Sir Isaiah Berlin's book *The Hedgehog and the Fox*:

Rousseau must have strengthened, if he did not actually originate, his [Tolstoy's] growing tendency to idealise the soil and its cultivators—the simple peasant, who for Tolstoy is a repository of almost as rich a stock of 'natural' virtues as Rousseau's noble savage. Rousseau, too, must have reinforced the coarse-grained, rough peasant in Tolstoy with his strongly moralistic, puritanical strain, his suspicion of, and antipathy to the rich, the powerful, the happy as such, his streak of genuine vandalism, and occasional burst of blind, very Russian rage against Western sophistication and refinement, and the adulation of 'virtue' and simple tastes, of the 'healthy' moral life, the militant, anti-liberal barbarism, which is one of Rousseau's specific contributions to the stock of Jacobin ideas. And perhaps Rousseau influenced him also in setting so high a value upon family life, and in his doctrine of superiority of the heart over the head, of moral over intellectual or aesthetic virtues.[1]

It is easy enough to indicate their common views on the virtues of breast-feeding or the futility of punishments and incentives as educational aids. Some critics, however, have tried to find passages in *Childhood*, *Boyhood* and *Youth* which might seem to derive from *Émile*, or to reveal similarities of form between the *Confessions* and Tolstoy's trilogy. On the whole these attempts have not been fruitful. The formalistic search for 'influences' tends to obscure the more important difference that Tolstoy is inclined to believe that the instinctive moral sense of good and evil in a child is the surest guide to the rightness of his feelings and actions, whereas Rousseau sets more store by the rational direction of the instincts and the rôle of the educator in guiding his charge along the right lines. Tolstoy has more faith in a boy's innate capacity for goodness, stresses more the virtues of altruism and good works, and is more critical of *amour de soi* as well as *amour propre*. In the context of his trilogy and especially *Boyhood* and *Youth*, we sense the presence of Rousseau most of all in the *penchant* for self-analysis and the urge to confess, to exaggerate one's own shortcomings, and to crave penitence.

If we have mentioned Rousseau, Karamzin, Dickens, Töpffer and Sterne, it is only to make the point that Tolstoy began his literary career in a cautious manner, by tilling familiar ground. One could go further and show how many now forgotten stories in the Russian literary journals of the late 1840s and early 1850s exploited the obviously fashionable theme of childhood. Boris Eykhenbaum[2] claims, for example,

[1] Isaiah Berlin, *The Hedgehog and the Fox* (London 1953), p. 43.
[2] B. M. Eykhenbaum, *Lev Tolstoi, kniga pervaya, 50-e gody* (Leningrad 1928), p. 93.

that Karl Ivanych, the German tutor in Tolstoy's story, must have reminded Tolstoy's readers of another German tutor, Adam Adamovich, in M. Mikhailov's story of the same name (1851). He suggests that Tolstoy may have discarded the episode in which he originally described Karl Ivanych returning home drunk, because of its similarity to an episode in Mikhailov's story. And he reminds us of Kulish's *History of Juliana Terentevna* in the August number of *The Contemporary* for 1852 à propos of which Tolstoy wrote in his diary: 'Read the new *Contemporary*; one good story, like my *Childhood*, but lacking in substance.'

It is probably true to say that a child is constantly aware of what is new and what is strange. 'The very notion of the ordinary', it has been said, 'is foreign to the child, to whom everyone encountered is unique.'[1] And yet there is a greater degree of affinity between childhood experiences than between those of adult life, and for that reason the literature of childhood is bound to share much common ground—a mother's love, play, lessons, heightened emotional sensibility, curiosity, vitality, the lack of inhibitions, the first awakenings of love or the growing awareness of other people. The generality of these experiences may have led Stephen Spender to say 'autobiographies of childhood are chiefly important for the light they throw on childhood in general, and they are not especially illuminating on the autobiography of particular individuals'.[2] The same may perhaps be said of autobiographical novels. It would be wrong to look to *Childhood* for a sharply delineated portrait of the young Tolstoy or of 'his childhood friend'. Nicholas is not especially individualised. He is not a prodigy, not deprived, maladjusted, unstable, eccentric. To the general experiences and emotions of childhood is added the particular dimension of a privileged social background—life on a country estate, domestic staff, a private tutor, hunting, social calls, dancing the mazurka. But the

[1] W. Allen, *The English Novel* (Harmondsworth Middlesex 1965), p. 164.
[2] Quoted by R. Pascal, *Design and Truth in Autobiography* (London 1960), p. 84.

focal point of the story is not so much the hero, although he is the centre of attention, but the pattern imposed on the material of childhood by an author writing at a given age from a given standpoint—namely, that childhood is an unforgettably happy, innocent and unique period of life, but that lurking behind its happiness is the inescapable and incomprehensible reality of death. These are Tolstoy's thoughts at the age of twenty-four. He has to superimpose them for most of the time on the feelings of a ten-year-old boy, whose outward way of life is not unlike his own but who is not just himself when young, in such a way that the boy does not think adult thoughts or know things he could not have known at his age. In rejecting a chronological survey from birth to adolescence in favour of the diary of a moment in time, the concentrated happenings of a mere two or three separate days, the very small slice of life, Tolstoy chose a new approach to an old subject, which was perhaps influenced by the belief, recorded in his *Recollections*, that one of the main features of his childhood life was an absence of the sense of the passing of time. The basic theme of happiness and the reverse side of the medal—death—is fitted into a clearly discernible pattern. The particularised narrative of a single happy day in a boy's life from dawn to dusk is followed by a cloying, sentimental chapter on childhood, culminating in a series of rhetorical questions written from the point of view of a disillusioned adult. The story is resumed from the child's point of view with the account of a second happy day, which in turn is succeeded by two carefully juxtaposed death scenes, which form the climax of the book. 'Maman', whose death has been foreshadowed by the boy's dream in Chapter 1, dies in dreadful agony. The physical horror and obscenity of death are unbearably painful for her son:

One of the last to approach and take leave of the dead woman was a peasant with a pretty five-year-old girl in her arms whom she had brought with her, goodness knows why. At that moment I accidentally dropped my wet handkerchief and tried to pick it up, but no sooner had I bent down than I was startled by a terrible, piercing cry of such horror that I shall never forget it if I live to be a hundred; a cold shudder runs through my body whenever I think of it. I raised my head—the peasant woman was standing on a stool by the coffin and struggling to hold the little girl in her arms. Throwing back her frightened little face and goggling at the dead woman, the child was waving her little arms as though to ward something off, and screaming in a terrible, frenzied voice. I uttered a cry which I think must have been even more terrible than the one which had startled me, and ran out of the room.

Only then did I understand the source of that strong oppressive smell which mingled with the smell of incense and filled the whole room, and the thought that the face which but a few days ago had been full of tenderness and beauty, the face of the woman I loved most of all in the world, could arouse horror, seemed to reveal the bitter truth to me for the first time and filled my soul with despair.[1]

By way of contrast, the death of Natalya Savishna, the simple uneducated nurse and housekeeper, evoked no such feelings of horror:

She quitted this life without a pang: she did not fear death but welcomed it as a blessing...She accomplished the greatest and best thing in life—she died without fear or regret.[2]

This is the burden of Tolstoy's story, although it may be doubted whether either death is really moving, since the characters are insufficiently alive for the emotions to be engaged. Nevertheless it is structurally significant that Natalya Savishna's life-history should round off the account of the final day, just as her death rounds off her life. Her achievement is the goal which Tolstoy himself sought most of his life, and indeed, many of his problems and his solutions to them are the direct outcome of his abnormal obsession with the fear of 'nothingness' and his determination to overcome it. Needless to say, it is an adult, not a child, who ponders over these two deaths and their significance.

When the adult intrudes with his mature reflections, the illusion of childhood immediacy, so vividly sustained throughout so much of the book, is shattered. While it is true that for

[1] Ch. 27.   [2] Ch. 28.

the purposes of fiction Nicholas has two ages, it is unfortunate that they are not kept more carefully apart, and that in the context of the two days of his childhood life he has to retail biographical facts about his parents which a ten-year-old boy could not have known, and reproduce the contents of letters not written to him or by him, or conversations which he could not have overheard. The changing focus of a person who is usually ten but sometimes twenty-four can be bewildering, particularly so since there are times when Nicholas, the boy, seems unusually mature for his age, and other times when his thoughts and actions strike one as infantile. Moreover, the form of fiction chosen by Tolstoy by its very nature imposes certain limitations and cannot allow him to develop those methods of characterisation which were later to distinguish him as a novelist. In the first place, since the boy is the narrator, he can only describe the people he comes into contact with from outside. He cannot paint psychologically interesting portraits of his father, mother or relations which have breadth and depth. He can only say what they are like on the surface. They only matter in so far as they matter to him. They can reproach him, or cause him joy or sorrow, or make him move from one place to another. But they cannot enjoy an independent existence or have a plot to themselves. Secondly, the narrator cannot be seen objectively from other points of view. We only know what he tells us about himself and what he cares to remember about other people's attitudes towards him. Thirdly, the choice of a one-day narrative technique allows little time to record and analyse growth and development and the whole process of growing up. These are not criticisms of Tolstoy's story but only indications that the attentuated autobiographical novel, while being the useful literary exercise he intended it to be, was not a genre well calculated to give scope to his greatest talents. Tolstoy's own criticisms of *Childhood* are perhaps too harsh. Speaking of the first part while still in the process of writing it, he complained in his diary: 'The thing seems to be too detailed, diffuse and lacking in life'; or again, 'The style is too careless and there are too few thoughts for me to be able to forgive the emptiness of content.'[1] It is a fact that writing did not come easily to him, but it is difficult to agree with these particular charges which he levelled against himself. If there is a wealth of detail, it is absorbing detail. The style is not only not diffuse, but on the contrary concise, economical and orderly. As he wrote in 1853: 'The manner adopted by me from the very beginning, namely of writing in short chapters, is the most suitable one. Every chapter should express just one thought or just one feeling.'[2] There is a pattern imposed by the structure of the story; and nothing that Tolstoy wrote could ever be devoid of life or content.

Maxim Gorky's *Childhood* provides an interesting contrast to Tolstoy's. A whole world separates the tragic catastrophes of his opening chapter from the trivial misfortune which befalls Tolstoy's young hero, angrily roused from sleep by a dead fly! Gorky's totally different background and experience of life, and the seamy and squalid realism of his narrative, gave the autobiographical novel a new content. Although he indulged in literary artifices, he was not writing with one eye on the conventions of a genre or the stages of development in the education of a self-centred boy. His own Maxim is not the focus of attention. It is his grandmother who plays the leading rôle, while a series of miniatures are grouped round two fullish-length portraits of his grandparents. His style is evolved from the spoken, not the written, word, and the book reads as if composed on the basis of the continuous oral telling and retelling of the boy's adventures. Gorky, like Tolstoy, is fond of musing, but he is goaded by the practical and utilitarian need to expose the sordid sides of Russian life in the belief that men can and must make the world a better place to live in.

In the age of the common man Gorky's *Childhood* perhaps commands a wider audience than Tolstoy's, and there is no doubt that some readers of Tolstoy's book feel a certain impatience with its over-conscious literariness, and the

[1] J.E. XLVI, 99 and 107.   [2] J.E. XLVI, 217.

occasional fulsome, rhetorical interjections or sentimental pastiches. Too many people cry too often, even Papa, Grisha and the German tutor. But much of its attraction for the modern reader must surely lie in the universal recognition of and response to the emotions recollected there: the capacity for love, the feeling of security, the flights of imagination, boundless enthusiasm and a sense of wonder, vanity and the desire to excel, the pleasure given by trifles and the importance attached to them, shyness, self-deceit, contempt for 'outsiders', fear of the unknown, the workings of conscience and a highly developed faculty of observation. No writer can be great without possessing powers of observation to an abnormal degree, but Tolstoy's particular gift was the ability to look inwards. Ilya Erenburg recalls an interesting passage from the diaries of A. N. Afinogenov: 'If the writer's skill consisted in the ability to observe, the best writers would be doctors and examining magistrates, teachers and train guards, Party committee secretaries and military leaders. But this is not the case, for the writer's skill consists in the ability to observe himself.'

It is typical of Tolstoy's style of writing to juxtapose a minute record of external detail with the thoughts it evokes in the observer's mind, exterior narrative shading into interior monologue. One need look no further for an illustration than the opening paragraphs of the first chapter of *Childhood*, where the description of Nicholas' waking is accompanied by his waking thoughts:

On the 12th of August 18—, exactly three days after my tenth birthday on which I had received such wonderful presents, Karl Ivanych woke me at seven in the morning by hitting a fly just over my head with a swatter made of sugar-bag paper fastened to a stick. He did it so clumsily that he caught the little ikon of my patron saint which hung on the headboard of my oak bedstead, and the dead fly fell right on my head. I put my nose out from under the bedclothes, steadied the ikon, which was still wobbling, with my hand, flicked the dead fly on to the floor and looked at Karl Ivanych with angry, though sleepy eyes. He for his part, wearing a bright-coloured quilted dressing-gown with a belt of the same material round the waist, a red knitted skull-cap with a tassel and soft goat-skin boots, continued to walk round the room, taking aim and swatting flies.

'I know I'm only young,' I thought, 'but why does he disturb *me*? Why doesn't he kill flies by Volodya's bed? There are plenty of them there! But no, Volodya's older than me. I'm the youngest. That's why he torments me. All he thinks of all his life', I muttered, 'is how to be nasty to me. He can see very well that he woke me up and frightened me, but he pretends not to notice...disgusting man. And his dressing-gown and skull-cap and tassel—they're all disgusting.'[1]

Two paragraphs from a long work of prose fiction can give only the barest impression of its author's style and method of characterisation, but it is no doubt the accumulation of such passages which has led to the common observation that in his first published work, Tolstoy combined the individualising detail of a Dickens or a Gogol with the psychological analysis of a Stendhal.

[1] Ch. 1.

3

THE SWORD AND THE PEN

Tolstoy entered the army proper in 1852, his previous service
having been as a volunteer. He did not resign his commission
until the end of 1856, but his war service effectively ended in
1855. These were eventful years for him, as he served succes-
sively in the Caucasus, the Danube and the Crimea during the
expeditions against Shamil, the Russo-Turkish War and the
siege of Sevastopol. Not that fighting was by any means a
full-time occupation. On the contrary, the story of these years
is the story of various leisure activities, reading and writing,
debauchery and long periods of idleness, with just sufficient
'action' to provide the raw material for his stories of contemporary life, the Caucasus and its inhabitants, the skirmishes
with the mountain tribesmen and the protracted defence of
Sevastopol.

I said earlier that Tolstoy's list of the works of literature
which impressed him most at this period of his life, as
recollected in old age, was sketchy and imprecise. A further
and more accurate source of information about his literary
tastes are his diaries and letters for the years 1852–5. Fiction
and history were his staple diet, seasoned with a little poetry.
Turgenev, Gogol, Pisemsky, Ostrovsky, Lermontov, Pushkin
and Griboedov are the Russian authors most frequently
mentioned. French names include—apart from the inevitable
Rousseau—Balzac, Sue, George Sand, Jean-Alphonse Karr and
Béranger. German literature is represented principally by
Goethe and Schiller, English and American by Dickens,
Thackeray, Samuel Warren, D'Israeli senior, Fenimore Cooper
and Harriet Beecher Stowe. Of the Russian historians, Tolstoy
makes particular mention of the general works of Karamzin
and Ustryalov, Mikhailovsky-Danilevsky on the Napoleonic
invasion of Russia, and Milyutin on the Franco-Russian war
of 1799. He also read Michaud's *Histoire des Croisades*. Generally
his comments on what he is reading are sparse and laconic.

This is particularly so of foreign literature, where a novel is often classified simply as 'good' or 'stupid'. Rousseau usually inspires him to greater length: 'Read *Profession de foi du Vicaire Savoyard*, and as always when reading it, it produces a great many sensible and noble thoughts in me. Yes, my main trouble is that I am too intelligent.' Scattered throughout the diaries are interesting *obiter dicta* about literature and about his own personality:

When you read a work, especially a purely literary work, the main interest is provided by the character of the author as expressed in that work. But there are some works in which the author disguises his viewpoint or changes it several times. The most agreeable are those in which the author, as it were, tries to hide his personal viewpoint and at the same time remains faithful to it whenever it does show through. The most colourless are those in which the viewpoint changes so often that it is completely lost.[1]

I read *The Captain's Daughter* and alas, I must admit that Pushkin's prose is now already out of date—not in its language, but in its manner of exposition. Now, quite rightly, in the new school of literature, interest in the details of feeling is taking the place of interest in events themselves.[2]

The common people are so superior to us by their life of toil and privation that it is somehow shameful for the likes of us to look for and describe what is bad in them, but it would be better to say of them, as of the dead, only what is good. This is the merit of Turgenev and the shortcoming of Grigorovich and his fishermen.[3]

In many of the diary entries which concern himself, there is the awareness that he is a man of exceptional gifts and outstanding intelligence, a man who needs a special yardstick to measure him, a man who craves popularity and literary fame, but who is at the same time acutely aware of his own deficiencies and over-inclined to dramatise and exaggerate his vices. At this early stage in his life one already finds in his diaries and note-books an anti-militaristic strain, an irreverent attitude to professional historians, a tendency to venerate the common people at the expense of his own class of society, and an

[1] J.E. XLVI, 182.   [2] J.E. XLVI, 187.   [3] J.E. XLVI, 184.

orientation towards the practical and the useful, which are such typical features of the mature man and artist, whether in his resolve to edit a journal to propagate morally useful writings or his desire to found a religion 'purged of faith and mystery, a practical religion which does not promise a future bliss but provides bliss on earth'.[1] Some of these aspects of Tolstoy's personality are apparent in *Boyhood* and *Youth*, the sequel to his *Childhood*, and we may take as the first of our three main themes in this chapter the recollections of the life he left behind him as processed and exemplified in literary form by these two stories (although *Youth* was not in fact published until 1857), and the Yasnaya Polyana-centred *A Landowner's Morning*.

Boyhood and *Youth* are the second and third parts of an uncompleted tetralogy (the fourth part, *Early Manhood* (*Molodost*), was never written). Four plans[2] survive of these four stages of 'development' or 'life', as they were later called. One states unambiguously: 'The main idea is—the feeling of love of God and of one's neighbour is strong in childhood; in boyhood these feelings are stifled by sensuality, self-assurance and vanity, and in youth by pride and a tendency to philosophise; in early manhood experience of life revives these feelings.'

Another plan lists seven basic ideas, not all of which were realised, but which indicate the trend of Tolstoy's thoughts and their edifying nature:

(1) To show the interesting side of the relations between the brothers.

(2) To distinguish in clear-cut fashion the characteristic features of each period of life: in childhood, warmth and sureness of feelings; in boyhood, scepticism, sensuality, self-assuredness, inexperience and pride (the beginning of vanity); in youth, beauty of feelings, the growth of vanity and unsureness of oneself; in early manhood, eclecticism of feelings, in place of pride and vanity—ambition, the recognition of one's worth and purpose, versatility, frankness.

(3) To show the bad influence of the vanity of one's teachers and the conflict of interests in the family.

[1] J.E. XLVII, 37.   [2] J.E. II, 241 ff.

(4) To develop in the work as a whole the difference between the brothers—the one with a bent for analysis and close observation, the other for the enjoyment of life.

(5) To show the influence of innate tendencies on character development.

(6) In the work as a whole to guide the characters through four fields—the feelings, the sciences, behaviour and money matters.

(7) To show the impossibility of loving one woman only.

This plan was to apply to four consecutive phases. As far as the second phase is concerned, it was faithfully followed. Compared with its predecessor, *Boyhood* is written in a minor key. A greater awareness of other people and a widening of the range of experience lead to greater personal unhappiness, a sense of injustice, religious doubts, petty misdemeanours and a lack of freshness and spontaneity—the result of an excessive preoccupation with the insoluble problems of life. The move to Moscow, pen-portraits of friends and relations, the life history of the German tutor, school lessons, minor peccadilloes, day-dreams, sexual awakening—such is the content of the story. Tolstoy, as was usually the case when he was in the process of writing, was dissatisfied with it. He complains at times of the slow action, the lack of unity and the absence of what he called 'a clear literary device'. Presumably he felt the need for the sort of taut framework provided by the two-day sequence in *Childhood*, and which was not provided, as he had hoped, by the contrasting characters of the brothers.

On the whole Tolstoy's criticisms—and this is not always the case—seem to me to be justified. *Boyhood* lacks the élan and charm of *Childhood* (perhaps the deliberate burden of its theme makes this inevitable). It is not so closely knit. Its character sketches, which are based more on narrative description than on dialogue or monologue, are not psychologically profound. The same is largely true of the next instalment *Youth*, which did not evoke much enthusiasm either from its author or from the critics. Its *raison d'être* is the hero's decision to put his philosophical ideas into practice, to strive for self-improvement, to try to become a new man. The horizons of his life are extended to include the university, where contact with a wide range of students makes him aware of the class structure of society, and engenders ambivalent feelings of contempt and admiration for students with a different background from his own. Throughout the story runs the alternating cycle of love of self and hatred of self; the sequence of resolution–failure–remorse–resolution with which readers of Tolstoy's life are only too familiar. Tolstoy himself felt that he was devoting more and more paper to creating less and less life. 'Diffuse' and 'flabby' are frequent, self-inflicted epithets of reproach. He deplores his tendency to deliberate and philosophise. In the brief assessments he made of each chapter of the story the words 'poor' and 'weak' occur commonly. No doubt it became increasingly difficult to keep all the parts of the projected tetralogy in view as the writing of it spread out over five years, and one senses a falling-off in inspiration with each new phase, a heavier and more sententious style and a more trivial subject matter. Not that the author ever lost sight altogether of his original plan. He does indeed use some easily recognisable devices to preserve an outer semblance of unity throughout a series of works in which the hero and his mental and spiritual growth provide the inner unity. Each story has a 'summarising' chapter, epitomising the ages of childhood, boyhood and youth respectively. The chapter on the storm in *Boyhood*, symbolising this turbulent period of life, is matched by the chapter on spring in the same relative position (Chapter 2) in *Youth*, giving force to his decision to begin life anew. The same people whom Nicholas met at his grandmother's name-day party in *Childhood* are visited by him in *Youth* in the course of his social rounds. The family split caused by his mother's death in the first story is healed by his father's second marriage in the third. The basic motifs of family ties, the relationship between brother and brother, brother and sister, father and son and the social etiquette of visiting and entertaining all give continuity and help to unite the three movements of the work. Artistically the same fondness for the use of physical gestures and mannerisms as an aid to characterisation, the penchant for systematisation and tabulation and the uniform manner of composing the numerous pen-portraits all wed a homogeneous style to a basically homogeneous content. Nevertheless, it is the first of the three stories which is aesthetically the most satisfying, despite the occasional passages in *Boyhood* and *Youth* which linger in the memory. In the following extract from *Youth*, Nicholas is lying on a verandah looking at the moonlit garden. In a typically Tolstoyan sequence a chain-like, rhythmically proportioned sentence packed with vivid realistic detail evokes a mood and conjures up a vision of an ideal woman who promises happiness, but a happiness which is dwarfed by the magnitude of the mysterious heavens, and beyond them the source of all creation. My translation, incidentally, tries to preserve what is so often lost in the standard versions—namely, sentence length and construction, the conscious repetition of key words (*lustre, sound, significance*, which are normally rendered by synonyms for the sake of variety), the double comparatives (*higher and higher*) and the humble and ubiquitous conjunction *and*:

At such times everything would take on for me a different significance: the appearance of the old birch trees with their leafy branches glistening on one side in the moonlight and their black shadows obscuring the bushes and driveway on the other, and the calm, rich lustre of the pond swelling steadily like a sound, and the moonlight lustre of the dewdrops on the flowers in front of the verandah which also threw their graceful shadows across the grey flower-bed, and the sound of a quail beyond the pond, and the voice of a man on the roadway, and the soft, almost inaudible scraping of two old birch trees against each other, and the hum of a mosquito above my ear under the rug, and the fall of an apple catching a twig and dropping on dry leaves, and the hopping of frogs which sometimes came right up to the steps of the terrace, their greenish backs shining mysteriously in the moonlight—all this would take on for me a strange significance, the significance of a beauty too great and a happiness somehow incomplete. And then *she* would appear with her long black plait of hair and her full bosom, ever pensive and lovely, with bare arms and passionate embraces. She would love me and I would sacrifice my whole life for one moment of her love. But the moon rose higher and higher, brighter and brighter in the sky, the rich lustre of the pond, swelling steadily like a sound, grew clearer and clearer, the shadows grew blacker and blacker, the light more and more limpid, and as I gazed upon and listened to it all, something told me that even *she* with her bare arms and ardent embraces was very far from being all goodness; and the more I looked at the high full moon, the higher and higher would true beauty and goodness seem to be, the purer and purer and the closer and closer to Him who is the source of all beauty and goodness, and tears of unsatisfied but tumultuous joy would fill my eyes.[1]

Tolstoy's contemporary, the radical critic Chernyshevsky, considerably influenced later critical thought by his sympathetic and perspicacious review article of 1856 devoted jointly to *Childhood* and *Boyhood* and to Tolstoy's war stories. He pointed to the author's 'remarkable powers of observation, acute analysis of the workings of the mind, precision and poetry in his pictures of nature, and his refined simplicity', while wisely adding that these same qualities could be found in Pushkin, Lermontov and Turgenev—to mention only his compatriots. More particularly he tried to put his finger on Tolstoy's individuality in three germinal sentences:

Count Tolstoy's attention is more and more directed to the way in which some feelings and thoughts develop out of others; he is interested in observing how a feeling, arising directly out of a given situation or impression and subjected to the influence of recollections and the force of associations furnished by the imagination, passes into other feelings, returns to its previous point of origin and then peregrinates over and over again, changing as it goes through a whole chain of recollections; how a thought, born of an original sensation, leads to other thoughts, is carried further and further on and merges day-dreams with real sensations, dreams of the future with reflections on the present. Psychological analysis can take various directions: one poet is interested primarily in character delineation; a second in the influence on his characters of social relations and the conflicts of life; a third in the connection between feelings and actions; a fourth in the analysis of passions. Count

[1] Ch. 32.

Tolstoy is primarily interested in the psychic process itself, its forms, its laws, the dialectics of the soul to give it a definition.[1]

Chernyshevsky's expressions 'the dialectics of the soul' and 'interior monologue' (which we meet for the first time in the same article) are still common currency over a century later in critical literature on Tolstoy. His highly appreciative article was no doubt welcome to Tolstoy, who was as sensitive to praise as to blame, and perhaps it helped to modify his unflattering opinion of this inelegant social radical. Chernyshevsky, however, was less fulsome in private than in public, and when it came to the subject of *Youth*, he had some very hard things to say in a letter to Turgenev:[2] 'Tolstoy...will write vulgar and stupid things unless he abandons his way of rummaging about in trivialities and stops being a little boy in his attitude to life...Read his *Youth*. You'll see what rubbish, what thin gruel it is except for three or four chapters...' (Chernyshevsky has in mind the chapters dealing with 'democratic' university students). The letter continues in an even ruder vein and leaves no doubt of his real feelings. While he attacked *Youth* on social grounds because of its preoccupation with upper class frivolities, right-wing critics were voicing their (more polite) objections to the excessively long periods in the same story, the abuse of the words *who*, *which* and *that*, or the 'illiteracy' of an officer sitting in a trench and writing to a friend. One has the impression not so much of frivolity or superficiality, as of a superfluity of undigested material. It is concentrated and opaque. It would have gained from greater selectivity. Perhaps the reason for *Childhood*'s greater appeal to the reader when compared with its sequel is the greater universality of childhood experience and the enchantment lent by distance. In *Youth*, on the other hand, one is more directly aware of a given social class and period. It is too long for a short story, and lacks sufficient character development and plot interest in the old-fashioned sense to enable it to support its weight.

[1] N. G. Chernyshevsky, *Pol. sobr. soch.* III (Moscow 1947), pp. 423 ff.
[2] N. G. Chernyshevsky, *Pol. sobr. soch.* XIV (Moscow 1949), p. 332.

At the very beginning of his literary career, in the Caucasus in 1852, Tolstoy planned the development of his creative work along two different lines—diachronically and synchronically, to use the terminology of linguistics. While envisaging in chronological sequence the various stages of development from childhood to manhood, he planned at the same time to write a novel about the day-to-day life of a landowner in the Russia of his day. The difference between these two projects he defined as follows:

Four Periods of Life [he calls it 'life', not 'growth'] will be *my* novel up to Tiflis. I can write about it, because it is a long way away from me. And as the novel of a clever, sensitive man who has lost his bearings, it will be edifying though not dogmatic. The Novel of a Russian Landowner, however, will be dogmatic.[1]

This statement of intent prepares one for the worst. As Proust put it, a work of this sort 'is like an object with the price ticket left on'. There are many allusions in his diaries and notebooks to the purpose of his novel, which some five years later was published as A Landowner's Morning—the first part of another uncompleted project. In one place he says that it will expose the evils of Russian administration. In another place he speaks of it as a work designed to solve problems. Elsewhere he elaborates his ideas with unmistakable clarity:

The basis of the Novel of a Russian Landowner: (1) The hero seeks to realise his ideal of happiness and justice in a rural way of life. Not finding it, and being disillusioned, he wishes to seek it in family life. His friend (a woman) suggests that happiness does not consist in an ideal, but in one's regular life's work, having as its aim the happiness of others. (2) There is no love; but there is the physical need for intercourse and the rational need for a companion for life.[2]

But perhaps the clearest statement of all comes in his so-called Introduction for the Author, not the Reader, which was probably written in 1853, when the work was still in its early stages.

The basic and fundamental feeling which will guide me throughout this novel is a love of the way of life of a country landowner. The

---

[1] J.E. XLVI, 150.   [2] J.E. XLVI, 146.

scenes in the capital, the provinces and the Caucasus must all be permeated with this feeling—with a yearning for this life. But the charm of the country life which I want to describe is not its tranquillity or its idyllic beauties, but the goal which it offers—the dedication of one's life to *good*—and its simple uncomplicated nature.

The main idea of the work is that happiness is virtue.

Youth feels this unconsciously, but various passions stand in its way as it strives towards its purpose. And only experience, mistakes and misfortunes compel it, once it has consciously grasped this purpose, to strive towards it and it alone, to be happy, to despise evil and to bear it calmly. On this basis the novel should be divided into three parts: Noble, but inexperienced enthusiasm of youth, errors, addictions to the passions. Reform. Happiness.

Secondary ideas: mainsprings of human activity: (1) good: (a) virtue, (b) friendship, (c) love of the arts; (2) evil: (a) vanity, (b) cupidity, (c) the passions: (a') women, (b') cards, (c') wine.[1]

This introduction continues to enlarge on the idea, to list the various characters and to outline the plot. Some starts were made and draft versions were written and discarded. The ideas already expressed were further complicated by their author's realisation, as he notes in his diary in Sevastopol during the Crimean War, that serfdom (or 'slavery' as he called it) was incompatible with the life of an educated landowner of his day. *A Landowner's Morning* is all that was published of the original project, a fragment of twenty chapters, in which a young Prince Nekhlyudov—a name to which Tolstoy was particularly partial in his fiction—begins by expounding his motives for leaving the university in order to 'do good' on his estate and ends up disillusioned as a result of what he sees and hears as he visits one peasant after another and observes the squalor of their lives and their indifference to his concern for them. The construction of the story is simple. Tolstoy first introduces Nekhlyudov in one sentence, immediately allows him to speak for himself in a letter to his aunt, reverts to author's narrative to enlarge on the appearance and personality

[1] J.E. IV, 363 ff.

of the prince and then uses the entries in his notebooks to motivate a series of visits to his peasants—one wants a plough-share, another has a horse to sell and a third is in need of grain. A bright spot in a generally gloomy picture is the clean, orderly and prosperous household of one of his peasant families; and Nekhlyudov is left in an introspective mood with a feeling of envy for their healthy, hard-working and happy son.

Tolstoy sensed that his tendentious story was a failure; but its significance has not been lost on socially-minded critics, and the claim has been made that it was the first work of Russian fiction to blame serfdom for the economic backwardness of the peasantry as distinct from its degrading effect on the human personality. In 1852 he had written in his diary: 'I feel positively ashamed to bother about such nonsense as my stories, when I have such a marvellous thing as my *Novel of a Russian Landowner*'.[1] But posterity has not shared this view. His novel is too close to him, too overtly didactic, to have much more than biographical interest.

Unlike *Boyhood* and *Youth* and *A Landowner's Morning*, Tolstoy's early military sketches have claimed the attention and won the affection of his readers, for while they were equally close to him, they show more attempt on his part to distance himself, to generalise his experience and to cast it into a literary mould. Tolstoy arrived in Starogladovskaya in the Caucasus in May 1851, and in the following month took part in his first military action as a volunteer. Next year, on the basis of recollections and diary entries, he wrote up his experiences, first in epistolary form (*A Letter from the Caucasus*), then, somewhat more obliquely, as *The Raid: The Story of a Volunteer*. Critics have drawn attention not only to Tolstoy's well-known fondness for grounding his fiction firmly in his own experiences and adventures, but also to the great vogue which the Caucasus enjoyed in Russia as a setting for prose and poetry, whether by Pushkin, Lermontov or Marlinsky, and to

[1] J.E. XLVI, 152.

the exceptional popularity of military tales with the reading public. Eykhenbaum recalls a story by the now forgotten Kostenetsky published in *The Contemporary* in 1850 and reviewed there in 1851, which Tolstoy must certainly have read. Its subject matter, its description of a campaign in the Caucasus and of the local terrain, its factual, unromantic tone and its discussion of the nature of bravery all suggest that it was not without its influence on Tolstoy. His choice of theme was a perfectly natural one, and the manner of its treatment not original, though relatively new. In autumn 1852, after several starts on his *Letter from the Caucasus*, Tolstoy noted in his diary that he wished to use his Caucasian material for publication in *The Contemporary*. 'I want to write some Caucasian essays to form my style and to get money,' he said;[1] and a few days later added details of what he planned to do if he met with an enthusiastic response from the editor of *The Contemporary*. His programme at first contained three sections, one on the manners and customs of the people, with stories of individual Cossack men and women, the second devoted to a trip to the Caspian Sea, and the third to war and the nature of bravery. Shortly afterwards a fourth section was added. It was to contain the stories he had heard from an old Cossack friend, Epishka, about his hunting expeditions, his campaigns in the mountains and the old Cossack way of life. The first two sections came to nothing. The fourth grew into *The Cossacks*, and the third into *The Raid*, the final version of which was written quickly in December 1852 and published in *The Contemporary* the following year.

The text which Tolstoy sent to the journal has not survived, but we know that the version actually published differed, much to the author's annoyance, from his own manuscript. Which changes were made by the editor and which by the political censors can only be conjectured. It should be noted, however, that English translations do not always correspond with what Soviet scholars have accepted as the definitive version of the story.

[1] J.E. XLVI, 145.

It is perhaps a commonplace that Tolstoy's early fiction grew out of his diaries. The following 'rule' which we read in these diaries makes the point unambiguously:

Copy out into the diary only the thoughts, information or observations relevant to proposed works. When starting each work look through the diary and copy out everything relevant into a special notebook.[1]

His diary for 1851 speaks of a raid on 3 July, his own cowardly behaviour, the officers' conversations about bravery and his own reflections on the nature of moral and physical courage.[2] It also contains brief pen-sketches of his comrades. With this material to 'copy out' and with a clear moral purpose and a fixed literary object in view, Tolstoy began to write the first of his tales of army life. In a short introduction (not always included in Soviet editions of Tolstoy's works) he poses a number of problems. What feelings prompt a man to kill another man? What is courage? What criteria determine whether an action is called brave or cowardly? The problems are taken up again in the form of a dialogue between the narrator (the volunteer of the sub-title) and a Captain Khlopov (obviously the Captain Khilkovsky who is described in Tolstoy's letters and diaries of the time). The narrator extracts a definition of bravery from the captain and compares it with one by Plato. The questions why people serve, how they behave before, during and after battle, whether war is ever justified, and whether feelings of hatred and revenge can ever be compatible with the harmony of nature provide the moral framework of the story. Different types of bravery are illustrated by the different characters, ranging from the sober to the swashbuckling, and the story is given a rather self-conscious' literary flavour by the references to Plato, Mikhailovsky-Danilevsky, whom Tolstoy happened to be reading, and Lermontov, as the creator of a type of literary hero on whom one of the characters models himself, illustrating incidentally the influence of literature on life. Tolstoy was re-reading

[1] J.E. XLVI, 218.   [2] J.E. XLVI, 65.

Lermontov while writing *The Raid*, and the idea expressed in one of his poems, also about a raid, that there is plenty of room for everybody in the world without the need to fight, is very closely echoed in similar words by Tolstoy who, like Lermontov, uses the expression '*Russian* courage' in the course of his generalisations. Tolstoy in fact was aware of his literary antecedents (perhaps too of La Rochefoucauld's maxims on courage and cowardice), aware that he was writing 'literature', not a war-correspondent's despatch.

If the moral framework of *The Raid* is provided by the theme of courage and its ambiguous nature, the technical framework is provided by the movement of the sun. As in *Childhood*, the events of two days are described. The opening of each chapter moves on the action by a few hours, e.g.: 'Next morning at 4 o'clock...' (Ch. 2); 'As soon as the bright sun appeared...' (Ch. 3); 'the sun had completed half its journey...' (Ch. 4); 'Towards seven that evening...' (Ch. 5); 'The troops were to start at ten in the evening...' (Ch. 6); 'We had been riding for more than two hours...' (Ch. 7). The description of nature is simple, concrete and free from literary conceits. Imagery is drawn from the vocabulary of lights and colours, the sun, the moon and the stars. Tolstoy's expert knowledge of flora and fauna enables him to particularise trees, plants and wild animals. The concrete, factual impression is further enhanced by the introduction of local dialect words for people, animals, weapons and the terrain—although this has a somewhat retarding effect on the narrative, since the words require explanatory footnotes. There is no introspection or interior monologue. The narrator himself is not obtrusive. The few characters are described externally and are not filled out.

Tolstoy marked his story like a schoolteacher. Some marks survive on the manuscript, the highest one (5+) occurring twice for emotional or potentially lachrymose scenes (the description of an old woman, the death of a young soldier) which he prided himself on having handled with restraint.

Chapter 11 is one such passage, and I quote it as an illustration of a young author's assessment of his own work:

Four soldiers were carrying the ensign on a stretcher and behind them a garrison soldier was leading a thin, sickly horse laden with two green chests in which the medical supplies were kept. They were waiting for a doctor. Some officers rode up to the stretcher and tried to cheer up and comfort the wounded man.

'Well, Alanin, old man, it'll be some time before you can dance a jig again,' said Lieutenant Rosenkrantz with a smile.

He evidently thought these words would keep up the good-looking ensign's spirits, but as far as one could judge from his cold and gloomy expression, the words did not produce the desired effect.

The captain rode up as well. He looked hard at the wounded man and there was an expression of sincere compassion on his usually cold and indifferent face.

'Well Anatoly Ivanych, my friend,' he said in a tender and sympathetic tone of voice such as I had never expected of him, 'it seems it's God's will.'

The wounded man looked round and a sad smile lit up his pale face.

'Yes, I didn't obey you.'

'Better say it's God's will,' repeated the captain.

The doctor arrived and took bandages, probes and other supplies from the orderly. Rolling up his sleeves, he went up to the wounded man with an encouraging smile.

'So they've made you a hole in a sound spot too, have they,' he said in a bantering, off-hand tone. 'Let's have a look.'

The ensign did as he was told, but there was bewilderment and reproach in the expression with which he looked at the jovial doctor, which the latter did not notice. He began probing the wound and examining it from all sides, but the wounded man, his patience exhausted, pushed the doctor's hand away with a heavy groan.

'Leave me alone,' he said in a barely audible voice. 'I'm going to die anyway.'

With these words he fell on his back, and five minutes later when I went up to the group which had formed round him and asked a soldier, 'How's the ensign?' they replied, 'On his last legs.'

In Tolstoy's scheme nought is reserved for certain infelicitous expressions which needed to be changed and for such word combinations as 'the sounds of a broken barrel organ', the logic presumably being that if the organ were broken no sounds could be produced! He was at pains, as his diary entries make clear, to try to steer a course between excessive generalisation and excessive detail, to keep a balance between a general idea and the concrete illustration of it, without the one appearing too obtrusive or the other too trivial or naturalistic. And he was careful not to abuse what he termed his 'satire'—his icono-clastic attitude towards 'the establishment'. 'I must be quick and get rid of the satire in my *Letter from the Caucasus*,' he wrote in his diary, 'for satire is not in my nature.' When writing the final draft of *The Raid* he commented, 'I don't like all the satirical part.'[1] Judging by the extant versions, the satirical element was certainly reduced with successive drafts. Nevertheless, despite his protestations to the contrary, it was, and continued to be, a powerful weapon in his literary armoury.

The Wood-felling was the second of Tolstoy's Caucasian tales.[2] Written intermittently over the years 1853–5, it was completed in Sevastopol and published in *The Contemporary* in 1855 under the initials L.N.T. In brackets were added the words 'dedicated to I. S. Turgenev'. A short fragment sub-titled *The Diary of a Caucasian Officer*, not actually used in the printed version of *The Wood-felling*, has survived separately. Here Tolstoy employed the same method as he had employed earlier in *The Raid*—namely, to preface his story with a general introduction, in this case a typical threefold classification of the types of warfare to be encountered in the Caucasus. This academic overture was discarded, and the narrator who tells the story in the first person and who is an officer cadet tem-porarily commanding a platoon in the North East Caucasus, sets the scene without any preliminaries. The time, the place and the occasion are defined. It is early morning, and time to set off on a wood-felling expedition. A soldier is introduced. He has forgotten his pipe. Whereupon Tolstoy immediately

[1] J.E. XLVI, 132.
[2] *The Memoirs of a Billiard Marker*, which Tolstoy professed to value more highly than *Childhood* or *The Raid*, but which Nekrasov rightly recognised as vastly inferior, was written in the Caucasus in 1853, but only published—reluctantly—in 1855.

abandons his story and launches into a long digression on the various types of Russian soldier. There are three in number, each type subdivided into two. (The magic number three had a peculiar fascination for him—if not types of warfare, then types of soldier.) The straightforward external description and characterisation of one soldier after another is followed by their semi-literate, jocular, but singularly unfunny conversation as they sit talking and warming themselves in front of the fire. Tolstoy then prods the action forward, making it follow once again the movement of the sun and introducing the precise but unadventurous double-barrelled adjectives of colour ('milky-white', 'purply-grey') so characteristic of his natural descriptions. A shell is fired at a few Tartars. The narrator sits down to talk to the company commander. For a moment Tolstoy comes into his own. The officer speaks French, but 'in spite of this his comrades liked him'. He seems to want to reply to the narrator's 'silent question'—and how often does Tolstoy make use in his fiction of the unspoken word, the silent glance, the thoughts that are going on behind the things that are said and done. The question too—why are you here? —is typical of Tolstoy. Why do people serve? Why do they come to the Caucasus? The themes so familiar from his diaries are adumbrated: the Caucasus as an escape, a refuge from financial difficulties or frustrated love; the difference between the traditional 'literary' picture of the Caucasus and its reality; the phenomena of cowardice and bravery. Characteristic too is the technique by which the themes are illustrated—the outward display of indifference to mask an inner trepidation. After this brief interlude the action is resumed. The Tartars fire back. The wood-fellers continue their work. The sun continues its journey. The compound hyphenated adjectives reappear. The pipe-smoking soldier is mortally wounded, and in the face of death recalls the trivial details of everyday life. The action is successful, but the soldier is dead. It is now evening and time to return—but not before the company commander explains that he cannot return to Russia until he has won the necessary promotion and decorations.

At this stage one might have expected the story to have been rounded off—the expedition over, the sun set, and end of a day in the life of a Caucasian officer. But a new chapter introduces one new character and then another, while in the following chapter, although it is the next-to-last, yet another officer makes his first appearance. In the meantime most of the men so carefully described and classified in the opening stages have been lost sight of altogether. The story as a whole is badly constructed, jerky and episodic, and it generates little interest in character or situation, although it has some memorable observations and comparisons ('We look very differently at the Caucasus when we are in Russia and when we are here...It's like reading poetry in a language you don't know too well; you think it's much better than it is'). Too many people have too little to do and say. The life and death of the pipe-smoking soldier, which could have been the focal point of the story, is not given sufficient prominence; it is overshadowed by descriptions of numerous peripheral officers and men and by *obiter dicta* on the Caucasus and the Russian character. Not but what Tolstoy tries hard to pull the various threads together by repeating words and sentences and returning at the end to his structural point of departure—soldiers sitting and talking round a camp-fire. But the impression remains of much extraneous material, of brief thumbnail sketches of individual soldiers, scraps of dialogue and examples of local dialect copied out with few changes from notebooks and diaries. In fact, when Tolstoy sent the story to *The Contemporary* he called it an 'article'. At the same time he asked Panaev to obtain Turgenev's permission for it to be dedicated to him: 'When I read my article through I found in it much involuntary imitation of his stories'.[1] Nekrasov was enthusiastic about it in his letter to Turgenev. 'It is a sketch of various types of soldiers (and officers), that is to say a thing hitherto unprecedented in Russian literature. And how splendid! The form of these sketches is completely your own, there are even expressions and comparisons which recall *A Sportsman's Sketches*—one officer is

[1] J.E. LIX, 316.

simply "A Hamlet of the Shchigrov Province" in army uniform'.[1] In a letter to Tolstoy, Nekrasov repeated that the form was reminiscent of Turgenev although 'all the rest belongs to you and couldn't have been written by anybody but you'. He emphasised the interest and *novelty* of the work. 'Don't despise sketches like this,' he wrote. 'Our literature has said nothing so far about the soldier except vulgar trivialities.'[2]

Nekrasov was surely right to press the comparison with Turgenev's 'form'. Certainly Tolstoy was a great admirer of Turgenev, and had noted at the time when he was starting work on *The Wood-felling*: 'Read Turgenev's *A Sportsman's Sketches* and it's somehow difficult to write after it.'[3] Eykhenbaum draws these comparisons:

The inability to 'link poetic scenes together' with which Tolstoy reproached himself, is overcome here à la Turgenev: a 'scene' is interrupted by Velenchuk's exclamation ('I've gone and forgotten my pipe. That's a blow, lads!'); then follows a long digression devoted to the classification and description of types of soldier, after which the 'scene' is resumed with the same exclamation. So it is in Turgenev—in *The Singers* or in *Bezhin Meadow*, the basic situation of which (conversation round a bonfire) is similar to that of *The Wood-felling*. Also à la Turgenev is the 'finale' of the story. A lyrical landscape recapitulating motifs from the opening gives way to a final compressed phrase abruptly changing the intonation and as it were restoring the reader to real life, thereby bringing the story to a close.[4]

These technical resemblances are certainly valid. On the other hand Turgenev did not break up his stories into chapters, nor did he pontificate or classify. Both authors shared a fondness for the careful reproduction of the speech habits of the uneducated classes, and both at this stage set more store by static character description and the stringing together of portrait sketches than by plot or dramatic interest. A significant and distinguishing factor about *The Wood-felling*, however, is its deflation of the

---

[1] J.E. III, 309 (quoted).   [2] J.E. III, 309 (quoted).
[3] J.E. XLVI, 170.
[4] B. M. Eykhenbaum, *Lev Tolstoi, kniga pervaya, 50-e gody*, p. 167.

romantic image: its substitution of real men Tolstoy knew, real conversations he had heard and real events he had experienced, for the literary stereotype of the Caucasus on which he had himself been nurtured. A fragment of Tolstoy's entitled *Notes on the Caucasus: A Trip to Mamakai-Yurt*—some lines of which are reproduced almost literally in *The Wood-felling*—points the contrast between the real and the imaginary. Recalling the words of Marlinsky and Lermontov, Tolstoy invokes the images of valiant Circassian men and fair, blue-eyed women, the mountains, rocks, snows and torrents, the plane trees, the cloaks, caps and daggers of his literary predecessors, while warning his readers that they will have to renounce these images in favour of some 'nearer to reality but no less poetic'.[1] In this respect Tolstoy can claim to have done for the army, war and the Caucasus what Turgenev did for the peasantry and what some writers of the 'natural school' had done for the lower classes of urban society.

The element of reportage, the eye witness account, the diary, the notes of a war correspondent which we find in *The Raid* and *The Wood-felling*, play an important rôle also in the three Sevastopol sketches. Tolstoy's efforts in collaboration with other officers to found a military journal to support the morale of the troops eventually came to nothing because of the Emperor's veto; but not before he himself had written two short pieces (*How Russian Soldiers Die* and *Dyaden'ka Zhdanov i kavaler Chernov*) which subsequently found their way into *The Wood-felling* and no doubt accounts to some extent for its uneven construction. Moving to Sevastopol towards the end of 1854, and being involved in action soon afterwards, he was able to direct his war material not to a soldiers' magazine but to the periodical which had launched him on his literary career. The three Sevastopol stories appeared in *The Contemporary* in the course of 1855 and 1856.

Sevastopol in December is a short 'article' which combines Tolstoy's first impressions of the town on his arrival with his memories of a spell of guard duty on the notoriously dangerous

[1] J.E. III, 216.

Fourth Bastion some months later. It reads like the notes of a soldier hankering to be a writer, but uncertain whether he is more than a war correspondent. After the first flush of excitement had worn off, Tolstoy soon began to doubt whether the army was his right vocation. 'A military career is not for me,' he wrote in spring 1855, 'and the sooner I get out of it to devote myself fully to literature, the better it will be.'[1] His diary for the same period tells of his literary plans: 'I will write of Sevastopol in its various phases, and the idyll of an officer's way of life.'[2] At the end of March 1855 he starts what he calls, significantly enough, *Sevastopol by Day and Night*—and once again one notices the importance of the day and of the diary in Tolstoy's early work. *Sevastopol in December*, as it was eventually called, begins with a conventional dawn scene, a kind of weather report; half-way through he reminds us that the weather has changed and gives another bulletin; in the final paragraph the sun has reached the end of its journey for the day. It is surely too much to read into this circular structural device an allusion to the fact that the city is surrounded. It is clearly a part of Tolstoy's literary stock-in-trade, regardless of the situation. The story jumps about as the nameless narrator jots down what he sees, walking about the town and its fortifications. There are no characters. There are no chapters. There is no particular topography. The narrator is talking to you as if you had been there too, and were sharing his reminiscences with him. The scene shifts from the bay and the people on the quayside—ordinary people going about their ordinary business—to a military hospital and the grim consequences of war. The tension is relaxed and you are in an inn, listening to officers and men talking and embellishing their stories to their own credit. You are taken on a tour of the defences, you see and hear action, and at the end you listen to a stirring coda lauding the epic spirit of Sevastopol and its Russian defenders, and the twin strains of the music of a regimental band and the firing of the guns.

In a letter to his brother, Tolstoy referred to a strong attack

[1] J.E. XLVII, 38.   [2] J.E. XLVII, 40.

of patriotism which affected him at the start of the Crimean War, and which is much in evidence in the first of the three Sevastopol sketches. At the same time there is a sober, realistic awareness of the skull beneath the skin, and a typically Tol-stoyan juxtaposition of the sombre thought of death and the joyful feeling of the beauty of the natural world. There is more than a touch of 'literariness' about *Sevastopol in December* as Tolstoy tries his hand at a long sustained sequence, with numerous subordinate clauses, ponderous repetitive syntax, frequent combinations of three adjectives and three nouns, balance, antithesis, repeated prepositions and a sentence exceed-ing a hundred words in length:

You will see the sharp curved knife enter the healthy white flesh; you will see the wounded man suddenly regain consciousness with terrible, heart-rending screams and curses; you will see the doctor's assistant toss the amputated arm into a corner; you will see another wounded man lying on a stretcher in the same room watching the operation and writhing and groaning not so much from physical pain as from the mental torture of anticipation; you will see terrible sights that rend your soul; you will see war not in its fine, orderly and gleaming ranks with music and prancing generals, but you will see war in its true aspect—blood, suffering and death.

But such an oratorical flight, inspired by the grim reality of a military hospital, is not typical of the work as a whole. The general tone is conventional and flat, although always concrete and individualised. Some local colour is introduced through the cautious use of soldiers' and sailors' jargon, local dialect and the mispronunciation of foreign words.

Much more consciously 'literary', however, is the second of the series, *Sevastopol in May*, which is less a communiqué and more a work of art, although both drafts were written in the surprisingly short space of eight days. Originally called *A Spring Night*, it combines his own observations of his fellow officers and men with the story of one night's action in May 1855. It is the first of Tolstoy's works to strike an uncompro-misingly hostile attitude to conventional thinking about war, and, within the limits of censorship, to expose and denounce militarism. It dispenses with a hero on the argument that 'my hero is truth', and tries to make a distinctive attitude to war and the professional soldier a unifying feature of the numerous detailed incidents and scenes. Structurally, the story is particularly interesting. There is more than a hint of sonata form about the opening statement of theme, the variations on it, the repetition of the statement (Chapter 14), more variations and a final coda. First comes a high-flown, rhetorical, declamatory introduction, with 'the angel of death hovering unceasingly' over the trenches:

Thousands of human ambitions have had time to be mortified, thousands have had time to be gratified and deceived, thousands to be lulled to rest in the arms of death. How many stars have been put on, how many taken off, how many Annas and Vladimirs, how many pink coffins and linen palls! And still the same sounds from the bastions fill the air, and still the French look out from their camp on a clear evening with involuntary trepidation and super-stitious fear at the black pitted earth of the bastions of Sevastopol and at the black figures of our sailors moving over them, and count the embrasures from which the iron cannon stick out menacingly; and still the sergeant look-out man watches through his telescope from the signal-station the brightly coloured figures of the French, their batteries, their tents, their columns moving up the Green Hill and the puffs of smoke in the trenches; and still with the same ardour a mixed crowd of people with even more mixed desires stream in from various corners of the earth to this fateful spot.[1]

The conclusion is brief and chilling. 'One of two things: either war is madness, or if people perpetrate this madness they are not the rational beings we consider them for some reason to be.' On this note the story proper begins, and the rhetorical flourishes give way to simple, factual narrative statements about the time, the place, the weather—and, of course, the sun. Tolstoy experiments with the character description of an officer from three different angles: omnis-ciently in his own author's comments; obliquely through the

[1] Ch. 1.

feelings of his friend, and his friend's wife, for him; and directly through his own day-dreaming. For thirteen chapters the narrative continues, introducing various officers, their thoughts, fears, presentiments, ambitions; describing a military hospital; recounting an action in which Praskukhin, an officer, is killed; and occasionally raising the tone to indulge in an exclamatory digression punctuated by rhetorical questions ('Vanity! vanity! all is vanity—even on the edge of the grave and among people ready to die for a noble conviction. Vanity! it seems to be the characteristic feature and peculiar malady of our time. Why did our predecessors not mention this passion ...[etc.]! Why are there only three kinds of people in our time...[etc.]? Why did the Homers and Shakespeares speak of love, glory and suffering while the literature of our time is only an endless story of "Snobs" and "Vanity"?') This self-conscious digression is typical of Tolstoy in a 'literary' mood—repetitions, exclamations, questions, classifications, literary allusions (he had just been reading Thackeray) and the constant preoccupation with 'our time'. But it is Chapter 14 which is particularly remarkable, and crucial both to the story's structure and its idea. It is probably without parallel in Tolstoy's fiction in that it consists of only one sentence—of well over a hundred words:

Hundreds of newly bloodstained bodies of people who, two hours before, had been full of various lofty or trivial hopes and desires lay with stiff limbs in the dewy vale of flowers which separated the bastions from the trenches and on the smooth floor of the mortuary chapel in Sevastopol; hundreds of people with curses and prayers on their parched lips crawled, writhed and groaned, some between the corpses in the vale of flowers, others on stretchers, on beds, or on the bloodstained floor of the ambulance station; and still, as on previous days, the dawn broke over Sapun hill, the twinkling stars grew pale, the white mists spread from the dark roaring sea, the rosy dawn lit up the east, the long purple clouds spread across the pale blue horizon; and still, as on previous days, the sun rose in power and glory, promising joy, love and happiness to all the awakening world.

It returns one's thoughts to the first chapter, as the thousands of ambitions become hundreds of bodies, hundreds of suffering victims; but out of the unspeakable darkness comes the never-failing light as dawn breaks on another day and life goes on, as it always will. To emphasise this movement, Tolstoy begins Chapter 15 with almost the same situation and vocabulary as he had used in Chapter 2—the regimental band playing, the men and women strolling up and down the boulevard. This echo principle is a common device in Tolstoy's writings, whether to pick up the threads after a long interval, or to underline a basic sameness in human reactions to similar situations. In Chapter 4 one officer contemplates the thought of death or injury in action. He wonders where he will be hit, and what the consequences will be if it is the leg or some other part of the body. In Chapter 12 the action has begun and another officer, waiting for the shell to explode, thinks the identical thoughts. It is hard to believe that the author was not aware that he was using much the same thoughts and words about two very different people. The important thing is that they are both human beings, and, confronted with a situation beyond their control, can be expected to show the same uncontrollable response.

Neatness of construction, interconnecting threads and the natural leading of one chapter into the next all confirm the artistry and balance with which Tolstoy treated his theme of the abnormality of war and the exploration of men's thoughts and behaviour in abnormal circumstances. In the case of one officer (Kalugin) it is the instinctive fear which overcomes a man in battle, the fear which Nicholas Rostov experiences in his first encounter with the enemy in *War and Peace*, the contrast between what a man really thinks and feels and what he would like other people to believe he thinks and feels. With another officer (Pesth) it is the instinctive desire to boast, to put the best possible construction on one's own actions in battle when in fact one can never really know what is going on on the battlefield and who is responsible for it—another theme to which Tolstoy is to return in *War and Peace*, which Stendhal had adumbrated in the context of Waterloo, and which Sholokhov was to endorse in *The Quiet Don* with true Tolstoyan force and irony. With a third officer (Praskukhin) it is the contrast between the simple outward action of a few seconds and the wealth of life lived inwardly during those few seconds. As he lies on the ground waiting for a shell to explode, one thought leads to another in a rapid chain-reaction of vivid reminiscences of his past life, as Anna Karenina's life is momentarily lit up like a candle before her suicide, and Dostoevsky's epileptics see their momentary visions before succumbing to their fits. The passage describing the death of Praskukhin is one of Tolstoy's early artistic triumphs:

'Who will it hit—Mikhaylov or me? Or both of us? And if me, whereabouts? If it's the head then I'm done for; but if it's the leg they'll cut it off, and I'll certainly ask for chloroform and I may survive. But maybe only Mikhaylov will be hit, then I'll be able to tell how we were walking side by side, and he was killed and I was splashed with blood. No, it's nearer me...it'll be me.' Then he remembered the twelve roubles he owed Mikhaylov, remembered also a debt in Petersburg which should have been paid long ago; a gypsy song he had sung the night before came into his head; the woman he loved appeared in his imagination wearing a bonnet with lilac ribbons; he remembered a man who had insulted him five years ago and whom he had not yet paid back; and yet—inseparable from these and thousands of other memories—the awareness of the present, the expectation of terror and death, never left him for a moment. 'But perhaps it won't explode,' he thought, and with a desperate resolve tried to open his eyes. But at that moment a red fire pierced his eyes through his still closed eyelids and something struck him in the middle of the chest with a terrible crash; he started to run, stumbled over a sword under his feet and fell on his side.

'Thank God, I'm only bruised!' was his first thought, and he tried to touch his chest with his hand, but his arms seemed fastened to his sides and his head seemed to be squeezed in a vice. Soldiers flitted past him and he counted them unconsciously: 'one, two, three soldiers, and an officer with his greatcoat tucked up', he thought: then lightning flashed before his eyes and he thought—are they firing from a mortar or a cannon? A cannon probably, there's another shot, and there's some more soldiers—five, six, seven soldiers passing by. He suddenly became terrified they would trample on him; he wanted to cry out that he was wounded, but his mouth was so dry that his tongue stuck to the roof of his mouth and a terrible thirst tormented him. He felt how wet he was about the chest, and this sensation of wetness made him think of water and he even wanted to drink what it was that made him feel wet. 'I probably hit myself when I fell and made myself bleed,' he thought, and as he began to give way more and more to the fear that the soldiers who were still flitting past would trample on him, he gathered up all his strength and tried to shout 'Take me with you', but instead gave such a dreadful groan that he was terrified to hear himself. Then some red fires began to dance before his eyes and it seemed to him that the soldiers were putting stones on top of him; the fires danced less and less, the stones they were putting on him pressed harder and harder. He made an effort to move the stones away, stretched himself, and no longer saw or heard or thought or felt a thing. He had been killed on the spot by a bomb-splinter in the middle of his chest.[1]

It is an ironical situation, since Praskukhin's comrade, Mikhaylov, who is unharmed by the shell which kills his neighbour, thinks *he* has been killed, while its victim, Praskukhin, believes he is only wounded—a situation deliberately in keeping with the author's ironical approach to war and his assumption that it is not what it appears to be. The prosaic thoughts ascribed to Praskukhin in the moment of death are on a far lower plane than the rhetorical passages which colour Chapters 1 and 14. The death scene is stripped of all noble or romantic allure, and we see only the basic human emotions of an ordinary man—fear, the desire to boast, and, above all, the desire to live. The laconic sentence which concludes the episode, 'He had been killed on the spot by a splinter in the middle of his chest,' like the bare statement of an official announcement, is put in sharp contrast with the wealth of hopes, fears and memories crowded into a few brief seconds, and is a chilling reminder that that is all that the outside world, his friends and relations, will ever know of his lonely and utterly incommunicable experience.

[1] Ch. 12.

While the abnormality of war is at once juxtaposed with the normality of another working day, it is only to emphasise that normal life for a soldier is a contradiction in terms. Normal life means artificiality, pretence; and Tolstoy immediately switches the focus to the official expression of sorrow which it was the duty of officers to assume; the lust for power ('everyone of us is a little Napoleon'); and the hankering after decorations. One officer who has just survived his ordeal is at pains to show that he understands French. Another fabricates stories of conversations he pretends to have had with the enemy officers. The impression is confirmed that war is stupid and unnatural and that soldiers act unwittingly when they are involved in it and hypocritically when they are not. The final chapter presents the same point of view in a different way—how absurd war is when men who have been on opposing sides immediately chat to each other and exchange presents and compliments; how nauseating it is when a little boy wanders about the battlefield kicking a headless corpse.

There are no heroes or villains in this story—only people doing good or bad things. It is perhaps the most successful of all Tolstoy's military tales and its sequel—*Sevastopol in August*—(the only one of the Sevastopol stories, incidentally, to be signed with his full name) is in many ways its artistic inferior. *Sevastopol in August* has a more recognisable plot, an obvious hero in Lieutenant Koseltsov, enthusiastic, generous, impetuous (not unlike Petya Rostov in *War and Peace*), who volunteers for action and is killed, and a simple structural device implicit in the contrast in character between Koseltsov and his sensitive, day-dreaming, Walter-Mitty-like brother, who is also killed in action. It exploits the familiar theme of courage, vanity, snobbery, ostentation and the basic urge for self-preservation, while striking a new note of shame and anger at the Russian defeat and the incompetence of the Russian military organisation in the Crimean campaign. There are two fine, moving and admirably restrained death-scenes and Tolstoy, as always, uses the interior monologue to good effect (particularly in Chapter 8). But the story as a whole is long and disjointed and too many unimportant people are introduced too late. It has been suggested that the influence of Thackeray, whom Tolstoy was reading enthusiastically at the time, may be felt here in the departure from the stricter structural form of the first two Sevastopol sketches, the greater spaciousness and the absence of the recurring motifs, echoes and associations which are particularly obvious in the second sketch. It has also been suggested that the fact that the two main characters are brothers is the first step in the direction of that unique combination of two genres—the battle and the family—which was achieved in *War and Peace*. But seven years were to elapse between the third Sevastopol sketch and the start of Tolstoy's first novel. In the meantime Tolstoy was to explore the third major theme of his literary apprenticeship—the theme of the refugee from society, the Caucasus as an escape from urban civilisation, and Rousseau's noble savage.

Although *The Cossacks* was not published until 1863, it was conceived and born in the Caucasus in 1852, written intermittently over a period of ten years on the basis of Tolstoy's notebooks, diaries and reminiscences of the Caucasus, and actually set in the year 1852. In its eventual form it is the story of Olenin, a rich young nobleman whose biography is in many respects strikingly similar to Tolstoy's. The victim of debts and an unhappy love affair, he sets out for the Caucasus with no clear purpose in mind except the vague hope of finding happiness, and making a fresh start. Enchanted by the free life of the Cossacks, he tries to forget his past and share the joys of an open-air life with people who are not tormented by the questions which beset an educated and privileged European. Riding, hunting, listening to tales of expeditions against the neighbouring hillsmen, talking, observing, drinking, he enjoys a temporary and unreflecting happiness in the company of men and women of a stronger, less inhibited nature than his own—the old Cossack veteran Eroshka, the handsome young 'brave' Lukashka, and Maryana, his beautiful and proud fiancée. Inevitably he falls in love with Maryana. But there is no place for him in the Cossack community. His love is rejected, he can find no niche, he is liked but not accepted by a society for which his education and upbringing have unfitted him and which cannot give him the lasting happiness and sense of purpose which he is seeking.

Like *A Landowner's Morning*, *The Cossacks* is only the first part of a projected novel which was never completed. It was hastily concluded, after a lapse of many years and many changes of plan, under the pressure to publish for financial reasons. The story of its gestation is long and complicated, and it is difficult, if not impossible, to follow all its stages of growth from the numerous drafts and notes which have survived in manuscript. We cannot reproduce here the attempts of Soviet textologists to piece the jigsaw together, but we can indicate the main directions of Tolstoy's thinking as he wrestled, at times despairingly, with his ambitious plans.

The germ of *The Cossacks*, and in particular, those parts of it which concern Eroshka, can be seen in Tolstoy's decision, recorded in his diary in 1852, to write a series of Caucasian sketches and to include in them the stories told to him by an old Cossack friend Epishka: '(a) about hunting, (b) about the old way of life of the Cossacks and (c) about his expeditions in the mountains.'[1] Another motive force was the desire on Tolstoy's part to give a more realistic picture of the Caucasus than that which had become imprinted on the minds of the reading public by the works of Lermontov and Marlinsky. The fragmentary Caucasian sketch of 1852 referred to above (*A Trip to Mamakai-Yurt*) spells out the conventional image of the Caucasus in words very similar to the thoughts ascribed to Olenin on his journey southwards. What is more important, Tolstoy registers his disapproval of this convention, as Olenin is later to do when he discovers that reality as processed by the romantic imagination does not correspond to the experience of his own senses. The intention of this early sketch, like the intention of *The Cossacks*, is to achieve truth—but without sacrificing poetry. Poetic experiments quite untypical of

[1] J.E. XLVI, 146.

Tolstoy are to be found scattered among the early drafts relating to *The Cossacks*: a lengthy poem about the Cossack woman Maryana (one of the extremely few examples from which to judge Tolstoy's indifferent gifts as a versifier); a fragment of *The Fugitive* (the title given to the first part of the 'Caucasian novel') written in rhythmical anapaestic prose and incorporating Cossack folksongs; and an isolated chapter entitled 'The Old and the New', also in rhythmical prose, and divided up in a way which might suggest stanzas of a future Caucasian poem. These experiments at a poem in prose were not continued, but some at least of the folksongs survived to the final version of *The Cossacks*.

A study of the discarded manuscript shows what difficulty Tolstoy had in deciding how to begin his story. Should he start with Maryana? If so, should she be married or single? Or should he begin with a scene at a military cordon and the murder of an Abrek tribesman? Or with the arrival of a Russian company in a Cossack village? Or with Olenin in Moscow before his departure for the Caucasus? Equally difficult was the problem of interweaving the two strands of Epishka's stories and the triangular relationship between Olenin, Maryana and Lukashka. Finally it was necessary to choose one of a number of possible resolutions of the conflict. Should Olenin marry Maryana? Should Lukashka murder Olenin and escape to the mountains? Should Olenin and Lukashka both die (a solution suggested to him by hearing a reading of *Antony and Cleopatra* in a Russian translation)? Should Olenin cease to love Maryana? Or should he be rejected by her and return to Russia? One plan envisaged that Lukashka should marry Maryana, that Olenin should court her and be wounded by Lukashka in a fit of jealousy; that he should then leave for Tiflis and an affair with a Russian aristocrat; return to the Cossack village for a liaison with Maryana in her husband's absence; and after the return and death of Lukashka should himself be killed by either Maryana or a soldier lover of hers. Further complications were introduced into the draft versions by the difficulty of deciding how much of

Epishka's character should be grafted on to Lukashka, whether Epishka himself should be rejuvenated and transformed into a man of thirty, how much history of the Cossack people should be included as narrative background, and to what extent Olenin's introspection should be recorded in epistolary form in a series of letters to a friend in Russia. As a result there are some awkward joins in the published text, some repetition, an isolated letter inserted unnecessarily towards the end, a certain inconsistency in the characterisation of Olenin and a somewhat uneasy vacillation between epic description and romantic self-analysis. Tolstoy professed himself 'Completely dissatisfied with my Caucasian story. I cannot work without an idea. But the idea that good is good in any sphere, that passions are the same everywhere and that the wild state is good is not enough.'[1] The choice of words in this sentence suggests very strongly the influence of Pushkin's poem *The Gypsies* on Tolstoy's original thinking. Pushkin's Aleko and Tolstoy's Olenin are both refugees from an urban civilisation which they leave without regret. Zemphyra and Maryana are both beautiful, unsophisticated children of nature. The old gypsy and the old Cossack, for all their obvious differences in temperament, epitomise the untutored wisdom which comes with experience and age. Both *The Gypsies* and *The Cossacks* paint a somewhat idealised picture of the primitive condition. But jealousy is the dominant theme of Pushkin's poem. In a fit of jealousy Aleko, unwilling to grant to others the freedom he demands for himself and unable to respect the unwritten law of the gypsies, kills his mistress and her lover, and the poem concludes: 'But there is no happiness even in your midst, poor sons of nature...there are fateful passions everywhere, and there is no defence against the Fates.' Is Tolstoy parodying a traditional romantic literary theme? Maryana proves to be inaccessible and remains faithful to her Cossack. It is not the old man but Maryana herself who pronounces judgment on the outsider. Eroshka, far from being a moral mouthpiece voicing a sermon on human behaviour, is a slightly comic and lecherous figure who loves

[1] J.E. XLVII, 152.

the stranger in the Cossack camp and has his own hedonistic views about women. The romantic image of the Caucasus is carefully deflated. But parody is surely too strong a word for what is rather an awareness of a literary prototype. Any Russian writing about the Caucasus was bound to have in mind the example of Pushkin, Lermontov and Marlinsky. The note in Tolstoy's diary about the strange and poetic union among the Cossack tribes of two opposites, 'freedom and war', exactly echoes the words of Lermontov: 'Their god is freedom and their law is war.'[1] Marlinsky's *Amalet Bek* crops up repeatedly in Tolstoy's manuscripts of *The Cossacks*. Inevitably their attitudes and responses coloured his own and gave him something to react against. But for him 'the fateful passions' do not dominate. They take their place beside the epic features of the fight, the hunt, the carousal, the tales of valour, the manners and customs of the people, the wealth of typical and significant detail, whether rifles or horses, sweetmeats or wines. His song is of arms—and the men and women.

What is sometimes regarded as a decisive turning-point in Tolstoy's work on his Caucasian story is the impact made on him by his encounter with Homer. Having read the *Iliad*, he decided he could not continue as before. 'Read the *Iliad*,' he notes in August, 1857. 'What a marvellous thing! Must revise the whole of my Caucasian story.'[2] This declaration of intent, however, should not be taken too seriously. Comparisons between the *Iliad* and *The Cossacks* are hardly more valuable than those between the *Iliad* and *War and Peace*. An epic or heroic poem in the classical, Homeric sense is essentially an adventure story told for entertainment, revolving round the superhuman deeds of men in battle. Much space is normally given to speeches and descriptive detail, and it is commonly written from a courtly point of view. It has supernatural elements in the form of gods, miracles and monsters. Invective and didacticism are foreign to it. It is not concerned with the

1 From the introduction to Lermontov's *Izmail-Bei*. See L. D. Opulskaya's article in her edition of *Kazaki* (Moscow 1963), p. 342.
2 J.E. XLVII, 152.

psychology of its heroes. While a valid point can be made about the 'affinity of temper and vision'[1] between Tolstoy and Homer, it would be difficult to prove that Tolstoy's revisions of *The Cossacks* were modelled on the *Iliad* in any significant way.

It would also be wrong, I think, to regard Tolstoy's story as a Cossack idyll. His letters of the Caucasus period are not unduly enthusiastic about the Cossack life—far less so than Olenin's letter to his friend—and while distance lent a somewhat idealistic and nostalgic enchantment, Tolstoy's essentially realistic picture did not exclude murder, theft, drunkenness and promiscuity. The Cossack way of life is not held up as an answer to Olenin's problems. As in most of Tolstoy's fiction, it is the questions which the Tolstoyan hero asks which are of greatest interest to the author. For this reason *The Cossacks* begins where it does—not with the Cossack community, or tribal warfare, but with Olenin in his Moscow setting—and ends with Olenin returning to his regiment, and not with a conventional dénouement. Perhaps, as Mr Bayley says, we are trapped by Olenin and cannot escape from him. Are we to have *The Cossacks*, he asks pertinently, or *The Cossacks as seen by Olenin*?[2] This is an important question; and the mixing of the epic and the subjective strains seems decidedly un-Homeric. The ubiquity of Olenin, however, and his search for happiness do provide a unifying, cohesive force to the story. What is happiness? Is it love for a woman? Is it work? Is it self-sacrifice?

'Happiness is this!' he said to himself. 'Happiness consists in living for others.' (Ch. 20)

'Self-renunciation is all stuff and nonsense. It's all pride, an escape from the unhappiness one has earned, a means to avoid envying other people's happiness. Live for others and do good! Why, when in my heart there is nothing but love for myself and the desire to love her and live her life with her?' (Ch. 33)

Whatever it is, Olenin does not find it. What he finds is the incompatibility of two ways of life with no common premises.

[1] G. Steiner, *Tolstoy or Dostoevsky* (New York 1959), p. 81.
[2] J. Bayley, *Tolstoy and the Novel* (London 1966), p. 263.

His is not so much a class problem—the conscience-stricken aristocrat unable to renounce his class—but the problem of a thinking man unable to renounce his mind. Even on his way to the Caucasus Olenin thinks how he will educate the wild Cossack girl of his dreams, teach her to speak French, to read the French classics, to learn foreign languages. Whatever the artificialities of the use of the French language in Russia and whatever the inadequacies of a Western-style education, Tolstoy, like Olenin, cannot escape the consequences of them. There is no intellectual fodder for Olenin in the Caucasus, only the 'wisdom' of an old man who tells him that it is not a sin to look at a woman and that when you are dead the grass will grow over you. Eroshka has many attractive sides to his character—warmth, humanity, courage, comradeship—but he is after all a rather comic reprobate. Lukashka is a simple, friendly and manly Cossack, but also a horse-thief and a gadabout. And needless to say Maryana never has any French lessons!

If *The Cossacks* is not an idyll, neither is it, as some Soviet critics claim, a demonstration of the natural superiority of that amorphous category, 'the people'. 'The idea of the superiority of the people, their consciousness, their labour-based morality over the moral worthlessness and degeneracy of the nobility is the main idea of the story,'[1] writes one recent critic. Lukashka is seen as 'a man of toil'. It is not quite clear by what criterion Mirsky regards the Cossacks as 'hopelessly superior'[2] to the much more moral, but civilised and consequently contaminated, Olenin, unless it be the very naïve one that if 'civilization' is bad, the lack of it must be good. Is work in itself morally good, regardless of the end to which it is directed? Is it 'right' to kill a man or steal a horse because it is 'natural'? Of course Olenin is not an exemplary human being. Of course Tolstoy scores many points against his own class and its idleness, extravagance, hypocrisy, spleen, and lack of

[1] R. B. Zaborova, '*Kazaki*' in *L. N. Tolstoi, Sbornik Statei* (Moscow 1955). pp. 135–61.
[2] D. S. Mirsky, *A History of Russian Literature* (London 1949), p. 257.

concern for social inferiors. But Olenin, although he is a nobleman, is also concerned with how to live and why. The Cossacks are not; at least not in Tolstoy's story, where no thoughts except *carpe diem* trouble their serenity and no tensions are allowed to develop. Olenin is weak, and inclined to an idle life. But he is not satisfied with it or with himself. By this criterion one would consider him at least the moral equal of his Cossack friends.

The Cossacks is an intriguing amalgam of styles and compositional devices, and characteristically Tolstoyan mannerisms. The opening paragraph pointedly divides the gentry from the working people. For the former it is still evening but for the latter it is already morning. A judicious *aperçu* of the self-centredness of human discourse paves the way for a short interior monologue in which Olenin reveals the narcissistic features common to many of Tolstoy's heroes. A switch to author's narrative enables Tolstoy to fill in Olenin's biography, which to all intents and purposes is Tolstoy's own. The device of allowing the hero to doze off at the start of his journey serves the double purpose of exploring his disconnected thoughts and memories (a somewhat similar trick is used in *A Landowner's Morning*) and of gently poking fun at the traditional literary image of the Caucasus. As Olenin approaches the Caucasus, romantic dreams give way to breath-taking reality as the beauty of the mountains is conveyed in a lyrically heightened passage which culminates in a rhetorical coda:

'Now it has begun,' a solemn voice seemed to say to him. And the road and the distant line of the Terek and the villages and the people—it all seemed a joke no longer. He would look at the sky and think of—the mountains. He would look at himself or Vanyusha and again—the mountains. Two Cossacks ride by, their holstered rifles swinging rhythmically behind their backs, a blur of colour from their horses' grey and bay legs...and the mountains. Smoke is rising from a village beyond the Terek...and the mountains. The sun has risen and is shining on the Terek, now visible beyond the reeds...and the mountains. A cart is coming from the village and women, beautiful young women, are passing by...and the mountains. Chechens are scouring the steppe and here am I driving along unafraid, with a gun, youth, strength...and the mountains.[1]

Chapters 4 to 9 are Tolstoy's concession to Homer. Olenin is temporarily discarded, to be replaced by an epic and heroic description of the works and days of a Caucasian village and the warlike prowess of Lukashka and Eroshka. The opening lines of Chapter 4 lower the tone abruptly, and the consciously contrived coda of the previous chapter is immediately followed by the sober narrative of *Sevastopol in December*, as geographical and ethnographical details are conscientiously retailed:

The whole stretch of the Terek, some fifty miles long, on which the villages of the Greben Cossacks are situated, is of a uniform character as regards both landscape and population...

As the background begins to be peopled with Cossacks the section builds up to an exciting climax in which Lukashka kills a Chechen tribesman and makes merry. It is now time to bring Olenin on the scene and to draw him into the lives of Eroshka, Lukashka and Maryana—the sub-structure of the plot. A memorable passage of natural description paints the joys of honest country toil so dear to Tolstoy's heart:

It was August. For days on end there had not been a cloud in the sky; the sun was unbearably hot and a warm wind had been blowing since morning, raising clouds of hot sand from drifts and from the road and carrying it in the air through the reeds, the trees and the villages. The grass and the leaves on the trees were covered in dust; the roads and dried-up salt marshes were hard and bare and re-sounded underfoot. The water in the Terek had long since sub-sided and had rapidly run away and dried up in the ditches. The slimy banks of the village pond had been trodden bare by cattle and all day long you could hear the splashing of water and the shouts of girls and boys. The sandy reed beds in the steppe were already drying up and during the day the cattle would run lowing into the fields. Wild animals wandered into the more remote reed beds and into the hills beyond the Terek. Clouds of mosquitoes and gnats swarmed over the lowlands and villages. The snowy mountain

[1] Ch. 3.

peaks were covered in grey mist. The air was thin and evil smelling. It was rumoured that Chechens had forded the shallow river and were prowling about on this side. Every evening the sun set in a glowing red blaze. It was the busiest time of the year. The whole population of the villages thronged the melon fields and vineyards. The vineyards, thick with twining verdure, lay in cool, deep shade. Heavy ripe clusters of grapes could be seen on all sides through the broad translucent leaves. Creaking carts laden with black grapes were strung along the dusty road leading to the vineyards. Clusters of them, crushed by the wheels, lay on the dusty road. Boys and girls in shirts stained with grape-juice ran after their mothers with grapes in their hands and mouths. Workers in tattered clothes with baskets of grapes on their strong shoulders continually passed one on the road. Cossack girls with kerchiefs tied over their foreheads were driving bullocks harnessed to carts laden high with grapes. Soldiers who met them would ask them for grapes and a girl would clamber up into the cart without stopping, take an armful of grapes and throw them into the skirts of a soldier's coat. In some yards the grapes were already being pressed. The smell of the emptied skins filled the air. You could see blood-red troughs under the sheds in the yards and Nogay workers with their trousers rolled up and their calves stained with juice. Pigs grunted as they gorged themselves on the skins and rolled in them. The flat roofs of the outhouses were strewn with black and amber clusters drying in the sun. Crows and magpies swarmed round the roofs picking up seeds and flitting from place to place.

The fruits of the year's labours were being joyfully gathered in and this year the fruit was unusually good and plentiful.[1]

This is a good specimen of Tolstoy's landscape painting, as crowded and animated as a Breughel, but with the stubborn repetition of a few basic motifs (a dozen mentions of grapes and clusters in fewer than a dozen sentences). It owes nothing to literary tradition or the Caucasian clichés of his predecessors. As a comparative beginner in the art of fiction, however, Tolstoy felt himself obliged to follow the technical example of earlier novelists, in some respects at least. His tribute to the current epistolary vogue was a stray chapter in the form of an

[1] Ch. 29.

unposted letter—an alternative device to interior monologue as a means of revealing Olenin's thoughts; while his subject required him to include some Cossack folksongs, of which he had heard and recorded no small number.

The Cossacks has all the ingredients of a successful story, combining as it does a basically interesting theme, exotic colour, stylistic variety and a wealth of unusual detail with a broad and sympathetic understanding of a wide range of characters, posing moral questions without passing moral judgments. It weaves together the themes of most of Tolstoy's earlier writings, and while it leads back to the trilogy *Childhood*, *Boyhood* and *Youth* inasmuch as it is concerned with a whole phase of development of a Tolstoyan hero, it also incorporates the experiences of the intervening years of Tolstoy's life and anticipates some important problems of his later fiction in which his semi-autobiographical characters grow older with their author. Turgenev and Bunin, Rolland and Hemingway, are but a few of the major novelists to have acknowledged its influence and appeal, and it marks an important milestone in its author's career as the first work by him to be translated into a foreign language and to achieve success abroad.

4

LITERARY DOLDRUMS

The years 1856–63 saw the publication of a number of stories which, with the exception of *The Cossacks*, did little to enhance Tolstoy's reputation. These were difficult years, when the transition from an irregular active life with no immediate concern for the need to make a living to the more humdrum social round of the town and the search for a regular and satisfying occupation produced an unsettling effect. On his return to Petersburg in 1856 he was enthusiastically received in literary circles and both right- and left-wing littérateurs fought to secure his services. He became attached to and later estranged from the devotees of art for art's sake. He maintained an uneasy personal relationship with Turgenev. In the intellectual debates between Slavophils and Westerners he gave his allegiance to neither side but was always ready to inveigh against any theory or philosophy presumptuous enough to offer formulae or solutions to life's problems. These years were the time of his travels through Europe, his short visits to Germany, France, Switzerland, Italy and England, his meetings with Froebel, Proudhon and Herzen. They saw what appeared to be his gradual retirement from literature and his devotion to the cause of educating his peasants at Yasnaya Polyana, founding a school and editing an educational journal. They were clouded by the death of his brother and the divorce of his sister. Above all they were marked by a diligent search for the 'ideal woman', a number of tentative love affairs with women of his own class and a passionate liaison with a married serf who bore him a son.

Tolstoy's diaries and letters give us a fairly clear, if incomplete picture of his mental and spiritual development at this time. Although he moved in the circles of the Moscow and Petersburg intelligentsia he was not himself an 'intellectual', and while he had certain convictions and beliefs, they did not tally with any recognisable conservative, liberal or radical viewpoint. If he associated more with the Slavophils, with

Druzhinin, Botkin and Annenkov and the right-wing elements of society, it was rather because he liked them as individuals than because he agreed with their politics. His views altered with the company he kept. He would change from a Westerner to a Slavophil and back in the course of an evening. Eykhenbaum once called him a nihilist of the right.[1] He liked upsetting other people's convictions. Although hostile to 'progress' in the sense of industrialisation, capitalist expansion or the building of railways, and to a system of priorities which put telegraphs, roads and ships before literature, he criticised the Slavophils for their 'backwardness' and expressed the fear that he might himself 'lag behind his age', 'not in the sense of not knowing what sort of hats and waistcoats are being worn but of not knowing what outstanding new book has been published and what problem is engaging Europe...'.[2] Indifferent or hostile to constitutional government and unimpressed by what he saw of parliamentary democracy in the West, he noted that 'all governments are alike in their extent of good and evil: the best ideal is anarchy'.[3] Nationalism he regarded as 'a unique obstacle to the development of freedom',[4] although he had his moments of jingoism during the Crimean War and again during the Polish insurrection of 1863. On one and the same page of his notebook he could write: 'The future of Russia lies with the Cossacks...freedom, equality and compulsory military service for everyone' and 'It is only necessary to put a uniform on a person, separate him from his family and beat a drum in order to make a beast of him.'[5] Contemptuous of aristocratic privilege and indolence, he could also write, in a positive sense: 'Aristocratic feeling is worth a lot.'[6] Congenitally hostile to the dogmas of Orthodoxy, he still classed himself as a believer and found inspiration, though not rational satisfaction, in the ritual of the Orthodox Church. In a letter to his neighbour Arseneva, whose ward he was and with whom he contemplated marriage, he wrote in 1856: 'You know that I

---

[1] B. M. Eykhenbaum, *Moi Vremennik* (Moscow 1928), p. 110.
[2] J.E. LX, 117.   [3] J.E. XLVII, 208.   [4] J.E. XLVII, 204.
[5] J.E. XLVII, 204.   [6] J.E. XLVIII, 3.

am a believer, but it is very possible that my faith differs greatly from yours, and this question should not be touched upon, especially by people who want to love each other. Religion is a great thing, especially for women...Guard it, never speak about it and fulfil its dogmas without going to extremes.'[1] Again he wrote: 'The nearness to death...is the best argument for faith...Better to accept the old, time-honoured, comforting and childishly simple [faith]. This is not rational, but you feel it.'[2] Instinct and intuition counted for much with him. His powerful mind seemed able to demolish any logical theory, but only to throw him back on irrational hunches, faith, or the activity of the heart which by their very nature defy logic. That he was in no doubt about the quality of his intellect may be seen from his correspondence with Arseneva. 'My strength is mind, your strength is heart...You will teach me to love, I will teach you to think.'[3] Small wonder that the marriage did not take place! Elsewhere he confessed to himself, 'The sort of mind which I have and which I like in others is the sort which does not believe in any theory...'[4] Caught between the Scylla of faith and the Charybdis of reason, he lived in a state of constant turmoil, unsure of himself and deeply suspicious of people who subscribed to any man-made philosophy. It was bad enough, no doubt, to have to believe in God when all your reason revolted against it; but it was much better than believing in Chernyshevsky.

If on his arrival in Petersburg Tolstoy was ambitious for literary fame and believed in the value of art for its own sake, it did not take him long to question his assumptions and take up a diametrically opposite stance. In 1855 he noted: 'My object is literary fame: the good which I can do by my writing.'[5] Four years later he wrote, albeit in a somewhat jocular vein, to his friend the poet Fet: 'I shan't write any more stories. It's disgraceful when you think—people are weeping and dying and getting married, while I go on writing stories about "how she loved him". It's stupid and disgraceful.'[6]

[1] J.E. LX, 128.   [2] J.E. XLVII, 207.   [3] J.E. LX, 116.

[4] J.E. XLVII, 212.   [5] J.E. XLVII, 60.   [6] J.E. LX, 307.

And, in a less playful tone, to the critic and author Druzhinin:
'Life is short, and to waste it in one's adult years on writing
the sort of stories I've been writing makes one ashamed. I can
and must and will do something...'[1]

It is difficult to say how much this change in attitude was due
to wounded self-esteem, the sense that his early success as a
writer had not been maintained, the knowledge that an editor
had actually returned a story as unfit for publication, and how
much to a nagging consciousness that he was not in fact 'doing
good' by his writing. At all events one gets the impression that
he was not only critical of his own efforts, but that his general
reaction to contemporary literature (with the exception of the
writings of his personal friends like Fet and Aksakov) was
uncharitable and at times decidedly cold. This is particularly
true in relation to Turgenev, a fact which no doubt may be
explained by his personal animosity towards him. *Asya* he
dismissed as rubbish. *Rudin* left no impression on him although
he later recalled hearing it read for the first time and referred
to it as 'a false and contrived thing'. A reading of *On the Eve*
prompted him to say to Fet: 'Writing stories generally is
futile, but even more so for people who are melancholy and
don't know what they want from life.'[2] Turgenev is accused
of banality, and lack of humanity and sympathy for people.
'The girl', he adds (i.e. the heroine of *On the Eve*) 'is hopelessly
bad. "Oh, how I love you...she had long eyelashes."'[3] But
still, surprisingly enough, he finds it better than *A Nest of
Gentlefolk*. *Fathers and Sons* he calls 'cold', and coldness is a
failing he could not overlook. In comparing Dickens on the
one hand and Thackeray and Gogol on the other, he draws
attention to the love with which Dickens handles his characters,
while 'Thackeray and Gogol are accurate, spiteful, artistic, but
not kind'.[4] Tolstoy read much Thackeray, but with little
comment. *Dead Souls* is praised because he finds there 'many
of his own ideas', but the later Gogol is severely criticised,
and, as a man, dismissed as 'simply worthless'. Ostrovsky's

[1] J.E. LX, 308.   [2] J.E. LX, 324.
[3] J.E. LX, 423.   [4] J.E. XLVII, 178.

Storm is labelled a 'lamentable work'. Even Pushkin is not spared. While re-reading his lyrics, poems and dramas and praising the *Gypsies* he notes: 'All the other poems except *Evgenii Onegin* are dreadful rubbish.' None of his criticisms, it will be seen, are helpful or illuminating. Whether positive or negative they are brief, impressionistic and categorical. His comments on his own stories are generally unflattering—again with little indication why. Special praise is reserved for George Eliot's *Scenes of Clerical Life* ('Fortunate', he says, 'are people like the English who imbibe with their mother's milk the Christian teaching, and in such a purified and exalted form as evangelical protestantism'),[1] for *Faust* and *Werther* and the *Iliad*, but not for *Adam Bede*. Shakespeare's *Henry IV* is dispatched with a devastatingly laconic 'No!'

Interspersed between the terse records of his likes and dislikes are many simple, sententious and acute *pensées*. 'The Gospel words "judge not" are profoundly true in art: recount, portray, but do not judge.'[2] 'The political excludes the artistic because, in order to prove, it must be one-sided.'[3] At this time, however, literary precept came more easily than literary practice, and on the whole the years 1856–63 were difficult and unhappy ones for Tolstoy. His position remained unestablished, he felt unsure of his vocation, critical, irritable and restless. Turgenev found him difficult to fathom, but summed him up (before their quarrel) in phrases which have the ring of authenticity: 'He is a strange man; I haven't met his like and I don't quite understand him. A mixture of poet, Calvinist, fanatic, and *barich* [a derogatory term for a young landowner], there is something reminiscent of Rousseau but more honest than Rousseau—highly moral, and at the same time unsympathetic.'[4]

During these difficult years, Tolstoy's literary output was not especially high. *The Cossacks* apart, his main published works, in chronological order of publication, were *The Snowstorm* (1856), *Two Hussars* (1856), *Meeting a Moscow Acquaintance in the Detachment* (1856), *Lucerne* (1857), *Albert* (1858), *Three*

---

[1] J.E. LX, 300. [2] J.E. XLVII, 203.
[3] J.E. XLVIII, 10. [4] *Nasha Starina*, *12* (1914), 1073.

Deaths (1859), *Family Happiness* (1859) and *Polikushka* (1863). In their different ways they are a very clear reflection of Tolstoy's beliefs, interests and prejudices, but from a literary point of view their compass is too small to accommodate the overt didacticism and moral pamphleteering which in diluted form in a larger work could be taken painlessly, and perhaps even enjoyed. In a word, they do not give sufficient rein to the reader's imagination. *The Snowstorm* grew out of an incident on a journey from the Caucasus. It is an unhappy amalgam of narrative description and recollections of childhood which come and go as the narrator dozes off on his journey through the night. (*The Cossacks*, it will be remembered, employs a similar device.) In the manner of Turgenev's *A Sportsman's Sketches* it paints largely sympathetic portraits of ordinary working people—the various peasant drivers who brave the storm. There is no suspense or excitement about the story, nor does the snowstorm lead to complications and adventures of the kind which Pushkin crowded with far greater economy into a much smaller space in his tale of the same title. Perhaps the only point of literary interest is the device, familiar enough in Tolstoy's later writing, of connecting the details of dreams with phenomena happening simultaneously in the outside world (a bell ringing outside appearing in the dream as a dog barking or an organ playing), and the moment of waking from a dream with the last sensation carrying over from the dream (the sensation of something pressing on one's foot being so strong that the dreamer rubs his foot immediately on awakening).

For his next published story Tolstoy took as his theme the contrast between the past and the present in the persons of a father and son of markedly different character, the younger generation suffering by comparison with the older. The basis of the story is a simple juxtaposition, neat and regular, and executed with an almost geometrical precision. The first eight chapters are devoted to the father, the second eight to the son. An amusing and ironical, if cumbersome and sententious, preface rings the praises of the good old days in a lengthy period, in fact one sentence, of a type which Tolstoy was particularly fond of using (for example in *The Decembrists*): 'In the 1800s, at a time when there were no railways, no highroads, no gaslight [etc., etc.]—in those naïve days when... when...when...[etc., etc.]—in the naïve days of Masonic Lodges, Martinists, the Tugenbund [etc., etc.]—there was a meeting of landowners in the provincial town of K.' Tolstoy had been reading *The Newcomes* shortly before, and the similarity with a passage from the 'Overture' to Thackeray's novel ('There was once a time when the sun used to shine brighter than it appears to do in this latter half of the nineteenth century...') is particularly striking. The second half of the story (Chapter 9) starts by picking up the preface to the first part in a style and idiom which immediately recall the construction of *Sevastopol in May*, and within this framework Turbin father and son, after an interval of twenty years, visit the same place, meet the same people and enact the same sequence of card-playing and philandering—but in a totally different spirit and with a totally different effect. The father is a handsome roué, gambler and seducer, but he is gallant, generous and charming. The son inherits the same weaknesses, but behaves in a mean, cold and calculating way. Tolstoy's English biographer, Aylmer Maude, draws attention to the English flavour of *The Two Hussars* when he calls it 'a rollicking tale with flashes of humour resembling Charles Lever's'[1] and it has been well observed that Turbin *père* is portrayed in a somewhat Dickensian manner, while Turbin *fils* is in the Thackeray vein. Translated into Russian terms, the father is a Pushkin hero, the son a Gogolian. 'One might say', observes Eykhenbaum, exaggerating his valid point for the sake of emphasis, 'that in *The Two Hussars* a comparison is drawn between Dubrovsky and Khlestakov.'[2] In its jocular, lighthearted tone, its wealth of plot interest, its absence of any serious thought, its surface level of description and its lack of psychological profundity, the story is hardly typical of its

[1] A. Maude, *The Life of Tolstoy* (Oxford 1930), I, 173.
[2] B. M. Eykhenbaum, *Lev Tolstoi, kniga pervaya, 50-e gody*, p. 252.

author—perhaps indeed one should call it an 'entertainment', and within its unpretentious limits a very successful one.

Less successful are Tolstoy's next two stories,[1] which have the common theme of the artist and society. *Albert* owes its origin to an encounter between Tolstoy and a gifted but drink-besotted violinist, which is elaborated into a conflict between the brilliant, unstable and childishly helpless artist-alcoholic and a Tolstoyan philanthropist, determined to save the artist for society and at the same time to reap the satisfaction of his own good deed. The trouble with the story, which came with difficulty and had five different titles at different stages of its composition, is that there is nothing to suggest the brilliance of the musician—merely the author's verbal assurance. In *Doctor Zhivago* Pasternak succeeded in creating a poet by allowing him to write great poems. In *Anna Karenina* Tolstoy managed to create a convincing portrait of a painter by showing how the ordinary trivial incidents of everyday life, his quarrels with his wife, his shopping at the tobacconist's, were intimately bound up with his own creative life. With music the problem is more difficult, as Thomas Mann found in trying to convince readers of *Doctor Faustus* that Leverkühn is a great composer, although the method Tolstoy was later to use with Mikhailov would appear to be equally applicable to the art of music—one can feel the temper and mood of the artist and something of his spiritual elation and depression. But in the last resort one has to take it on trust that a fictional painter or composer or violinist is a great artist. Tolstoy's Albert is a man of 'intuition', not of theories or ideas; whatever he says or does or whatever he plays is done instinctively. So far so good. But what does he do when he is not playing? He drinks. There is no other dimension to his life. In an early draft Tolstoy had envisaged broadening the scope of the story by introducing an artist and a connoisseur of music to discuss Albert's case and debate his usefulness to society in words reminiscent of the questions put to the poet by the crowd in Pushkin's poem.[2] But the final

---

[1] *Meeting a Moscow Acquaintance in the Detachment*, which appeared in 1856, failed to make any impression at all.   [2] *The Poet and the Crowd* (1828).

version is less ambitious. Tolstoy himself was very dissatisfied with it, but sent it nevertheless to *The Contemporary*. Nekrasov decided he could not publish it for the following reasons: 'The thing mostly to blame for your failure is the unsuccessful choice of subject which, quite apart from the fact that it is very hackneyed, is almost impossibly difficult and thankless. While the seamy side of your hero is plain for all to see, how can you express in a tangible and convincing manner his brilliant side? And if that is not there, there is no story...'[1] Tolstoy duly revised the story and Nekrasov published it with grave misgivings, which were justified by its cold reception. Equally coldly received by critics and readers alike was *Lucerne*, which focuses on the attitude of society to the artist rather than on the personality of the artist himself. Its overt tendentiousness and irascibility really puts it beyond the range of *belles lettres* into the category of polemical journalism. Its origin can be found in a diary entry for 7 July 1857 when Tolstoy was staying at a Swiss tourist centre, and in a long letter to his friend Botkin. The diary reads:

Walked to *privathaus*. On the way back at night—cloudy, with the moon breaking through—heard several marvellous voices. Two bell towers on a wide street. Little man with guitar singing Tyrolean songs—superb. Gave him something and invited him to sing opposite the Schweizerhof. He got nothing and walked away ashamed, the crowd laughing as he went...Caught him up and invited him to the Schweizerhof for a drink. They put us in a separate room. Singer vulgar but pathetic. We drank. The waiter laughed and the doorkeeper sat down. This infuriated me—swore at them and got terribly worked up...[2]

The incident is inflated into a story and then deflated again into a paragraph at the end of it, as though implying that the content of the story could really be expressed in a few lines and emphasising for the reader's benefit that 'this is fact, not fiction':

On the 7th of July 1857 a poverty-stricken strolling player sang and played the guitar for half an hour in front of the Schweizerhof

---

[1] Nekrasov to Tolstoy, 16 December 1857.   [2] J.E. XLVII, 140.

Hotel in Lucerne where the very rich people stay. About a hundred people listened to him. The singer asked them all three times to give him something. Not one of them gave him anything, and many people laughed at him.

The very rich people being mainly English, Tolstoy prefaces *Lucerne* with a withering denunciation of their arrogance, complacency, insensitivity, and cold, silent awareness of their own superiority. 'And yet not all these frozen people are stupid and unfeeling,' he adds in a moment of generosity; 'then why do they deprive themselves of one of life's greatest pleasures— the enjoyment that comes from the intercourse of man with man?' The trouble with these national generalisations, and in the same context the pointed contrast between the irregularity of the beauty of nature and the artificially straight, man-made quay built to please the English, is not whether they are true or false, but that they are gratuitously disbursed by the author and do not emerge as deductions which the discriminating reader can make from the characters themselves and their mutual relationships. Tolstoy's peculiar gifts of vital characterisation and searching mental and spiritual analysis are hardly put to use at all. It is true that the narrator allows himself a certain vindictive delight in describing the pleasure of deliberately not making way for a complacent Englishman but jostling him with his elbow—a psychological moment which brings to mind a similar scene in *Notes from the Underground* where the hero asserts his individuality by crowding off the pavement a man who has offended him—Tolstoy's healthy anger contrasting typically with the poisonous spleen of Dostoevsky's 'underground man'. But psychologically the story does not register, and one's reactions are purely mental ones to the logic or otherwise of the statements put out. Is it true that this incident would have been impossible in any French, German or Italian village? Could a hundred people, even though they were English, remain almost completely silent throughout a meal? What basis of comparison is there between a luxury hotel in Switzerland and a cheap Paris *pension* as a criterion for judging the respective habits and manners of the English and the French? These *ex cathedra* statements are the prerogative of the journalist, not the artist. There is no characterisation. The singer is given no identity. He has virtually nothing to say. The incident over, there is some tedious moralising and rhetoric to the effect that the ways of God are inscrutable, and that the poor downtrodden singer may perhaps be happier than the rich well-fed tourist, and that the author has no right to pity the singer or be angry with the aristocracy. Needless to say, the story was not well received by Tolstoy's friends, the Botkins and the Annenkovs, who could hardly be expected to sympathise with his contemptuous attitude to educated Westerners. Turgenev very shrewdly summed up *Lucerne* as a mixture of Rousseau, Thackeray and the short Orthodox Catechism—'Go your own way and go on writing,' he said, 'only not moral-political sermons like *Lucerne*, of course!'[1] If the story is still remembered today, it is as the first piece of Tolstoy's fiction which is unambiguously, consistently and irascibly hostile to the West European *bourgeoisie*.

Three Deaths reads like a parable illustrating a simple idea, expressed by the familiar Tolstoyan device of contrast. In his own words:

My idea was: three creatures died—a lady, a peasant and a tree. The lady is pathetic and repulsive because she lied all her life and lied on the point of death. Christianity as she understands it has not solved the problem of life and death for her. Why die when you want to live? With her mind and her imagination she believes in the future promises of Christianity, but all her being kicks against it and she has no other consolation (except a pseudo-Christian one). She is repulsive and pathetic. The peasant dies peacefully just because he is not a Christian. His religion is different, although from habit he observed the Christian ritual. His religion is nature, which he lived with. With his own hands he felled trees, sowed rye and cut it, and slaughtered sheep. Sheep were born, children were born, old men died—and he fully understood this law and never transgressed it like the lady, but looked it fairly and squarely in the face. *Une brute*, you say, and what's wrong with being *une brute*? *Une brute* is

[1] *Tolstoi i Turgenev: Perepiska* (Moscow 1928), p. 40.

happiness and beauty, harmony with the whole world, not discord, as with the lady. The tree dies peacefully, nobly and beautifully. Beautifully because it does not lie, does not break down, is not afraid, has no regrets. This is my idea...[1]

Three Deaths is a fairly faithful illustration of this idea. The overt class message is not likely to convince those who do not believe that because a person is a 'lady' she is for that reason more likely to be mendacious and repulsive, or that because a man is a peasant he is *ipso facto* likely to have a more beautiful and harmonious soul. The story is too short for the characters to be developed, and one has to accept the author's word that the one has more inner peace of mind than the other for the reasons implied. The religious message that the letter of Christianity is mortifying but the pagan spirit of 'natural' religion is quickening evokes a more sympathetic response than the thesis that 'ladies' are nasty because they are 'ladies'. But Leskov handles it more artistically, because more discreetly, in his powerful story *At the End of the World*. The death of the tree is an embarrassment. How can a tree die nobly and fearlessly? Or ignobly and with trepidation? In fact Tolstoy, in recapitulating his idea in the letter quoted above, appears to have forgotten that he had described the tree as 'tottering on its roots in fear'. The background to the story, as befits its sympathy for the natural life, is the seasons of the year. It is autumn, cold, grey, damp and nasty when the peasant dies and when nature is dying with him. It is spring when the lady dies, and all that is natural bursts into life. Although the story is so short, there is no mistaking Tolstoy's stamp on every page. The husband of the dying woman thinks of the consequences for himself of her death. The dying peasant who gives his new boots away, instinctively acts for the good of others. The unavailing presence of the doctor and the priest at the woman's bedside emphasises Tolstoy's prejudice against the ritual practices of sacred and secular healers—the negative side of his positive belief that in the important crises of life and death,

[1] J.E. v, 301.

help comes not from without but from within. The opportunity is not missed to draw attention to the fact that the husband addresses his wife in French, not Russian. It is a measure of the artistic limitations of this story that Tolstoy, who rightly believed that a work of literature should not be able to be summarised but is capable of being expressed only in the way in which it has been expressed, should have been able to condense the full essence of *Three Deaths* into a dozen lines of summary without much sacrifice or distortion.

Tolstoy's next published work of fiction, *Family Happiness*, was written against the background of a topical social problem which was very close to his heart—the place of women in society and in the home. The novels of George Sand, the writings of Proudhon and Michelet, and Tolstoy's own courtship of Arseneva all served to remind him that he was not married but would like to be, and that he must first clarify his ideas about the nature of love, the purpose of marriage and the rôle of the ideal husband and wife. 'Il faut que tu crées ta femme,' wrote Michelet. Tolstoy agreed. His letters to Arseneva (1856), with whom he seriously contemplated marriage, are the best source material for *Family Happiness*, although a good case has been made out to support Tolstoy's liking for the climate of ideas generated by Proudhon's *De la Justice dans la Révolution et dans L'Église*, parts of which are devoted to marriage, and Michelet's *L'Amour*, both of which appeared in the year (1858) when Tolstoy was making his first start on *Family Happiness*, and both of which defend marriage against the recently fashionable advocacy of 'free love'. The letters to Arseneva, which advise her among other things to go for a walk every day and to put on her corsets and stockings by herself, and which reproach her for her bad taste in hats, also plan the details of the ideal married life with scrupulous and pedantic care. They recommend where to live in summer and winter, how many rooms an apartment should have and on what floor, what the husband should do to make his peasants happy, what he should teach his wife, and how she should divide her time between music, reading, and helping her husband... With these plans in mind, Tolstoy embarks on his first attempt at treating the theme of love in fiction, and not surprisingly does so in a calculating, static and predictable manner, making his characters play to the rules of the game as *he* understands them. The story is told in the first person, and takes the form of the reminiscences of a married woman—her courtship, marriage, brief idyllic happiness, estrangement, and eventual reconciliation based on the subordination of selfish love to the wider ideal of duty to the family ('love of my children and the father of my children'). The woman emerges a little more fully than the man—she may have owed something to Esther in *Bleak House*,[1] as well as to Arseneva—and it is a remarkable achievement on Tolstoy's part to have conveyed the innocent awakening of a young girl's love in a manner which many women readers have found truthful and convincing. But it is poetry of atmosphere rather than subtlety of characterisation which one remembers in the early chapters of the story, which have a greater charm than the later schematised version of married life; for after all, Tolstoy had courted Arseneva, not married her. The following passage is the prelude to a moonlight walk which Masha, the narrator, takes with her future husband and her chaperone:

'Just look what a night it is!' Sergei Mikhailych called out from the drawing-room, as he stood by the open French window looking into the garden.

We joined him, and it really was such a night as I have never seen since. A full moon shone above the house behind us so that it was not visible, and half the shadow cast by the roof, the pillars and the verandah awning lay slanting and foreshortened on the gravel path and the round lawn. Everything else was bright and bedecked with the silver of the dew and the moonlight. The broad path through the flower beds—on one side of which the shadows of the dahlias and their supports lay aslant—ran on, all bright and cold and with its rough gravel glittering, until it vanished in the mist. The roof of the conservatory shone bright through the trees and a gathering mist rose from the glen. Bright too were the branches of the lilac

---

[1] I. Katarsky, *Dikkens v Rossii* (Moscow 1966), p. 299.

bushes, already partly leafless. One could make out every single dew-drenched flower. Light and shade so mingled together that the avenues seemed to be not paths and trees, but transparent houses, swaying and vibrating. To our right, in the shadow of the house, everything was black, indistinguishable and uncanny. But all the brighter and more conspicuous in the darkness was the fantastic, leafy crown of a poplar tree which for some reason was oddly poised there aloft in the bright light close to the house, and had not vanished far away into the retreating dark blue sky.

'Let's go for a walk,' I said.

Katya agreed, but told me to put on my goloshes.

'There's no need to,' I said. 'Sergei Mikhailych will give me his arm.'

As if that could stop me getting my feet wet...[1]

Typical of Tolstoy is the juxtaposition of light and darkness, the repeated emphasis on a single word—in this case 'bright'—the careful description of shadows and of what they obscure or leave revealed, the simple, spontaneous remarks punctuating a lyrical narrative which never soars too high but keeps close to the earth which is the source of Tolstoy's power—and the occasional, quiet flash of humour. There are many such passages in the first half of *Family Happiness*, but they are less frequent in the later stages where interest in mood and its associations with nature gives place to a predetermined transition from one state to another. The dialogue becomes at times inept, and there are some embarrassing passages which might have been culled from an old-fashioned schoolgirl's magazine: when, for example, the wife is momentarily tempted by the prospect of a society liaison:

I was so longing to throw myself headlong into the abyss of forbidden pleasures which was suddenly opening up and drawing me in...

'I am so unhappy,' I thought, 'let more and more misfortunes fall upon my head.'

He embraced me with one arm and bent over my face. 'Let shame and sin be heaped still higher on my head.'

[1] Ch. 3.

'Je vous aime,' he whispered in a voice which was so like my husband's. I thought of my husband and child as erstwhile dear creatures with whom all was now over. But suddenly round the corner I heard the voice of L.M. calling me. I pulled myself together, snatched my arm away and without a glance at him, almost ran after L.M.[1]

This is hardly sounding the depths of a woman's heart. Nor is the motivation for the heroine's renunciation of society a convincing one. Why does she return to her husband? Is it a change of heart, or simply a sense of pique at being out of her depth? Or just a desire for peace and quiet? The husband, too, seems tired. There is a flavour of Turgenev at his most wistful —the past is gone, youth is over, there is no excitement in store but only the desire for a quiet life in which passion is replaced by habit. Will the woman be satisfied? She ought to be, according to the plan. But the story breaks off where it should really start. Towards the end it shows all the signs of hasty composition. Some of its episodic characters are denoted merely by initials. It has no complexity or natural growth; and while its beautiful evocation of the raptures of youthful, romantic love more than compensates for its sketchiness and didacticism, the story as a whole left Tolstoy so dissatisfied that he did not wish to publish it. Was fiction, he wondered, his real calling? Were there not more urgent jobs to be done? In 1860 he wrote to Fet:

There is nothing to prevent lovers of the classics, of whom I am one, seriously reading poems and stories and seriously discussing them. But now we need something else. We don't need to learn, but we do need to teach Martha and Taras at least a little of what we know.[2]

There was an interval of nearly four years before Tolstoy, by this time a married man, ventured into print again with *The Cossacks* (begun ten years previously) and *Polikushka*, which he started in Brussels in 1861, the year of the emancipation of the serfs. In between, his literary efforts had been devoted more or less exclusively to his educational journal *Yasnaya Polyana*.

[1] Ch. 8.   [2] J.E. LX, 325.

And because of his school activities and his close daily contact with peasant children it was only fitting that his next work of fiction should be devoted very largely to the peasantry. *Polikushka* in fact is Tolstoy's first story to have a peasant as its central figure. He is a serf with a tarnished reputation, entrusted by his mistress, who has tried to reform him, with the responsible task of collecting a sum of money from a neighbouring town. He loses the money on the journey home and commits suicide. His baby child is accidentally drowned in its bath. His wife goes out of her mind. Threaded into the plot is the story of another peasant, whose nephew is the victim of the recruiting system and whom he is too mean to buy off. He finds the money, returns it to the mistress and is presented with it, not as a reward but in the belief that it is 'unlucky money'. The peasant is so troubled by his dreams and so persuaded that 'money causes sin' that he uses it to ransom his nephew and reunite him with his family. The story may be read in different ways, for it is neither moralistic nor overtly didactic like the stories of the later 1850s. Those who regard it as a salutary illustration of the theme that money is the root of all evil are rebuked by Tolstoy's former secretary, Gusev, who declares categorically that the basic theme is 'the moral oppression of serfdom'.[1] But this contention ignores the universal applicability of the mental anguish of a man who feels he has let down a person who has helped and trusted him. A Soviet Polikushka might have done the same thing if his 'benefactor' had been his factory manager. The ownership of one person by another, disgraceful as it is, is not the real cause of human misery—not but what a reading of *Polikushka* strengthens one's antipathy to the evils of serfdom, the squalid lives of its victims and the iniquities of the recruiting system. But here the emphasis is surely on the moral dilemma of trust seemingly betrayed, and this is enhanced by the detachment with which Tolstoy writes without betraying his own sympathies and without apportioning vices and virtues, praise and blame, in a schematic and preordained manner. The

[1] N. N. Gusev, *L. N. Tolstoi, Materialy k biografii 1855–1869* (Moscow 1957), p. 586.

tragedy is not the inevitable outcome of serfdom (Rebecca West once somewhat flippantly observed that it could have been avoided if there had been a reliable postal service) but it is enacted against an unlovely background where the peasant Dutlov is, if anything, a more unattractive character than the mistress of the village. Virtually unnoticed by the critics, it won the qualified praise of Turgenev in a letter to Fet and the unqualified disapproval of Fet himself. Turgenev wrote:

After you had gone I read Tolstoy's *Polikushka* and marvelled at the power of his great talent. Only an awful lot of material is wasted and there was no need for him to have drowned the son. It's terrible enough without that. But there are some truly wonderful pages.[1]

Fet, on the other hand, complained:

Everything about *Polikushka* is crumbling, putrid, poverty-stricken, painful...it is all accurate and truthful, but so much the worse for that. It is the deep, broad foot-mark of a giant, but a foot-mark which has turned off into a bog. I am not against the subject, but against the absence of any ideal purity. Venus, arousing desire, is evil. She should only sing of beauty in marble. The stench itself should acquire fragrance in the creative process, after passing through *Das Labyrinth der Brust* of the artist. But *Polikushka* smells of its corrupted environment...[2]

Tolstoy replied:

You are right of course. But there are not many readers like you. *Polikushka* is drivel on the first subject that comes into the head of a man who 'wields a good pen'.[3]

Fet's strictures hardly deserve attention, but it is surprising that none of these writers saw fit to comment on Tolstoy's unusual experiment of describing Polikushka and his background not in standard literary Russian but in a language more appropriate to the manner in which one peasant might talk about another. In his earlier tales Tolstoy had frequently couched the dialogue

[1] A. Fet, *Moi Vospominaniya*, Pt. 2 (Moscow 1890), p. 7.
[2] Unpublished letter. Quoted by N. N. Gusev, *L. N. Tolstoi, Materialy k biografii 1855–1869*, p. 610.
[3] J.E. LXI, 17.

of his soldiers in non-literary form, but this is the first important example of his adapting his own narrative style to the character and milieu he is describing. Patchy and uneven, *Polikushka* is nevertheless a powerful and moving story, the very objectivity of which immediately places it on a higher artistic plane than *Albert* or *Lucerne*.

It is very probable that in the same year as *Polikushka* was published, Tolstoy also wrote *Strider*, which did not, however, appear until 1885. This unorthodox and imaginative story of the life and death of a horse, the central part of which is related by the horse itself, is poignant and affective. The consequences of being different (a piebald and a gelding), the themes of alienation, injustice and the inconstancy of love inevitably arouse pity; while the vision of human beings and their system of private property, incomprehensible from a horse's point of view, provides the sort of opportunity for trenchant and well-aimed satire which some earlier writers found in the juxtaposition of European and oriental civilisations based on widely different conventions.

Tolstoy's marriage to Sonya Behrs which had taken place the year before these last two stories were written, was the most important event in his life, and gave to his writing a new lease of creative energy which lifted it onto an incomparably higher plane. Secure in the newly found stability of married life, and with his educational experiments for the moment at an end, he slowly emerged from the literary doldrums, ready to start work in earnest on the masterpiece which was to occupy him more or less exclusively for the next six years.

5

'WAR AND PEACE'

The foundations of *War and Peace* rest in the deep and lasting interest in history which Tolstoy acquired as a young man. In his early twenties his reading included the standard histories of modern Europe, but it was Russian history, and especially that of his own century, which fascinated him most. Not that he was favourably impressed by much of what he read. The official Russian historian Mikhailovsky-Danilevsky's works on Napoleon's invasion of Russia and Thiers' volumes on the same period provoked him to write as a young man of twenty-four: 'To compile a true and accurate History of Europe in this century—there is a task for a life-time.'[1] As his reading continued, he became more convinced of the inadequacy or inaccuracy of much of what he read and of the enormity of the gulf separating the truth of history from the truth of the historian, until eventually he conceived the idea of making his own contribution, not by trying to correct the historical record, but by writing a historical novel on a nineteenth-century Russian theme. 'The first germ of an interest in history', he was later to say, 'arises out of contemporary events,'[2] and in his first novel he intended to write about one of his own contemporaries returning home after thirty years of exile in Siberia for his part in the abortive Decembrist rising which ushered in the reign of Nicholas I. 'My Decembrist', he said, 'is to be an enthusiast, a mystic, a Christian, returning to Russia in 1856 with his wife and his son and daughter, and applying his stern and somewhat idealised views to the new Russia.'[3] In fact only three chapters of this novel, *The Decembrists*, were written before Tolstoy abandoned it to turn his attentions to an earlier generation and the weightier theme of Napoleon's invasion of Russia.

The earliest plans and drafts of *War and Peace* date back to

[1] J.E. XLVI, 141.
[2] Quoted by A. Maude, *Life of Tolstoy*, I, 265. [3] J.E. LX, 374.

1863, but six years were to pass before the final volume appeared in book form. In 1873 Tolstoy drastically revised his novel and discarded some of the philosophical and reflective passages altogether. Others, including the second epilogue, were removed piecemeal and reassembled for publication as a separate volume. All the numerous passages in French were translated into Russian. In 1886 Tolstoy's wife (presumably with his tacit acquiescence, though certainly not with his active approval) undid her husband's work and produced a version which is virtually the same as the 1868–9 edition. This has become the definitive text.

The first chapters of *1805*, as the book was originally called when it began to appear in serial form, are entirely devoted to the domestic life of the Rostovs, the Bolkonskys and the Petersburg nobility, and give no hint of the vast scope of what was to come—the battles of 1805, Schöngraben and Austerlitz, the Tilsit interlude, the renewal of hostilities between France and Russia, the campaign of 1812, the battle of Borodino where Prince Andrew Bolkonsky is fatally wounded, the capture of Moscow by Napoleon, the retreat from Moscow and the partisan warfare, the death of Petya Rostov and the expulsion of the French from Russian territory. Seven years pass and the family dramas of the Rostovs and the Bolkonskys are played out. Parents die, children grow up, Nicholas Rostov marries Princess Mary Bolkonsky, Natasha Rostov marries the Tolstoyan 'seeker' Pierre Bezukhov. Life meanders on until Tolstoy interrupts its flow with a long and polemical disquisition on history, free will and historical inevitability.

Needless to say, the course of the novel fluctuated considerably in the process of writing. Prince Andrew himself was an afterthought. As late as 1866 the title was to be *All's Well That Ends Well*. A draft version of that year spares Andrew's life. He recovers from his wounds. But when he comes to a full realisation of Natasha's love for Pierre he sacrifices his own feelings for her so as not to stand in his friend's way. Likewise Sonya, the Rostovs' ward, is moved by Andrew's sacrifice to surrender her claims to Nicholas so that he may be free to marry

Princess Mary. Petya is not killed in battle. There is no hint of Karataev, the peasant agent of Pierre's regeneration. Finally the two couples marry on the same day before Nicholas and Andrew rejoin their units and go with the Russian army to Paris. This is merely one of many discarded attempts to tie the domestic knots and resolve the personal dilemmas of the two major families in *War and Peace*; and it was Tolstoy's apparent preoccupation with purely domestic scenes, especially in the opening chapters of *1805*, that gave rise to the belief that he originally intended to write a sort of family chronicle, a Charlotte Yonge family novel with a military background, but that he changed his purpose and consciously elevated his work into a historical novel which duly became a national epic. The evidence, however, seems to be against such a change of plan. Historical figures, including Napoleon and Alexander, had been introduced into draft versions at a very early stage, while the first drafts of some of the battle scenes were already being written in 1863. The theme of war, the campaign of 1812 and the historical rôle of the leaders of nations and armies all occupied Tolstoy's thoughts from the very first.

The study of the genesis and evolution of the novel, the sources Tolstoy used and the uses to which he put them in transforming history into fiction is an important aid to understanding Tolstoy's technique as a novelist. I have treated these problems elsewhere at some length,[1] and here they will be merely indicated without elaboration. The numerous draft versions and plans of *War and Peace* are considerably longer than the finished novel itself. This is partly the result of the difficult transition from the Decembrist theme to that of the Napoleonic wars and Tolstoy's need to decide when and how to begin his story; partly too of his preoccupation with problems of genre—precisely what type of work was he trying to write? —but particularly of his restless urge to redefine his characters and their mutual relationships with ever greater artistry and precision.

[1] *Tolstoy's 'War and Peace': A Study* (Oxford 1962).

When Tolstoy began what was probably his first attempt at writing the first chapter of his work he gave it the title *Three Eras*—a fact which suggests that he was still thinking in terms of his discarded fragment *The Decembrists*. The three eras were to be 1812, 1825 and 1856. But the first date, 1812, soon became 1811, then 1808 and finally 1805, and when *The Russian Messenger* published the first thirty-eight chapters of the book in 1865, it did so under the title *1805*. Tolstoy wrote an unpublished foreword to these chapters which explains his reasons for pushing the action backwards in time and reveals his ultimate intentions:

In 1856 I began to write a story with a definite tendency, the hero of which was to have been a Decembrist returning with his family to Russia. From the present I moved involuntarily to 1825, the period of the delusions and misfortunes of my hero, and I abandoned what I had begun. But even in 1825 my hero was already a grown-up man with a family. In order to understand him, I had to carry myself back to his youth, and his youth coincided with Russia's glorious period of 1812. Once again I discarded what I had begun, and took as my starting-point the year 1812, the smell and sound of which can be apprehended by us and are dear to us, but which is now so far removed from us that we can think about it calmly. But for a third time I abandoned what I had begun, not now because I needed to describe my hero's early youth: on the contrary, in the midst of the semi-historical, semi-public, semi-imaginary great typical faces of a great period, the personality of my hero receded into the background, and the young and the old, the men and the women of that time interested me equally and came to the fore. I turned back a third time, from a feeling which might seem strange to the majority of readers, but which, I hope, will be understood by those whose opinion I value: I did so from a feeling not unlike shamefacedness and which I cannot define in one word. I felt ashamed to write about our triumph in the struggle against Bonapartist France without having described our failures and our shame. Who has not experienced that secret but unpleasant feeling of shamefacedness and mistrust when reading patriotic works about 1812? If the cause of our triumph was not accidental, but lay in the essence of the character of the Russian people and army, this character ought to have been expressed still more clearly in the period of failures and defeats. And so having gone back from 1856 to 1805, I now intend to lead not one, but many heroes and heroines of mine through the historical events of 1805, 1807, 1812, 1825 and 1856.[1]

This intention was not realised, but that is no reason to doubt the truth of Tolstoy's explanation. It helps to account for the extraordinarily complicated and lengthy task of getting the book launched after more than a dozen false starts. One version begins with a society ball; a second with a name-day party; a third with a private dinner-party; a fourth with a military scene; a fifth with a historical introduction. Ultimately Tolstoy arrived at the soirée in Anna Scherer's salon which we are familiar with in the novel as it now exists; and there is no doubt that the choice was a good one. One can understand Tolstoy's reluctance to begin with a camp or battle scene in which the heroes of the novel would have to make their first appearance outside their normal milieu, and in which there would be no obvious place for the civilian Pierre or the equally important womenfolk. Given the fundamental importance in the context of the work of Napoleon's invasion of Russia it seems logical to begin with an expression of differing opinions about the man and his achievements, ill informed and ludicrous as some of these opinions are. And given the desirability of this divergence of views and a superficially serious level of discussion, coupled with the wish to introduce as many important men and women characters as possible in the early pages of the book, the choice of a distinguished salon providing the semblance of up-to-date serious discussion in the midst of tittle-tattle and the mobility created by the constant arrivals and departures, is an improvement over the more static and archaic setting of the Rostovs' or the Bolkonskys' private homes or the restricted intimacy of Prince Andrew's town flat. But perhaps the decisive reason for Tolstoy's choice of this particular opening was the opportunity it gave him to start off in a gently satirical vein and to poke fun

[1] J.E. XIII, 54.

at the pretentiousness of the *haut monde* and the intellectual poverty of the 'important' people who imagined themselves to be in the vanguard of public opinion. The contrast between the natural and the conventional is an important theme of *War and Peace*. In the scene in Anna Scherer's salon we have the first hint of the antithesis of the 'natural' Pierre and the 'unnatural' Francophile society in which, reluctantly and against his better judgment, he moves and has his being.

If it was difficult for Tolstoy to write his opening scenes, it was equally difficult for him to envisage their continuation within the conventional framework of the novel. Explaining the reasons for his numerous false starts, he says:

Above all I was hampered by traditions both of form and content. I was afraid to write in a language which would not be the same as everybody else's; I was afraid that what I wrote would not fit into any category, whether novel, short story, poem or history; I was afraid that the need to describe important people of 1812 would compel me to be guided by historical documents and not the truth...[1]

Tolstoy's confusion over genre was further confounded by the feeling that he was writing a history, but not a historian's history, still less a history of 'kings and battles'. 'Neither Napoleon nor Alexander, Kutuzov nor Talleyrand will be my heroes: I shall write a history of people freer than statesmen, a history of people living in the most favourable conditions, free from poverty, free from ignorance, independent people...'[2] And yet he explicitly refused to call his work a 'novel', or a 'historical chronicle' and could think of no more satisfactory description of it, once written, than that it was 'what the author wished and was able to express in the form in which it is expressed'.[3] Many years later he said to Goldenveizer:

I think that every artist is bound also to create his own form... Turgenev and I were once recalling all that was best in Russian literature and it proved to be the case that the form of all these

---

[1] J.E. XIII, 53.   [2] J.E. XIII, 73.   [3] J.E. XVI, 7.

works was completely original. Not to mention Pushkin, take Gogol's *Dead Souls*. What is it? Neither a novel nor a long short story. Something completely original. Then there is Turgenev's *A Sportsman's Sketches*, the best thing he ever wrote. Dostoevsky's *House of the Dead*, my *Childhood* (sinner that I am), Herzen's *My Past and Thoughts* and Lermontov's *Hero of our Time*...[1]

Or again:

From Gogol's *Dead Souls* to Dostoevsky's *House of the Dead*, there is not a single prose work rising above mediocrity in the recent period of Russian literature which quite fits into the form of a novel, a poem or a story.[2]

Tolstoy denied that his work was a novel for the following reasons, which he put forward in the proposed introductions to *1805* which were never published:

In publishing one part of my work without a title and without a definition of the genre to which it belongs, that is, or in not calling it a poem, or a novel, or a long short story or a story, I consider it necessary to give a few words of explanation why this is so and why I cannot define what part of the whole is comprised by what is published here.

The proffered work most nearly approaches a novel or a long short story, but it is not a novel because I cannot and do not know how to set fixed limits to the characters I have invented, like marriage or death, after which the interest of the narrative would cease. I could not help realising that the death of one character only roused interest in others and that marriage was for the most part the start and not the finish of the plot's interest. Again, I cannot call my work a long short story because I simply cannot make my characters act merely with the object of providing or clarifying some idea or group of ideas.[3]

In another variant of the same introduction he qualifies what are substantially the same reasons with the words: 'We Russians generally speaking do not know how to write novels in the sense in which this genre is understood in Europe.'[4]

[1] A. B. Goldenveizer, *Vblizi Tolstogo* (Moscow-Leningrad 1959), p. 116.
[2] J.E. XVI, 7.   [3] J.E. XIII, 55.   [4] J.E. XIII, 54.

Although Tolstoy was concerned about the lack of an obvious climax to his work and the number of what might be called culminating points in it, the reasons he gives cannot disqualify it as a novel. It is impossible to define in the abstract what a novel should be like. One can only observe what extended works of prose fiction are like and have been like. And there is no doubt that *War and Peace* has many of the characteristic features of earlier European novels. It has its love stories, happily crowned by marriage. It has many standard situations of entertainment and adventure: a girl's first ball, an attempted abduction, a duel, a wager, a gambling scene, a hero believed dead but in fact alive, a heroine who attempts suicide in a moment of despair. It has to do with basic human emotions and conflicts, passion, jealousy, courage, thirst for adventure. It has its fair share of journeys, meetings and partings. Coincidences play an important part in the development of its plots. This is not to imply that *War and Peace* is like any novel in particular, but that it has enough recognisable thematic and other points of contact to establish it as belonging to that loose and ample genre. It is only when one tries to label it historical, epic or psychological that one is conscious of unnecessarily restricting its vast scope. If *War and Peace* marks a new stage in the history of the Western European novel, it is because of its concern with historical, social, ethical and religious problems on a scale never attempted in any previous novel. It has considerable psychological subtleties—but no more so than the novels of Stendhal. Turgenev or Jane Austen wrote far more economically and with greater wit. Smollett, Fielding or Sterne had more humour, more 'entertainment value'. Balzac had more historical colouring, more period detail. Emily Brontë had greater depths of imagination. Many a second-rate author had extolled historical deeds of national heroism or created memorable characters. But in Tolstoy there was a unique combination of intelligence, imagination and seriousness of purpose; profundity of thought and profundity of emotion. His novel engages the mind and the heart, it brings into play the animal and rational sides of the reader. Its content is richer, fuller and more varied than that of any other novel before it. It is in these attributes, and not in the qualities which do or do not make it an epic novel or an historical novel or a family chronicle, that we must look for the greatness and originality of Tolstoy's achievement.

Concern with questions of genre, tradition and form undoubtedly made Tolstoy's task more difficult. But it was problems to do with characterisation which were ultimately responsible for much of the re-writing of *War and Peace*. Should old Bolkonsky have a son? If so, should he die at Austerlitz? Or at Borodino? Or should his life be spared? What should he be like? He is not mentioned at all in the very interesting draft plan which has survived and which provides the earliest detailed notes on nearly all the main characters in the novel, in several cases grouped under headings such as property, social status, love relationships, mental faculties, family and even 'poetry'. The entry for Natasha shows that in the case of his heroine Tolstoy had all the essential features clear in his mind when he began writing and that he adhered to them faithfully to the end. The same is largely true of the other women characters and of such men as Berg or Nicholas Rostov who had little or nothing of Tolstoy in them. On the other hand the draft sketch of Peter, as he was then called, who has most of Tolstoy in him and for that reason is more mobile and elusive, corresponds much less closely to the finished portrait. Of the future Natasha it is said:

Natalya. Fifteen years old.
Terribly generous.
Believes in herself. Naughty, and always gets away with it, a nuisance to everybody and loved by everybody.
Ambitious.
Has a command of music, understands and feels it acutely.
Suddenly sad, suddenly terribly happy. Dolls.
Love: crying out for a husband, two even, needs children, love, bed.
Foolish but nice, uneducated, knows nothing and always knows how to hide it.

In love with teacher, Boris, doll Bibi, friendship with Sonya.
First ball, in love with Tsar. Country, Mikhail ['Anatole' has been crossed out by Tolstoy], love, fall. Horror and cheerfulness. Concert. Relations of half friendship with Arkady. With Pyotr. Wants to kill herself. He is wounded. She runs away from him. Explanation. Wedding-clothes.

The entry for Nicholas (Nicholas Tolstoy as he is called) is brief and recognisable:

Property Lives very comfortably in father's style, but economical.
Society Tact, gay spirits, unfailing courtesy, all the talents to a limited extent.
Poetry Understands and feels everything to a limited extent.
Intellect Limited, talks commonplaces admirably. Fashionably excitable.
Love No binding loves. A little intrigue. A little friendship.

These are the first rough notes about Peter:

Property Father wealthy. Son squandered everything given him, debts paid twice, refused. Generous, a gambler, knows poverty, keeps his wits about him.
Society Knows people, can easily deceive, and laughs. Can play any part—nobleman, beggar. Despises contacts, everything himself. More than usually ambitious. Doesn't know duty and always does the opposite. Doesn't acknowledge order of things. Cruel and kind *ad infinitum*.
Love Loves quickly, passionately, and at once hates the person loved. Despises women. Can't bear company of women—all fools.
Poetry Passionately fond of music, voice not good. Sings ['dances à la russe' has been crossed out by Tolstoy]. In love, remembers nothing before success, passionately fond of Russia, loyal in friendship.
Intellect Quick at understanding everything. Eloquent in all ways. Farsighted. So much a philosopher that he's afraid of himself. Often speaks of immortality, and tormented by the question. Jealous of Napoleon.
Family Father—minister, Frenchman. Brother—diplomat, whom he hates, cousin a Volkonskaya on mother's side. Mother née Ofrosimova.[1]

[1] J.E. XIII, 14 ff.

In the case of the men, the entries are usually followed by a brief account of what they were doing between 1811 and 1813, an indication of their age, and in particular some reference to their attitude to Napoleon. With the women, the notes are generally shorter and no attempt is made to fit them into the context of Napoleon's invasion. While it is one thing to have a general conception of the characters in one's mind, it is quite another to arrange their entrances and exits and their mutual relationships so that they lead their own lives and do not merely dance to their creator's tune. In his endless revisions Tolstoy was guided by a few simple principles which he evolved for himself and which are typical of his approach to characterisation, which is the province above all in which he was to excel. Generally speaking he preferred to introduce his characters in situations and environments which were typical of their normal, everyday lives. He liked to do so too, where possible, in an indirect or oblique manner. In one version of the opening chapters of the book, the Viscount de Montemart is telling a story in Anna Scherer's salon before an assembly of guests who have been given only a perfunctory introduction. Tolstoy intended to interrupt the viscount's story to tell the reader more about the main characters who form the audience, and indeed began to do so. Later, however, he crossed out his narrative description and scribbled in the margin: 'who listens and how'.[1] In the revised text he concentrates essentially on what the audience are *doing*. The viscount's story fades into the background, while the reaction, or lack of reaction, of the people who are listening comes to the fore. As Tolstoy said at the age of twenty-two, echoing an observation of Lessing in the context of Homer: 'It seems to me that it is really impossible to *describe* a man, but it is possible to describe the effect he produces on me.'[2]

Again, he believed that it was crucially important that the first meeting between two people whose fate was to be closely linked together (as for example Prince Andrew and Natasha) should be handled with more than usual care, and this belief dictated a number of his significant revisions.

[1] J.E. XIII, 210.   [2] J.E. XLVI, 67.

In one early draft of their first meeting at Otradnoe, Prince Andrew is virtually swept off his feet by Natasha. He is infatuated by the sight and sound of the little girl dressed up as a man (a detail not included in the end). When she looked at him at supper 'he felt the blood rushing to his face, his lips and eyes felt strange, he blushed and felt as embarrassed as a little boy'. This is in marked contrast to the unfavourable impression made by Natasha in a later text. This time Prince Andrew, on arriving at Otradnoe, sees and hears a girl who takes no notice of him. Later that day he sees the same girl at dinner, but pays not the slightest attention to her, dismissing her as 'provincial'. Tolstoy then intended that Prince Andrew should leave the same evening, his business completed, but this phrase is crossed out and the text continues with Andrew, as in the final version, overhearing Natasha and Sonya talking in the moonlight, and leaving next morning before the girls are up. The final version, although it follows the night scene closely, expands and deepens the first impression which Natasha has made on Andrew. When he first sees her, the sight of her disturbs him and stimulates thought and feeling. But it does not overwhelm him. This is a compromise, but an effective and convincing one.

As for Natasha's impressions of Prince Andrew, Tolstoy was equally uncertain how best to represent them. The first version is a compromise between a positive and negative reaction, both of which were recorded and then deleted. The positive reaction read: 'In the evening Natasha told Sonya as she recounted to her friend her impressions of the day that Prince Bolkonsky was such a charming creature that she had never seen nor could ever imagine anyone comparable. He and Nicholas, nobody else.' The negative reaction, likewise crossed out, was: ' "No, I don't like him, I don't like him," said Natasha that evening about Prince Andrew. "There is something proud, something dry about him." ' This version as amended sticks to the middle of the road, and Tolstoy is content to let Natasha tell her mother that Prince Andrew is the sort of man she likes.

In the final version, Tolstoy changes his mind again and

there is no reference at all to the impression Prince Andrew makes on Natasha. After all she is very young, and still, as she thinks, in love with Boris; and Andrew, depressed and pre-occupied as he is, hardly appears as a gallant cavalier. The version as we now have it deserves to be quoted as a good example of Tolstoy's restrained lyricism and psychological grasp of a critical moment in the lives of two people as yet unconscious of their destiny:

During the dull day, in the course of which he was entertained by his elderly hosts and the more important of their guests [the old count's house was crowded on account of an approaching name-day], Prince Andrew repeatedly glanced at Natasha, gay and laughing among the younger members of the company, and kept asking himself: 'What is she thinking about? Why is she so glad?'

Alone in new surroundings, he could not get to sleep for a long time that night. He read, put the candle out, then lit it again. The shutters were closed on the inside and the room was hot. He was cross with the stupid old man [as he called Rostov] who had made him stay by assuring him that some necessary documents had not yet arrived from town, and he was cross with himself for having stayed.

Prince Andrew got up and went to open the window. As soon as he opened the shutters the moonlight, as though it had long been watching and waiting for this moment, burst into the room. He opened the window. The night was fresh, still and bright. Right in front of the window was a row of clipped trees, black on one side and bright silver on the other. Under the trees grew some kind of lush, wet, bushy vegetation with odd silvery leaves and stems. Beyond the black trees was a roof sparkling with dew, to the right a big bushy tree with dazzling white trunk and branches and above it a nearly full moon in a nearly starless, pale spring sky. Prince Andrew leaned his elbows on the window, his eyes fixed on the sky.

Prince Andrew's room was on the middle floor. People were also still awake in the rooms above him. He heard female voices overhead.

'Just once more,' said a female voice overhead, which Prince Andrew recognised at once.

'But when are you coming to bed?' replied another voice.

'I'm not, I can't sleep, what's the use! Just one last time.'

The two female voices began to sing a musical phrase—the end of some song.

'Oh, how lovely! But now we must stop, it's time for bed.'

'You go to sleep, I can't,' replied the first voice, closer to the window. She was evidently leaning right out for he could hear the rustle of her dress and even her breathing. Everything was stock-still, just like the moon and its light and the shadows. Prince Andrew, too, dared not stir for fear of betraying his involuntary presence.

'Sonya, Sonya!' the first voice began again. 'Oh, how can you sleep! Just look how lovely it is! How lovely! Do wake up, Sonya,' she said almost with tears in her voice. 'There never, never was such a lovely night before.'

Sonya made some reluctant reply.

'No, just come and see what a moon! Oh, how lovely! Come here, darling, come here. Do you see? I'd like to squat down like this, put my arms round my knees, strain as hard as possible—you need to strain hard—and fly away. Like this . . . !'

'Don't, you'll fall out.'

He heard the sound of a scuffle and Sonya's disapproving voice: 'It's gone one o'clock, you know.'

'Oh, you only spoil it all for me. Go on then, if you want.'

Again all was silent, but Prince Andrew knew that she was still sitting there, and sometimes he heard a soft rustle and sometimes a sigh.

'O God! O God! What does it mean?' she suddenly exclaimed. 'Well, to bed if I must!'—and she slammed the window to.

'I might as well not exist for her!' thought Prince Andrew as he listened to her voice, for some reason expecting and fearing that she would say something about him. 'There she is again! You'd think it was on purpose,' he thought. And such an unexpected turmoil of youthful thoughts and hopes contradicting the whole course of his life suddenly sprang up in his soul that, unable to explain his condition to himself, he lay down and fell asleep at once.[1]

Of particular importance to Tolstoy was his firmly held belief that once his characters were on stage they must be made to behave with complete consistency and inner plausibility.

[1] *War and Peace*, II, 3, 2.

Speaking in his old age to Goldenveizer, he emphasized that 'when psychological mistakes are made, when the characters in novels and stories do what, from their spiritual nature, they are unable to do, it is a terrible thing'.[1] While he devoted much care to achieving character consistency, he was equally assiduous in improving his account of the mutual relationships between his men and women, especially their love relations. He was continually looking for ways of increasing the dramatic elements of a situation at the expense of the static or narrative. He strove after greater restraint in handling sentimental and potentially lachrymose scenes, especially death scenes; and he made determined efforts to prune his text of improprieties and naturalistic excesses which are completely absent from the novel we now know. Finally it should be added that many of the changes made in the process of writing *War and Peace* concern style in the narrower sense of syntax and vocabulary. English translations cannot really reproduce the balance, symmetry, parallelism, rhythm and harmony of Tolstoy's language, which did not come spontaneously but only as the result of laborious endeavour and constant re-writing over a period of several years. Only by comparing the finished product with the raw material can one appreciate the force of the saying that genius is an infinite capacity for taking pains.

There can be few novelists who have been as industrious as Tolstoy was in assembling source material for their fiction and providing a detailed and seemingly authentic historical and military framework for their characters. In his library at Yasnaya Polyana the works of the Russian historian Mikhailovsky-Danilevsky, the official historian of the wars of 1805, 1806–7 and 1812 and a participant in the 1812 campaign, outnumber those of any other author. The three-volumed history of 1812 by Bogdanovich, also a royal commission, and Thiers' *Histoire de l'Empire*, as pro-Bonapartist as the Russians are anti-Bonapartist, are also to be found on the shelves. There are numerous memoirs of Russians and foreigners: of Sergei

[1] A. B. Goldenveizer, *Vblizi Tolstogo*, p. 113.

Glinka, the jingoistic editor of *The Russian Messenger*, who himself gets a brief mention in *War and Peace* and whose *Notes on 1812* provide the main basis for the scene in the Sloboda Palace in 1812 when nobles and merchants assemble to hear the Emperor's manifesto; of Radozhitsky, an artillery officer; and of Perovsky, whose account of his own interrogation by Davout and his last-minute reprieve forms the gist of the scene in the novel when Pierre is similarly interrogated with his life hanging in the balance. The memoirs of the young student Zhikharev provided Tolstoy with much material for the description of the reception and banquet in honour of Bagration at the English Club in Moscow as well as for the character of M. D. Akhrosimova. He made extensive use of the *Correspondance diplomatique* and the *Soirées de Saint Pétersbourg* by Joseph de Maistre, the Savoyard ambassador to the court of Alexander I. He singled out Bernhardi's German biography of General Toll in four volumes as one of his three main period sources, and the marked passages, marginal notes and turned-down pages of his own copy provide an easy clue to the sections which he found most useful. His library also contains copies of early nineteenth-century periodicals and of patriotic novels about Napoleon and 1812 by the minor Russian novelists Zotov and Zagoskin. Not actually in the library, but known to have been used by him as source material, are the memoirs of the partisan poet and hero of 1812, Denis Davydov; the works of Count Rostopchin, governor-general of Moscow in 1812; Korf's *Life of Speransky*, the most influential of Alexander I's ministers in the early years of his reign, who entertains Prince Andrew to dinner in *War and Peace*; the memoirs of Napoleon's aide-de-camp General Rapp and of the duc de Raguse; and the interesting letters written by M. A. Volkova to V. I. Lanskaya between 1812 and 1818, the style and sentiments of which are imitated in Princess Mary's correspondence with Julie Karagina in the novel.

Tolstoy did not of course approach his task in the manner of a modern historian, and the sources he chose were not beyond reproach. Much of his material was blatantly chauvinistic, whethcr pro-Russian or pro-French. He read his history as an ordinary, well-educated dilettante might, going to the standard authorities and preferring biographies of people close to the events he described and memoirs of eyewitnesses. And he saw nothing wrong in borrowing liberally from people who were in a better position than he was to record external facts, even though he disagreed wholeheartedly with their interpretations. The amount of verbatim borrowing in *War and Peace* is relatively small, and occurs when Tolstoy is reproducing the text of letters, documents, communiqués and recorded conversations between historical personages. On the other hand, there is a considerable amount of near-literal borrowing, where the body of the original is faithfully reproduced but where 'stage directions' are added and Tolstoy fills in the reactions of the speakers in a dialogue to what is being said, describes what they did with their eyes, lips and bodies and indicates the poses they adopted.

For example:

MIKHAILOVSKY-DANILEVSKY	TOLSTOY
...ling up to Kutuzov and seeing that ...rifles stood stacked, the Emperor ...xander asked him: 'Mikhail ...ionovich, why aren't you advanc-...?' 'I'm waiting', answered Kutu-..., 'for all the columns to be ...med up.' The Emperor said: 'You ...ow, we are not on the Empress's ...ld where a parade does not begin ...il all the troops are assembled.' ...,' answered Kutuzov, 'that is just ...y I'm not starting because we are ...: on the Empress's Field. However, ...ou order it. . .'[1]	'Why aren't you starting, Mikhail Larionovich?' said the Emperor hurriedly to Kutuzov, glancing courteously at the same time at the Emperor Francis. 'I'm waiting, Your Majesty,' answered Kutuzov, bowing respectfully. The Emperor, frowning slightly, bent his ear forward to show that he had not quite heard. 'Waiting, Your Majesty,' repeated Kutuzov (Prince Andrew noticed that Kutuzov's upper lip twitched unnaturally as he said the word 'waiting'). 'Not all the columns have formed up yet, Your Majesty.' The Tsar heard, but obviously did not like the reply; he shrugged his rather round shoulders and glanced at Novosiltsev who stood by him, as if complaining of Kutuzov. 'You know, Mikhail Larionovich, we are not on the Empress's Field where a parade does not begin until all the troops are assembled,' said the Tsar with another glance at the Emperor Francis, as if inviting him, if not

Mikhailovsky-Danilevsky, *Opisanie pervoi voini Imperatora Aleksandra s Napoleonom 1805 godu* (St Petersburg 1844), p. 181.

TOLSTOY

to join in, at least to listen to what he ᵥ
saying. But the Emperor Francis continued
look about him and did not listen. 'That is j
why I'm not starting, Sir' said Kutuzov i
resounding voice, apparently to preclude
possibility of not being heard and again son
thing in his face twitched. 'That is just why ᴵ
not starting, Sir, because we are not on par:
on the Empress's Field', he said clearly ᵃ
distinctly. . . 'However, if you order it. . .'¹

A study of Tolstoy's adaptation of Zhikharev's version of the
dinner for Bagration is particularly illuminating. Tolstoy takes
from his source² such details as the number of people present;
the clumsy embarrassed movements of Bagration as he enters
the club; the verses presented to him on a silver salver; the
verbatim text of these verses; the band striking up its patriotic
strains; the seating of the guest of honour; the toasts and the
hurrahs and the words of the cantata composed in Bagration's
honour. For himself he describes the footmen as well as the
guests. He fills in the conversation of the various groups
standing and waiting for Bagration to arrive. He describes
Bagration's physical appearance in much greater detail than
Zhikharev. And he gives some space to the reactions of Count
Rostov and his son to the occasion.

An interesting example of a near-literal borrowing, which is
particularly important in defining the use which Tolstoy made
of his source material, is his assimilation of the actual words
and images of another author's narrative. Speaking of
Napoleon's armies, Thiers said that they *'semblaient couler
comme trois torrents inépuisables'*.³ Tolstoy takes this casual
comparison and rings the changes on the basic words *couler,
torrents, inépuisables*, not even forgetting the *trois*. Thus 'he was
looking through his field glasses at his troops as they *swept* like
torrents out of. . .the wood and *poured* across the three bridges

¹ *War and Peace*, I, 3, 15.
² S. P. Zhikharev, *Zapiski sovremennika*, Pt. I, *Dnevnik studenta* (1955), p. 195.
³ Quoted by B. M. Eykhenbaum, *Lev Tolstoi, kniga vtoraya, 60-e gody*,
   (Leningrad and Moscow 1931), p. 339.

...one after another, *inexhaustibly* they continued to *stream* out of the wood...'. The French *torrent* is literally rendered by the Russian *potok*, the adjective *inépuisable*, 'inexhaustible', becomes a gerund *ne istoshchayas'*, 'inexhaustibly'; the simple verb *couler* suggests to Tolstoy three compound verbs of cognate meaning, *vyplyvat'*, *razlivat'sya*, *vytekat'*, which add weight and variety to the original. The figure three is transferred from the torrents to the bridges. Thiers provides other good passages to which Tolstoy applied this method, which is not literal translation, but magnification of the original image through the translation and permutation of the roots of the original words. The freedom with which Tolstoy treated his material is well illustrated again in his use of Baron Korf's *Life of Speransky*. He takes all the details he needs of Speransky's domestic life, his family, dinner-table, guests, and after-dinner talk, but refuses to be influenced by Korf's warm and sympathetic attitude to the subject of his biography. Temperamentally hostile to the politician, the political reformer, the constitution-maker in the abstract, he cannot bring himself to sympathise with the concrete figure of Speransky, who emerges in the novel as cold, bureaucratic and unsympathetic. But most of the 'factual' details of Tolstoy's portrait come from the work of one of Speransky's warmest admirers.

Taken all round there can be very few scenes in *War and Peace* of a military or historical nature which cannot be tracked down to an original source in Russian, French or German historical, biographical or memoir literature. The fact that this is so gives the student a unique opportunity to explore the creative process of transfer and adaptation which is such an essential part of Tolstoy's equipment as a novelist.

Much has been written in English on the sources for Tolstoy's non-historical characters, and a considerable literature has been devoted to Tolstoy's ancestors, family and friends, who were to a greater or lesser extent the prototypes of the men and women of *War and Peace*. He had many models to copy. His task was not to create characters out of the void or to try to portray individuals from a very different background to his own, but to select and reject from real life the models of people near and dear to him, adding here, subtracting there, blending one trait with another. Invention was almost a term of abuse with him, and his common criticism of a piece of writing he does not like—'it's all invention'—contrasts sharply with Dostoevsky's—'I am a novelist so that I can invent.' For Tolstoy it was not the product of the imagination, but the reality of life which presented the writer with his most difficult challenge. As he said at the age of twenty-three: 'The word is far from adequate to convey the things of the imagination, but to express real life is harder still.'[1] Tolstoy created people; but he did not invent characters and situations out of his head. He brought to life in his novel the material he had assembled from the lives of real people. His was an intensifying rather than an inventive genius.

Characterisation is Tolstoy's true forte as a novelist. His great men and women are highly individualised but they all share a basic denominator of human experience which is common to all men and women regardless of class, country, age and intellectual attainments. This is not true, however, of the historical characters, with the exceptions of Napoleon and Kutuzov. The generals and statesmen, for the most part, are flat and static figures. Little or nothing is revealed of their private lives. We do not see them in intimate relationships with other people. Their lives, their hobbies, their personal dramas are a closed book to us. This may not have been accidental, for Tolstoy seemed to believe, with Prince Andrew, that 'a good commander must be limited. God forbid that he should be humane, love anyone, pity anyone or think about what is right and what is not.'[2] Tolstoy could not see the falseness of this belief, for there were no generals and statesmen at Yasnaya Polyana.

With the fictional characters, his treatment was very different. We have seen that he began by drawing thumbnail sketches of his future heroes and grouping their main characteristics under

---

[1] J.E. III, 216.   [2] *War and Peace*, III, I, I.

various headings. Where Pushkin tended first to jot down the
details of his plots and Dostoevsky to formulate his ideas,
Tolstoy began with the personalities of his men and women—
the fact, for example, that Natasha is 'suddenly sad, suddenly
terribly happy' or that Nicholas is 'very good at saying the
obvious'.[1]

Natasha's most striking features—her vivacity, impetuous-
ness and craving for love—are all revealed in one brief chapter
in the first part of the first book of the novel, which, for its
superb effortlessness, simplicity and charm, deserves to be
quoted in full:

When Natasha ran out of the drawing-room, she only ran as far as
the conservatory. There she stopped, listening to the conversation
in the drawing-room and waiting for Boris to come out. She was
already growing impatient, and stamping her foot, was on the
verge of tears because he did not come immediately, when she
heard the young man's discreet footsteps, neither hurried nor
languid. Natasha rushed and hid herself between the flower-tubs.

Boris stopped in the middle of the room, looked round, brushed
a speck of dust from the sleeve of his uniform and went up to the
mirror to examine his handsome face. Natasha peeped out from her
hiding-place with bated breath, waiting to see what he would do.
He stood for a while in front of the mirror, smiled and walked
towards the other door. Natasha was about to call out to him, but
changed her mind.

'Let him look for me,' she said to herself. No sooner had Boris
gone than Sonya came in through the other door, flushed, tearful
and muttering something angrily. Natasha checked her first
impulse to run out to her and remained in her hiding-place, watching,
as though from under an invisible cap, what was going on in the
world. She was experiencing a peculiar new pleasure. Sonya was
muttering something and looking round towards the drawing-
room door. Then Nicholas came out.

'Sonya! What's the matter? How can you?' Nicholas said as he
ran up to her.

'It's nothing, it's nothing, leave me alone,' sobbed Sonya.

'No, I know what it is.'

[1] J.E. XIII, 16-18.

'Well, if you know, well and good, you can go back to her.'

'So-o-onya! Look here! How can you torture me and yourself like that for a mere fancy?' said Nicholas, taking her hand.

Sonya did not take her hand away, and stopped crying. Natasha, not stirring and scarcely breathing, watched from her hiding-place with shining eyes. 'What will happen now?' she thought.

'Sonya! There is nothing else I need in the whole world. You alone are everything to me,' said Nicholas. 'I'll prove it to you.'

'I don't like you to talk like that.'

'Well, I won't. Only forgive me, Sonya!' He drew her towards him and kissed her.

'Oh, how nice,' thought Natasha, and when Sonya and Nicholas had gone out of the room, she followed them and called Boris to her.

'Boris, come here,' she said with a sly and meaningful look. 'There's something I have to tell you. Over here,' she said and led him to the place between the flower-tubs in the conservatory, where she had been hiding. Boris followed her with a smile.

'What is the *something*?' he asked.

She became embarrassed, looked round, and, seeing her doll which she had thrown on a tub, picked it up.

'Kiss my doll,' she said.

Boris looked kindly and closely at her eager face, but did not answer.

'Don't you want to? Well, come here then,' she said, and going deeper in among the plants, threw down the doll. 'Closer, closer!' she whispered.

She caught hold of the officer's cuff, and a grave and frightened look came over her flushed face.

'Do you want to kiss *me*?' she whispered, almost inaudibly, glancing up at him with a smile and almost crying with excitement.

Boris blushed.

'How funny you are,' he said, bending down to her and blushing still more, but waiting and doing nothing. Suddenly she jumped up onto a tub, to be higher than he was, and, embracing him so that her slender bare arms clasped him above the neck, tossed back her hair and kissed him full on the lips.

She slipped down between the flower-pots on the other side of the plants and stood there, hanging her head.

'Natasha,' he said. 'You know I love you, but...' 'Are you in love with me?' Natasha broke in.

'Yes I am, but please don't let's do what we did just now...In another four years...then I'll ask for your hand.'

Natasha thought for a moment.

'Thirteen, fourteen, fifteen, sixteen,' she said, counting up on her slender little fingers. 'All right! That's settled then?'

And a smile of joy and contentment lit up her eager face.

'Settled!' said Boris.

'For ever?' said the little girl. 'Till death itself?'

She took his arm, and with a happy face walked calmly by his side into the sitting-room.[1]

The main characters, once conceived, are all introduced at a very early stage. They are introduced with a minimum of biography or 'prehistory'. We are not told what Pierre did in Paris, or why Prince Andrew married Lise, any more than we are told about the past history and formative influences of people we meet for the first time in real life. The amount of physical description is minimal, but such as there is is typical and important, and likely to recur. It is generally true that the people of lesser importance are described in greater external detail. What Tolstoy does with his major characters is to draw attention to the expression on their faces, their eyes, their smile, their way of looking or not looking at a person; and above all to the impression they make on one another. Napoleon's eyes, significantly enough, are not described. They are merely big.

The visual quality of Tolstoy's characterisation is particularly apparent in *War and Peace*. Sounds can be 'transparent'. Colours and shapes have positive and negative values. White is a symbol of lifelessness and artificiality (Napoleon's hands, Hélène's shoulders)—not of purity or perfection. Pierre is dark blue and red in Natasha's eyes—colours which have a deep, rich and 'positive' significance. Again, Natasha thinks of Pierre as 'square-shaped', which might suggest the virtues of simplicity, solidity and dependability. Karataev is the epitome of roundness. There is 'something round' even in his smell. It is interesting that the symbols of the square and the circle,

[1] *War and Peace*, I, I, 10.

uncomplicated and elementary, have, so to speak, a morally positive charge for Tolstoy.

If Pierre is red, blue and square to his future wife, he is also decidedly unhandsome. Here one senses Tolstoy's subjective attitude to physical beauty which often varies in inverse proportion to moral goodness. Pierre and Princess Mary, who are both 'good' people, are both ugly. Tolstoy was acutely aware of his own unprepossessing features, and no doubt at heart had a higher appreciation of his moral worth than he cared to disclose in his diaries. Significantly, the handsome Kuragin and the beautiful Hélène are both creatures of more than dubious morality.

If on the visual plane there is a correlation between ugliness and virtue, beauty and vice, there is on the level of the spoken word a connection between the language used by a character—whether Russian or French—and his or her moral bearing. French, when used of or by a Russian, very often has a suggestion of sophistication, artificiality, even mendacity; to speak Russian means to be simple, natural and true. Sometimes Tolstoy uses a French word and gives its Russian equivalent in brackets immediately after it: 'Boris Drubetskoy, *en garçon* (a bachelor) as he put it, having left his wife behind in Moscow, was also at the ball.'[1] This affectation of a French phrase when a Russian equivalent exists, goes down as a black mark against Boris. Equally ironical is the use made of individual French words in the Russian text of the scene between Pierre and Captain Ramballe in Moscow in 1812, when the two are discussing love: 'It was obvious that *l'amour* which the Frenchman so loved was not that low, simple sort of love which Pierre had once felt for his wife, nor that romantic love which he felt for Natasha...'[2] Pierre's feelings, whether for Hélène or Natasha, were sincere and natural, even if in the first case they were misguided; they were therefore Russian. Ramballe's concept of *l'amour*, on the other hand, is something unnatural and affected, and the French word is retained. When the conceited Anatole Kuragin visits the unpretentious Princess

[1] *War and Peace*, III, 1, 3.   [2] *War and Peace*, III, 3, 29.

Mary as a prospective suitor, he is made to think in French:
'La pauvre fille. Elle est diablement laide.'

The use of French in a Russian setting is an important means
of characterisation, not merely a device to create an aura of
period authenticity. Indeed, I doubt whether Tolstoy worried
unduly about capturing an authentic period flavour, or about
his characters belonging unmistakably to the historical environment in which they are placed. It seems to me that there is nothing about his men and women specifically representative of
their own age which is not also representative of Tolstoy's
generation. They are the products of a class and a way of life
which had not materially altered when he began to write.
That they experienced the impact of a great patriotic war is a
fact which distinguishes their lives from the lives of Tolstoy's
contemporaries, but the development of their characters
cannot be explained solely in terms of that particular war.
Pierre in *War and Peace* might ask different questions from
Levin in *Anna Karenina* or put the same questions in a different
way, but his spiritual journey is fundamentally the same.
Prince Andrew's reactions to war could have been those of
one of the many obscure defenders of Sevastopol. Natasha's
progress to motherhood, while not identical with Kitty's, is
not peculiar to the first, rather than the second, half of the
nineteenth century. My own opinion is that there is comparatively little specifically historical or period detail in *War
and Peace*. Tolstoy believed that the age he was writing about
'had its own characteristics which resulted from the alienation
of the upper class from the other classes, the religious philosophy
of the time, the peculiarities of education, the habit of using
French etc.', and that this was the character he had given to it
in his novel. One critic disagreed so strongly that he said very
pertinently that as you read and re-read *War and Peace* you
cannot help asking yourself—where did Gogol's Russia come
from?[1] Merezhkovsky[2] believed that the background of *War*

[1] *'Voina i Mir': Sbornik pamyati L. Tolstogo*, ed. T. I. Polner and V. P. Obninsky
(Moscow 1912).
[2] D. Merezhkovsky, *L. Tolstoi i Dostoevsky, zhizn' i tvorchestvo'* Petersburg
1909), pp. 165 ff.

and Peace was essentially Tolstoy's own background, the background too of *Anna Karenina*. He felt that there was no vital difference in historical colouring between the battles of Austerlitz and Borodino on the one hand and the Sevastopol sketches on the other; that Prince Andrew could hardly be thought of as a contemporary of Karamzin's *Poor Lisa* (1792) —'one feels that he had read Byron, Lermontov, Stendhal, Flaubert and Schopenhauer'—and that Pierre as well as Levin might have been Tolstoy's own contemporary. As for the domestic life of a Russian nobleman during the Napoleonic wars, the only significant period detail, Merezhkovsky asserted, is the glass entrance-hall with its two rows of statues in niches in the old Count Bezukhov's town house in Moscow. This last charge can easily be refuted; but the fact remains that Tolstoy was not really very interested in the sort of period detail and historical *couleur* which one finds, say, in a Balzac novel. It is hard to visualise exactly what the Rostov and the Bolkonsky houses and rooms looked like from what we are told of them. Descriptions of food and dress are meagre. There is little from which to conjure up pictures of towns, shops, churches, streets or vehicles. But there is an immense inventory of human nature.

Tolstoy's heroes and heroines have all the virtues—and some of the failings—of a closely knit family. They know each other instinctively. A gesture is more significant than a spoken word. There is a strong sense of belonging, of participating in each other's thoughts and feelings, of intuitive understanding. They do not have to prepare what they are going to say. Indeed they can take each other for granted to the extent of following their own train of thought, without paying attention to the conversations in which they are engaged:

They [i.e. Nicholas and Natasha] hardly gave one another time to ask and answer questions about the thousands of trifling things which could interest nobody but themselves. Natasha laughed at every word he said or she said herself, not because what they were saying was funny, but because she was happy and unable to control her joy which expressed itself in laughter.

'Oh, how nice, how splendid!' she said to everything. Under the influence of the warm rays of love, Rostov felt for the first time in eighteen months that the childlike smile which had disappeared when he left home now spread over his face and soul.

'No, listen,' she said, 'you're quite a man now, aren't you? I'm terribly glad you're my brother.' She touched his moustache. 'I want to know what you men are like. Are you like us or not?'

'Why did Sonya run away?' asked Rostov.[1]

The normal process of articulation between people who are close to one another is apt to be much more disjointed than formal discourse, and this fact is sometimes conveyed in *War and Peace* by the casual, apparently fortuitous beginnings and endings of conversations which are struck up or broken off at random, petering out into three dots. Somewhat similarly, important conversations between people of the same background may often be of a casual and abrupt nature as, for example, the dialogue between Levin and Oblonsky in the barn in *Anna Karenina*, which is entered into on the spur of the moment and sounds authentically unpremeditated.

Tolstoy often composed the dialogues between his favourite characters with an eye for the unconstrained, unpredictable and erratic nature of the thought processes of people who do not have to try to impress each other. Equally relevant to the composition of the novel and the methods of characterisation is the extensive use Tolstoy makes of interior monologue as a more personal and vivid alternative to third-person narrative description of people's thoughts and feelings. A good example is the passage where Natasha, aged sixteen, is wondering whether to marry Boris. She runs into her mother's room, talks to her, runs back to her own room, cannot sleep, and lies on her bed thinking and looking at Sonya:

'Sonya?' she thought, looking at the sleeping, curled-up little kitten with her enormous plait. 'No, how could she! She is virtuous. She is in love with Nicholas and doesn't want to know anything else. And Mamma—even *she* doesn't understand. It's astonishing how clever I am...and how nice she is...' she went on, speaking

---

[1] *War and Peace*, II, I, I.

of herself in the third person and imagining that it was some very clever, the cleverest and the best man speaking about her. 'She has everything,' went on this man. 'She is exceptionally pretty and agile—she swims and rides splendidly. And her voice! It really is a wonderful voice.'[1]

This is an interesting passage, because it shows how the simple interior monologue can be expanded and made more subtle by the introduction of a second voice—a trick which is repeated in very similar words ten chapters later. Tolstoy has said that Natasha was pretty. He could have added in so many words that she was vain. But vanity, unlike good looks, is an inner characteristic and one that is best expressed through the workings of the mind.

Another interesting example of interior monologue as a revelation of character occurs in the scene where Anatole Kuragin, an unwilling suitor, visits Princess Mary, a lady over-anxious to be wooed. The two people's thoughts are laid bare, but no words are spoken. Externally the emphasis is laid, in Princess Mary's case, on her peculiar hair style, specially arranged for the occasion, and the agitation suggested by her clumsy, heavy tread. Anatole, for his part, stands suavely at ease, 'silently beaming at the Princess and obviously not thinking about her at all'. No words are exchanged, but what is at first conveyed by gestures and appearances is later communicated internally by thoughts and feelings:

'But am I not too cold with him?' thought Princess Mary. 'I try to be reserved because in the depths of my soul I feel too near to him already: but then he can't know all I think about him and may imagine that I don't like him.'

And Princess Mary tried, but could not manage to be nice to her new guest.

'La pauvre fille! Elle est diablement laide,' thought Anatole.[2]

Their unspoken words reinforce the impression of them created earlier by the descriptive narrative and add a happy touch of variety to the more conventional methods of characterisation.

---

[1] *War and Peace*, II, 3, 13. [2] *War and Peace*, I, 3, 4.

It is a commonplace that Tolstoy's principal heroes develop with the course of the action, without however betraying their true selves (with a minor character such as Dolokhov one can detect a false note, but Natasha does not lose her buoyant step, even when she is attending the dying Prince Andrew). Tolstoy achieves this development by showing how, at every stage in their lives, the likelihood of change is always present, so that they are never static, apathetic or inert, but constantly liable to respond to some new external or internal stimulus. Often the stimulus is provided by a person from the opposite camp—a 'negative' character, a selfish, complacent or static man or woman. These people act as temptations to the heroes; they are obstacles in their path which have to be overcome. Pierre, for example, is momentarily blinded by the apparent greatness of Napoleon. He is trapped into marriage with Hélène, with whom he has nothing in common, and is in danger of being drawn into the Kuragin net. After their separation he is reconciled with her again, only to bemoan his fate once more as a retired gentleman-in-waiting, a member of the Moscow English club and a universal favourite in Moscow society. Prince Andrew, like Pierre, is deceived by the symbol of Napoleon, and like Pierre he finds himself married to a woman who is as much his intellectual inferior as Hélène is morally beneath Pierre. Natasha for her part is attracted at first by the social climber Boris Drubetskoy and later infatuated with the same Anatole Kuragin who had actually begun to turn Princess Mary's head. Julie Karagina looms for a while on Nicholas' horizon. From all these temptations and involvements the heroes and heroines are saved, not by their own efforts but by the timely workings of Providence. Prince Andrew's wife dies. Pierre is provoked by Dolokhov into separating from his wife, and after their reconciliation he is eventually released by Hélène's death. Natasha is saved from herself by the solicitude of her friends. By chance Princess Mary catches Anatole unawares as he flirts with Mlle Bourienne. It seems as if fate is working to rescue them from the clutches of egocentricity. But there are also obstacles against which they have to contend without any help from Providence. Tolstoy made it a main object of his characterisation to show his positive heroes at all important moments 'becoming' and not just 'being', beset with doubts, tormented by decisions, the victims of ambivalent thoughts and emotions, eternally restless. Princess Mary has to overcome her instinctive aversion to Natasha. Nicholas has to wage a struggle between love and duty until he finds in the end that they can both be reconciled in one and the same person. Pierre's inner disquiet and spiritual striving express his determination, now weak, now strong, to overcome in himself the very qualities of selfishness and laziness which he despises in other people. The lives of Pierre, Prince Andrew and his sister, Natasha and her brother, are lived in a constant state of flux. Movement is of their essence. Externally their eyes, their lips, their smile are mobile and infectious; their expressions constantly alter. Internally their thoughts are in a state of turbulence and their mood is liable to swing violently from one extreme to another—from joy to grief, despair to elation, enthusiasm to boredom. There are times indeed when two incompatible emotions coexist uneasily and the person does not know whether he or she is sad or happy.

By contrast, the minor figures in *War and Peace* are not shown in the critical stages of their change and development. Even Sonya's conflict (she is described in an early portrait sketch in typically Tolstoyan fashion as 'generous and mean')—the conflict between her loyalty to the family and her love for Nicholas—emerges rather through Tolstoy's description of it than through the inner workings and sudden vacillations of her mind. Vera and Berg, Akhrosimova, Bolkonsky and many other lesser figures, however vital and many-sided they might be as individuals, are fundamentally static characters who are fully grown from the beginning. The ability to respond to change, the qualities of restlessness, curiosity, flexibility and dynamism are essentially the perquisites of the main heroes of the novel—in particular Pierre and Natasha—who perhaps reflect most faithfully the changes in Tolstoy himself and those closest to him at Yasnaya Polyana.

The illusion of movement—and of the reality of life—which is such an obvious feature of *War and Peace* is aided by the constant interaction of all the elements which make up the novel: men and women, nature, and the world of inanimate objects. Very seldom is a person seen or described in isolation, just as in real life human beings cannot be divorced from the infinite number of animate and inanimate phenomena which make them what they are and determine what they do. Tolstoy likes to show the interdependence and interpenetration of men and nature. The stars, the sky, the trees and the fields, the moonlight, the thrill of the chase, the familiar objects of the home all affect the mood and the actions of the characters no less than the rational processes of the mind or the persuasions of other human beings. That this is so in life is a truism. But few authors have had Tolstoy's power to show the multiplicity of interacting phenomena in the lives of their imaginary men and women.

Natural description with Tolstoy is essentially an element of characterisation, not a thing in its own right. Pierre looks at the comet and thinks of his love for Natasha. Prince Andrew gazes at the sky and a series of thoughts are evoked in him. But neither the comet nor the sky is described except in the most general terms. Again, the oak tree which Prince Andrew sees on his way to and from Otradnoe corresponds to a definite mood within him: nature is in harmony with his soul, now dead and now alive:

It was already the beginning of June when Prince Andrew on his return home drove back through the birch wood where the gnarled old oak had made such a strange and memorable impression on him. The harness-bells sounded even more muffled in the wood than they had done six weeks before; now everything was thick, shady and dense, and the young firs, dotted about in the forest, did not jar on the general beauty but toned in with the general mood as their fluffy young shoots showed a tender green.

It had been hot all day. A storm was brewing somewhere but only a small cloud had sprinkled the dusty road and the sappy leaves. The left side of the wood was in dark shadow; the right side glistened in the sunlight, wet and shiny, and swayed gently in the breeze. Everything was in bloom; the nightingales trilled, their song reverberating far and wide.

'Yes, here in this wood was the oak tree I agreed with,' thought Prince Andrew. 'But where is it?' he thought again, gazing at the left side of the road and, without recognising it, looking with admiration at the very oak tree he sought. The old oak tree, quite transfigured and spreading out a canopy of dark sappy foliage, stood rapt, hardly wavering in the rays of the evening sun. Gnarled fingers, old scars, old doubts and sorrows—nothing of this was in evidence now. Through the hard, century-old bark sappy young leaves had broken through even where there were no twigs, so that it was impossible to believe that the old veteran had produced them. 'Yes, it is the same oak,' thought Prince Andrew, and all at once an unreasoning, spring-time feeling of joy and renewal came over him. All the best moments of his life suddenly rose at once to his memory. Austerlitz and the lofty heavens, and his wife's dead, reproachful face, and Pierre on the ferry and the girl thrilled by the beauty of the night, and the night itself and the moon—all this suddenly rose to his memory.

'No, life is not over at thirty-one,' Prince Andrew suddenly resolved once and for all.[1]

Just as there is a close connection between nature and man, so also is there an organic relationship between man and the particulars of his domestic environment. When Nicholas Rostov comes home on leave, many objects are mentioned in rapid succession—streets, shops, lanterns, cabs, the broken plaster on the cornice of his house—but they are details which give rise to positive or negative responses in the mind of the impatient and agitated Nicholas. Adjectives like 'insufferable', 'familiar', 'still and uninviting', 'the same old', tell us little about the streets and the house. There is no accumulation of detail for its own sake. Such detail as there is is there because it evokes a response, and the scene is written, one feels, with the response in the front of the author's mind and the objects in the back. The door-handle of the Rostovs' house is not a wooden one; it is not a glass one; it is just the 'same old one'.[2]

[1] *War and Peace*, II, 3, 3.   [2] *War and Peace*, II, 1, 1.

The sense of movement, interaction, change, and—by contrast—continuity is always present in *War and Peace*, and the characters seem to flow on like a river between two arbitrarily chosen points in its course. Watching the currents and the eddies, one is unconscious of the river's source and mouth. But if Tolstoy was not interested in where his characters came from, he could not fail as a novelist to suggest where they were going. He had to try and resolve their conflicts and bring them to a state which, though not final and irreversible, was a new and higher stage in their life's development. The peace of mind which Prince Andrew attained before his death might not have lasted long if he had lived. Pierre's uneasy religious equilibrium might not have been of long duration. The submissive part assigned to the male in Tolstoy's essentially matriarchal world might have palled on him. Natasha might have tired of her new domestic role. The mere fact that we can easily foresee new threats to their security, new stimuli and new responses, is proof of Tolstoy's unwillingness to set a seal on his characters or to tie all the knots tight. But although there is not, and cannot be any absolute finality about the state to which his men and women are brought, there is nevertheless a harmony, charity and sense of purpose in their lives when we leave them which represent the highest ideals of which they are capable, given the personalities with which they have been endowed and the beliefs of the author who created them.

The study of the architecture of *War and Peace* is a relatively new occupation. For a long time it was the fashion to talk of the untidiness and sprawling nature of Tolstoy's and Dostoevsky's novels, and to contrast their alleged shapelessness and formlessness with the harmony, economy and aesthetically satisfying order of Turgenev's. But this opinion, which was given a wide currency by Henry James, completely fails to do justice to Tolstoy's diligent and sophisticated craftsmanship. In his own letters and diaries one meets in a literary context such words as 'links', 'ties', 'couplings', or 'connections', and more specifically an allusion to the need for criticism to guide readers through the 'endless labyrinth of connections which is the essence of art'.[1] *War and Peace* is full of such connections. It seems to me that the principle on which it is composed is to think of people and phenomena in terms of their opposites and then to contrive the juxtaposition and interaction of these opposites. The principle operates, in the long view, as a series of sharp contrasts between two dissimilar groups—family and social—which, as groups, each reveal a corporate uniformity. Within these contrasted groups, and in the short view, there is individuality and variety. But ultimately the individual, however many-sided his personality, remains basically true to his group and does not transfer his allegiance to the other side. The flow of the novel is maintained by this constant juxtaposition of contrasting groups, the individual members of which are in continual contact as they move to and fro and mix with each other. But group solidarity triumphs. The individual is only free within the limits of the group.

The basic contrast in *War and Peace* is the one inherent in the title, taking war to mean military actions, and peace to mean non-military actions whether in peace-time or in war. The two basic states of existence, whose juxtaposition throughout the novel is very obvious, provide Tolstoy with a useful outer framework. The arrangement of the war material follows the lines not of a just and unjust cause, but of 'good' and 'bad' men. 'Good' in the military context means unpretentious, uninflated, aware of one's own limitations, spontaneous, non-conformist; 'bad' in the same context means arrogant, self-opinionated, disingenuous, hidebound, lustful for power. On both sides in the struggle there is cruelty; on both sides magnanimity; on both sides muddle and confusion. But where Tolstoy draws the line is between the man who does not pretend to be in control of the situation, and the man who believes that he is.

Similarly, at the basis of the construction of the peace scenes in the novel is the contrast between 'good' families and 'bad'.

---

[1] Letter to N. N. Strakhov (April 1876), J.E. LXII, 269.

The Bolkonskys and the Rostovs are patriotic in the best sense of the word—not jingoistic or even anti-French necessarily—but devoted to their country and its finest national traditions. To the Kuragins and the Drubetskoys on the other hand, Russia is not as dear as their own private pleasure or their own personal ambition. The former are never wholly wrapped up in themselves. They are capable of giving as well as receiving. The latter are the incarnation of egoism. Here again we have two groups, fairly homogeneous and totally unlike each other, whose interaction (Vasily's and Anatole's designs on Princess Mary, for example, or Anatole's attempted abduction of Natasha) weave another strand into the fabric of the novel.

Within the 'good' families of the Russian aristocracy, there is a further sharp division between the earnest, intelligent Bolkonskys and (Vera apart), the gay, impulsive, somewhat scatter-brained Rostovs, a contrast of thought and feeling. Pierre moves between the two homes, attached by marriage to Natasha Rostova, and linked by his first marriage with the 'unnatural', sensual, Kuragins. He is the keystone of the arch in the building of *War and Peace*.

If the main groups are homogeneous but contrasting, there are gradations, variety, growth and development in the members of the groups. Prince Andrew is a very different man in 1812 from what he was in 1805. But even in 1805 he was a Bolkonsky, not a Kuragin. He always belonged to 'us' and not to 'them'. Similarly Natasha, stripped of her vivacity and brought to a somewhat sober motherhood, remains a Rostov—simple, natural, direct, untroubled by serious thoughts. However great the apparent change in character, it is not big enough to place men and women outside the group to which they belong and always will belong. Contrast between groups; change and development of individuals within these groups: such are the constants and variables in Tolstoy's method of composition.

The constructional device of antithesis, so favoured by Tolstoy, may be seen to operate not only in contrasting groups, but also in contrasting scenes which directly succeed one another. Nicholas in raptures over Natasha's singing gives way to Nicholas in despair as he confronts his father with the news of his gambling debts. The carefree scene of Natasha dancing at 'Uncle's' house is followed in the next chapter by a reminder of all the cares and troubles of the Rostov household. The gaiety in the Rostov ballroom as the sixth *anglaise* is danced gives place to gloom almost at once as the dying Count Bezukhov has his sixth stroke. Pierre goes out to take the life of Napoleon. Instead he saves the life of a child. He loses his faith in humanity as he watches prisoners being executed, only to have it restored by his meeting with Karataev which takes place immediately afterwards. The sudden *peripeteia*, the rapid alterations of mood, help to create the illusion of movement which is the very essence of *War and Peace*. Tolstoy's own words in one of the philosophical digressions—'there can be no beginning to an event, for one event always flows uninterruptedly out of another'—can well be applied to his novel. It has no real beginning or ending. The illusion of movement is enhanced by the short chapters and the rapid alterations of scene—Moscow, Petersburg, the country, the army. No single episode is dwelt on at great length, while the longer scenes (the battles) are enacted with considerable mobility; only historical and philosophical digressions hold things up. The sense of movement is further intensified by the constant arrivals and departures of the characters. Nobody stays in any one place for long. There is no obvious climax to the book, but there is a series of culminating points, some in the military action, some in the stories of the lives of the characters, which keep the narrative moving from one low peak to the next.

Another device which Tolstoy commonly uses to sustain the flow of movement of the narrative is the constant repetition of identical or closely related situations and thoughts which establish links or 'connections' as Tolstoy would call them, or, as they have been called in the context of another Russian novel, 'situation rhyme'.[1] They cast the mind back momen-

[1] J. M. Meijer, *Situation Rhyme in a novel of Dostoevskij* ('s-Gravenhage 1958).

tarily, and provide the cohesion vital for a work of this length. In spring 1809 on his way to his Ryazan estates and shortly before his first meeting with Natasha, Prince Andrew crosses the same ferry he had crossed with Pierre on that momentous occasion the year before when they had spoken of God and a future life. When Nicholas goes to Moscow on leave in 1806 he offers his driver a three-rouble tip when the sledge is only three houses away from his own door. When he goes home on leave again (this time to Otradnoe) he again gives his driver a three-rouble tip at the last post-station. On the former occasion he feels that 'all was the same at home'; on the latter occasion the feeling that 'everything is just the same, so why did I hurry?' is uppermost in his mind. Precisely halfway through the novel, after Natasha's unhappy experience with Anatole Kuragin and the first awakening of Pierre's love for her, Pierre looks up to the skies and sees the brilliant comet of 1812 (Tolstoy mistakenly allows him to see it in 1811!). After the French have entered Moscow, Pierre again looks at the skies and sees the same comet 'which was connected in Pierre's heart with his love'. On his return from Otradnoe, and his first meeting with Natasha, Prince Andrew sees the same oak tree, now in leaf, which he had noticed on his journey there, as yet untouched by spring. Situations rhyme; thoughts reverberate and echo. Prince Andrew's musings after Austerlitz on the unimportance of everything he understands and the importance of the incomprehensible 'Great All or Nothing' are recalled during the scene with Pierre on the raft, while the latter's thoughts on the meaning of life recur throughout the novel in similar forms and sometimes even in identical images and words.

Another link in the chain which holds the novel together is the fact that clues to the eventual outcome of a situation or relationship are sometimes given at a very early stage—long before that situation or relationship has begun to be determined. In the chapter in which Princess Mary is introduced, she hears the praises of her future husband Nicholas sung in a letter from her friend Julie. When Nicholas meets Mary for the first time at Bogucharovo 'the meeting immediately struck him as a romantic event'. Nicholas' first reaction to the news of Natasha's engagement to Prince Andrew is that the marriage will not take place. The ground is prepared very early on for the Natasha–Pierre relationship by emphasising their mutual attraction and the animation they both feel in each other's company. Tolstoy felt obliged to hint at the likely outcome of a situation well in advance, so that when the expected happens (and there are really very few surprises) the conjectures of the attentive reader may be rewarded. He sows the seeds early and they all come to flower.

It was Tolstoy's belief that the vast majority of ordinary men and women, for all their differences and individual idio-syncrasies, are creatures of habit and routine who react in a recognisable and essentially similar way to the basic situations of life. This belief is reflected in his writings by something of a standard approach to the description of human responses to such universal happenings as love and death. One finds not only in *War and Peace* but also in *Youth* the state of being in love described as an inability on the part of the person in love (Pierre in *War and Peace*) to get up and take his departure. There is a similarity between the scene in *War and Peace* where Countess Rostova learns of the death of her son, Petya, and that in *Childhood* when the grandmother learns of her daughter's death. Both scenes have this in common that the two women address other children as though they were talking to the ones who had just died. One notices a standard approach to the portrayal of profound emotional disturbance in an almost obsessive concentration on the movements of the human jaw. Not only does Prince Andrew's jaw quiver at moments of agitation. The same is true, in *War and Peace* alone, of Natasha, Nicholas, Pierre, Captain Tushin, a doctor, a Frenchman and others too. There is a stock Tolstoyan descrip-tion of the fear–courage ambivalence displayed by men in the face of the enemy, and Nicholas Rostov, in his baptism of fire at the Enns bridge, shows the same fear of death and love of life, the same awareness of the contrast between the beauty of nature and the ugliness of suffering, the same momentary fear of being thought a coward as was shown earlier by the obscure heroes of the Sevastopol sketches:

Preoccupied with his relations with Bogdanych, Rostov stopped on the bridge, not knowing what to do. There was no one to hew down (as he had always imagined there would be in a battle), nor could he help to fire the bridge because he had not brought any burning straw with him like the other soldiers. He stood gazing round, when suddenly he heard a rattle on the bridge like nuts being spilt, and the hussar nearest to him fell against the rails with a groan. Rostov ran up to him with the others. Again someone shouted 'Stretchers!' Four men seized the hussar and began to lift him.

'Ooh! Leave me alone, for Christ's sake,' cried the wounded man; but they lifted him up and put him on the stretcher all the same.

Nicholas Rostov turned away and gazed into the distance at the waters of the Danube, at the sky and the sun, as though searching for something. How beautiful the sky looked, how blue, how calm and how deep! How bright and majestic the setting sun! How soft and glossy the water looked, glistening in the far-away Danube! And more beautiful still were the blue mountains far beyond the Danube, the monastery, the mysterious ravines and the pine forests veiled to their summits in mist. There was peace and happiness... 'If only I were there,' thought Rostov, 'I would wish for nothing else, nothing at all. There is so much happiness in me alone and in that sunshine, while here it's groans, sufferings, fear and this hurry and confusion. There they are shouting something again, and all running back somewhere, and I'll run with them, and there it is— death—above me and all round me...Another moment and I shall never again see that sun, that water, that ravine...'

Just at that moment the sun began to disappear behind the clouds; more stretchers came into view before Rostov's eyes. And the fear of death and of the stretchers, and the love of life and of the sun all merged into one feeling of sickening agitation.

'Lord God in your heaven there, save, forgive and protect me!' whispered Rostov.

The hussars ran back to their orderlies, their voices grew louder and calmer, the stretchers disappeared from sight.

'Well, friend, so you've smelt powder?' Vaska Denisov shouted just above his ear.

'It's all over, but I'm a coward, yes, a coward,' thought Rostov, and with a deep sigh he took his horse Rook, which stood resting one foot, from his orderly and began to mount.[1]

Tolstoy's version of the falsification of facts by even the bravest of those who fought at Schöngraben, and his account of Prince Andrew's reactions to imminent death in battle as a smoking shell spins near to him both remind one very much of scenes from the same Sevastopol sketches. Psychological reactions to battle are, in Tolstoy's experience, remarkably uniform; but it is also the case that his battle scenes themselves are composed in a fairly uniform manner. Their standard ingredients are general confusion coupled with the particular exploits of individual brave men—the single battery keeping up a lone fire, the single officer charging with standard in hand, isolated acts of daring and initiative unforeseen in the debates at Headquarters. The description of actual fighting is not extensive (in the case of Borodino, only three chapters are strictly concerned with the fighting itself), while scenes of camp life, army headquarters and regiments in reserve, or descriptions of attitudes of mind predominate. It would be wrong to imply that the three big battles in *War and Peace* all conform to the same general pattern. Schöngraben and Borodino were, if not victories, at least triumphant pages in Russia's military history. Austerlitz on the other hand was a disaster, and is treated with even greater irony and venom. Nevertheless the three battles as described by Tolstoy have much in common, and the very fact of their common denominator is further evidence of that sameness of approach which is characteristic of the structure and composition of significant episodes—and not only military episodes—in Tolstoy's fiction.

Take for example the not infrequent sleep and dream scenes in *War and Peace*. Here the standard compositional device is to direct the sleeper's thoughts to a point where they can sensibly coincide with the words of the man who wakes him. Pierre, on his retreat from Borodino, sleeps the night in the carriage in the

---

[1] *War and Peace*, I, 2, 8.

yard of an inn at Mozhaisk. Thoughts run through his mind which are channelled into the mouth of a speaker and led up to the point where this voice in his sleep tells him 'to unite the meaning of everything in his soul':

'Unite everything?' said Pierre to himself. 'No, not unite. You cannot unite thoughts, but you can *harness* all these thoughts. Yes, you must *harness* them, you must *harness* them,' Pierre repeated to himself...'Time to harness, time to harness, Your Excellency! Your Excellency, you must harness, it's time to harness,' repeated someone's voice...[1]

Another recognisable feature of Tolstoy's composition is his fondness for describing his characters reacting to new situations in terms of old ones with which they are thoroughly familiar. Nicholas Rostov, a keen sportsman, sees battle in terms of a hunt. When he runs away in battle, Tolstoy likens him to a hare fleeing before the hounds. Captain Tushin, a pipe-smoker, sees the enemy's guns as pipes. This is in keeping with the underlying philosophy that gives shape to Tolstoy's novel, that over the larger issues of life there is a basic sameness about the pattern of human behaviour, and that human beings, conditioned as they are by habit, milieu, and social and class prejudices, tend to follow a more or less predictable human course. Despite the frequency in the novel of the word *svoistvenny* ('peculiar to'), denoting the distinguishing features of an individual, it is the expressions such as 'the same as ever', or 'as is always the case', denoting habit and conformity, which predominate in *War and Peace*.

The time sequence in Tolstoy's longest novel is not entirely orthodox. Sometimes he departs from a strictly chronological narrative of events, as when Prince Andrew's story is at one stage carried so far forward that the author has to go back nearly two years in order to recover Pierre and bring his story up to date. Occasionally Tolstoy varies the narrative sequence by relating the conclusion of an episode before the events leading up to that episode. The account of Petya's death and

[1] *War and Peace*, III, 3, 9.

the rescue of Pierre from captivity comes before the description of the prisoners' march and the death of Karataev *en route* which, chronologically speaking, came first. Kuragin's courting of Mary in December 1805 is described before the November events at Schöngraben.

Of a rather different nature are the temporal lapses and inconsistencies of which Tolstoy is occasionally guilty. Sometimes they are due to the failure to synchronise dates given in West European sources according to the Gregorian calendar with the Julian calendar chronology of his Russian sources. At other times they are merely careless slips, as when Tolstoy refers to the cloudless June night in Petersburg very shortly after the *soirée* at Anna Scherer's which took place in July, 1805, or when Pierre sees the comet of 1812 in 1811. Rather more surprising is the erratic rate at which people grow up. In 1805 Natasha is thirteen. Less than a year later, in 1806, she smiles 'as only fifteen-year-old girls smile'. In 1809 she is only sixteen. Vera, on the other hand, who was seventeen in 1805, has reached the age of twenty-four by 1809. I see no subtle significance in these blunders, unlike the Soviet critic[1] who argues that Tolstoy's time is 'open', and that his characters have their own rhythm and tempo; that they are meant to traverse their paths at different speeds; that the eternally youthful Natasha cannot be expected to grow four years older in four years; and that since conventional time scales restrict the novelist, each character is given *his own* time. That Tolstoy, like lesser men, was not infallible can be seen also from his odd grammatical errors, the difficulty he sometimes had in distinguishing the gerund from the participle, or the occasional gallicisms which creep into his Russian syntax and vocabulary. 'I like what is called incorrectness, that is to say what is characteristic,'[2] he said on the subject of language. But we need not always take him at his word or make a virtue of his fallibility!

Not a few criticisms have been levelled against Tolstoy's

[1] Birman's article in *Russkaya literatura*, III (1966).
[2] Letter to Tishchenko, 1886.

language and style, especially in the early stories and in parts of *War and Peace*. Professor Davie[1] reminds us of Turgenev's reproach that 'the fear of phrases has driven Tolstoy into the most desperate phrases'. He reproduces some of Merezh-kovsky's[2] examples of Tolstoy's clumsiness in *War and Peace*:

What crime can there be [says Pierre Bezukhov] in my having wished—to do good? Even though I did it badly, or only feebly, yet I did something for that end, and you will not only not persuade me of this, that that which I did was not good, but not even that you did not think so.

This translation could certainly be improved, but the point is basically valid. Merezhkovsky also suggests that in trying to be too simple, Tolstoy was at times reduced to *simplesse* and artificiality, and there is evidence to support his argument. For himself, Professor Davie is offended by Tolstoy's excessive addiction to classification and analysis, and argues, contro-versially, that his prose fails him 'when he is analysing a person's mood or action and finding hypocrisy beneath it', maintaining that he not only took over some of Rousseau's ideas, but also, and to his own detriment, inherited 'the very construction and measure of Rousseau's sentence'. This original idea deserves further exploration, but it cannot be made on the basis of existing translations. From the point of view of language and style, Tolstoy has been better served by his translators than many of his fellow-countrymen. Nevertheless, standards fall a long way short of perfection. Clumsiness and *simplesse* apart, no English version of *War and Peace* has really succeeded in conveying the power, balance, rhythm and above all repetitiveness of the original. Perhaps it is repetition which is the most characteristic single feature of Tolstoy's prose style. Take, for example, the following typically Tolstoyan sequences. The subject of the first one is Pierre, and he is scrutinising his feelings for his first wife Hélène (the italics here and in the passages which follow are mine):

[1] D. Davie, *Russian Literature and Modern English Fiction* (University of Chicago 1965), p. 184.
[2] D. S. Merezhkovsky, *Tolstoi as Man and Artist* (London 1902).

'But how often have I *felt proud of* her, *felt proud of* her majestic beauty, her social tact,' he thought, '*felt proud of* my house in which she received all Petersburg, *felt proud of* her unapproachability and beauty. So this is what I *felt proud of!* I thought I did not *understand* her. How often when considering her character have I told myself I was to blame for not *understanding* her, for not *understanding* that constant composure…'[1]

Or again:

…thought Prince Andrew, as he waited among a number of important and unimportant people in Count Arakcheev's *reception-room*.

During his service, chiefly as an adjutant, Prince Andrew had seen the *reception-rooms* of many important men, and the different types of these *reception-rooms* were well known to him. Count Arakcheev's *reception-room* had quite a special character. The faces of the unimportant people waiting their turn for an audience in Count Arakcheev's *reception-room*…[2]

Here the Russian *priemnaya* recurs five times in as many lines— a fact which is glossed over in the Maudes' English translation by omitting it once, calling it a 'waiting room' once, an 'ante-room' twice and simply a 'room' once. Similar examples could be found in almost every chapter of the book.

Single-word repetition is easy to reproduce in a careful translation; more apt to be overlooked are the devices used to achieve balance and rhythm. In this respect Tolstoy was particularly addicted to a classical rhetorical arrangement of his material in groups of three—three adjectives, three nouns, three verbs, three prepositions. In the following description of the preparation for the Olmütz review I have added numerals and italics:

Now thousands of feet and bayonets, with colours flying and at the officers' command, (1) halted, (2) turned and (3) formed up at intervals, wheeling round *other* similar masses of infantry in *other* uniforms; *now* could be heard the rhythmic hoof-beats and jingling of the smart cavalry in (1) blue, (2) red and (3) green braided

---

[1] *War and Peace*, II, 1, 6.   [2] *War and Peace*, II, 3, 4.

uniforms with smartly dressed bandsmen in front on (1) black,
(2) roan or (3) grey horses; *now*, deploying itself *with its* brazen
clatter of cannons, (1) polished, (2) shining and (3) swaying on their
gun carriages and *with its* smell of linstocks, the artillery crawled
up between the infantry and the cavalry and took up its appointed
positions. *Not only* the generals *wearing* full parade uniforms with
their thin and thick waists drawn in to the utmost, their red necks
propped up by their collars and *wearing* scarves and all decorations;
not only the elegant, pomaded officers, *but every* soldier with his
(1) fresh, (2) washed and (3) shaven face, and his weapons polished
and shining to the last degree, *every* horse, groomed till its coat shone
like satin and every hair of its wetted mane lay smooth—all felt
that something (1) serious, (2) important and (3) solemn was
happening.[1]

Running through the syntax of Tolstoy's narrative passages is
nearly every device of arrangement and balance known to
Cicero and Demosthenes. There are the 'threes', the 'not
only...but also', the 'either...or, neither...nor'; there is the
fondness for 'in the first place', 'in the second place', 'in the
third place'; there is the frequency of 'some said', 'others said',
'yet others said'; and there are the divisions of people and
opinions into parties, groups and categories. The effect is of a
powerful, overwhelmingly direct attack which is characteristically and unmistakably Tolstoyan.

Even more difficult to convey in translation are the words
and phrases which do not belong to a neutral, literary
language and which taken collectively, constitute the distinguishing features of an author's style. There are a good many
examples in Tolstoy's vocabulary and syntax of archaic
linguistic mannerisms derived from an official 'civil service'
style of writing known to philologists as the 'language of the
chancelleries'. They occur at random in the author's narrative,
in certain documents such as Kutuzov's letter to old Prince
Bolkonsky, and in the mouths of statesmen such as Kochubei
or Arakcheev. Tolstoy knew how to impart to his characters
and situations the appropriate, stylised linguistic flavour. The

[3] *War and Peace*, I, 3, 8.

language of the freemason who introduces Pierre to his masonic lodge has a strong Church Slavonic tang. A sentimental Karamzinian aura pervades Julie's correspondence with Princess Mary. There is a popular gnomic element in Karataev's speech, salted as it is with expressions of folk wisdom. The language of the soldiers and peasants in *War and Peace* is rich in colloquial words and idioms. The passages devoted to hunting, bee-keeping or horse-breeding are sprinkled with local dialect words which will not be found in dictionaries of standard literary Russian. In short, Tolstoy consciously, but with restraint, employs a wide variety of linguistic idioms, but at the same time avoids an excess of obscure jargon or recondite professional terminology, the over-naturalistic reproduction of peasant speech, the proliferation of dialect forms or the flirtation with neologisms, one or other of which extravagances mar some of the works of Gogol, Leskov, the writers of the 'natural school' of Russian fiction and many early Soviet novelists. The hallmark of Tolstoy's style is lucidity, and such lucidity demanded caution and moderation in departing from the best standards of Russian spoken by the educated people of his own class and day—the basis of the language of *War and Peace*.

The spoken language of the principal characters in the novel is not generally marked by any special idiosyncrasies or even by any individal colouring. Prince Andrew and Pierre, Nicholas and Natasha are immediately recognisable by the sort of things they say, but their actual words might well have been taken, one imagines, from the day-to-day language of Tolstoy and his family in the 1860s. An exception might be made for Prince Andrew, whose gallicisms obtrude from time to time. But he, like the others, is—surprisingly enough—a person of few words. The main characters in the novel are given relatively little direct speech. When they speak they do so briefly. More is said about them than they say themselves, and still more is expressed through interior monologue or through the author describing their thoughts and feelings. It is the minor characters who are allowed idiosyncrasies of language, favourite words, witticisms and stylised mannerisms, and these subtleties of language—when Prince Vasily visits old Prince Bolkonsky at Bald Hills he finds his archaisms and gallicisms so obvious that he tries to imitate them himself—are a real, if minor, part of Tolstoy's art, which only a Russian can fully appreciate.

The language of *War and Peace* is not rich in imagery. Metaphor and metonymy are quite rare, and even similes, which are Tolstoy's commonest literary image, are not especially prominent when viewed against the novel as a whole. The objects of his similes are drawn for the most part either from the animal world, the processes of nature and the daily round of country life, or from the physical world with its mathematical laws. In the former case they reflect the author's profound knowledge and observation of rural life, and stem directly from his own experience; in the latter they savour more of textbooks of elementary physics or mechanics and suggest the influence of Tolstoy's learned, scientific friends of the 60s, an influence which is geared up and put to the service of a providential, determinist philosophy. The one group of similes has to do with ants, bees, flies, hares and hounds, herds of cattle, rams, wounded animals, the action of water, and household objects such as spinning wheels and looms. The subject matter of the other group is mass and momentum, velocities, parallelograms of forces, attraction, gravity, heat, engines, clocks, watches and mathematical equations. Seldom is a startling image produced, but the comparisons are thoughtful and unstereotyped. At times they run into many lines—in one case two whole pages!—and inevitably bring to mind the epic similes of Homer and Virgil. It is possible that a complex extended simile such as the one comparing Moscow to a queenless hive is a conscious imitation of an epic device, a prose counterpart of the bees simile in the *Georgics* or in *Paradise Lost*. Less obviously inspired are the frequent comparisons of battle scenes, acts of war and troop movements with fishing, hunting and agriculture, or the actions of society men and women at soirées and dinners with simple domestic or rural activities.

They are both comparisons and contrasts: comparisons of two superficial likes, but with ironical allusions to the distance separating abnormal and unnatural things like war or high society and the natural, simple activities of normal country life. It has been well pointed out[1] that the simile of the guests 'shaken together like rye in a shovel' at the English Club dinner to honour Bagration, or the comparison of Pierre, confronted by his deceitful wife, to a hare crouching motionless before the surrounding hounds, have the effect, among other things, of contrasting the false social world with that of the land and the rural life. And there is no doubt that irony, which lies concealed in these images, is a sharp weapon in Tolstoy's hands. Doctors, diplomats and historians were among his favourite targets. Writing of the causes of the French Revolution as retailed by history textbooks, he says:

Louis XIV was a very proud and self-confident man; he had such and such mistresses and such and such ministers, and he ruled France badly. His descendants were weak men and they too ruled France badly. And they had such and such favourites and such and such mistresses. Moreover certain men wrote some books at that time.[2]

This passage is a good illustration of a naïve oversimplification; Tolstoy refuses to view a thing in the conventional light and contrives, in the words of the Formalist critic Shklovsky, 'to make it appear strange'. Shklovsky regarded Tolstoy as an exponent of 'the device of making it strange', which meant, simply speaking, removing a word or object from its conventional context, calling it by a different name, refusing to recognise it, pretending it is something else, doing anything with it, in fact, to rescue it from being a verbal cliché with no power to evoke a response. Perhaps the classic example of this 'device'—this ironical oversimplification as I would call it —is the description of the opera in Moscow as seen through Natasha's eyes, which begins:

The floor of the stage consisted of smooth boards, at the sides was some painted cardboard representing trees, and at the back was a

---

[1] G. Steiner, *Tolstoy or Dostoevsky*, p. 85.
[2] *War and Peace*, Epilogue, 2, 1.

cloth stretched over boards. In the centre of the stage sat some girls in red bodices and white skirts. One very fat girl in a white silk dress sat apart on a low bench, to the back of which a piece of green cardboard was glued. They all sang something...[1]

To Natasha, newly arrived from the country, the artificiality of operatic convention seemed ludicrous and grotesque, and these deflationary sentences with their ironical naïveté well convey her mood.

But the English reader is likely to be less interested in Tolstoy's language than in the ideas he seems to be expressing, and to offer one's own interpretation of these ideas, subjective as it must be, should require no apology. There is a marked tendency among Soviet critics of the 50s and 60s to interpret *War and Peace* very largely in terms of class and country. They see it on the one hand as showing the cleavage between the people (*narod*) and the aristocracy (*znat'*), and the moral superiority of the former over the latter, on the other as an expression of patriotic pride in the glorious achievements of the Russian nation and its moral superiority over the French invaders and the pro-French elements within its midst. The assumption underlying most modern Soviet interpretations of the ideas which Tolstoy is said to be expressing in his novel (leaving aside for the time being the theoretical digressions on war and the philosophy of history), can be stated briefly in general terms. Very simply it is this: that the more the gentry subscribe to the simple, natural, popular (*narodny*) way of life of the Russian nation, the more they narrow the gap between themselves and the *narod*; and the more they renounce the emptiness of society life for the full domestic round of work and family responsibilities, the more comprehensible to themselves and the more satisfying their lives become. It is part of this design that Pierre's spiritual transformation should be brought about by the peasant Karataev; that Prince Andrew should be a different and better man in the company of the allegedly simple 'Russian' Pierre or the 'popular' Captain Tushin than in the salons of Petersburg; that Natasha and

---

[1] *War and Peace*, II, 5, 9.

Nicholas should both have the national love of song and dance and the ability to feel at home with 'uncle'; that Natasha and Pierre, Nicholas and Princess Mary, should find salvation in family life and in the country, the epitome for Tolstoy of all that is simple, 'popular' and good; that not only the untypical Karataev but numerous representatives of the common people should be treated with warmth and sympathy and should constitute a necessary and beneficial part of the lives of the gentry. It is part of the design also that many of the main heroes should be shown to advantage in the close company of the common people—Pierre and Karataev, Princess Mary and her 'God's folk', Nicholas and Lavrushka, Prince Bolkonsky and Tikhon. Finally, it is Tolstoy's achievement to have equated what is 'popular' with what is Russian, and what is Russian with what is good; and conversely to have equated 'anti-popular', foreign and bad. The French are the invaders. They are alien. The Russians are their innocent victims. They are 'our people', nobly and successfully defending the motherland against the nineteenth-century equivalent of the fascist aggressors. Kutuzov is simple, wise, 'Russian'—and successful. Napoleon is arrogant, stupid, 'French'—and unsuccessful.

The victory of the Russian army over the French culminates in the moral triumph of the Russian man; he is victorious not only by force of arms, but also by virtue of his moral superiority. Similarly, the Russian aristocracy is divided between the 'positive heroes', who, whatever their external façade, are at heart as Russian as Pushkin's Tatyana, and the 'negative' characters, the victims of Tolstoy's ironical denunciation—the Kuragins, Drubetskoys and their ilk—who by their sophisticated way of life, their French speech, and their Frenchified salons belong unambiguously to the other camp.

This interpretation—oversimplified and inevitably distorted a little in my impressionistic rendering of it—contains a mixture of truth and untruth, some factual errors and some errors of emphasis. The basic concept of the aristocracy as a negative, and the common people as a positive, pole cannot be substantiated. The aristocracy as a class are not painted black.

Some of its members are good people, others are bad, while others again have good and bad qualities equitably shared. Nor is it true to say that the 'positive' members of the aristocracy become better in proportion as their lives bring them into closer contact with the people. Prince Andrew's journey is not to the people through the people. He is made to see the folly of military and worldly success not just through his encounter with Captain Tushin but through his experiences of the horrors of war and the uncertainties of love. His fluctuating moods and changing assessments of what is important, and what is not, derive from his mature observations of war and the happiness, disappointment and renewed happiness of his association with Natasha—rational and emotional factors which have nothing to do with considerations of class. Similarly Pierre never becomes identified with the *narod*. There is nothing simple or traditionally Russian about his way of life. The peasant Karataev exerts a positive influence on him; but so too does Natasha, who, for all her love of national songs, games and dances, is hardly one of the common people.

The Russian–French polarity is also a false one. Pierre is not anti-French. He was educated in France, speaks French as well as, if not better than, Russian and never talks disparagingly of French culture and civilisation. He is even given a French name. He hates Napoleon, not because he is French, but because he appears to be an arrogant *poseur*. He dislikes the salons of Petersburg and Moscow, not because of their imitation of French manners and their veneration for things foreign, but because of their artificiality and veneer. The use of French by native Russians is unnatural and unnecessary, and an obvious target for Tolstoy's satire. But this does not mean that the French language in itself is unnatural and artificial. The Rostov family, warmly and sympathetically presented as typically Russian gentry, are not anti-French, although they are intensely patriotic in time of war. Prince Andrew is steeped in French culture, as any well-educated man of his time was bound to be.

Tolstoy's attitude to the French in *War and Peace* (Napoleon

and French militarism excepted) is friendly rather than hostile
—in marked contrast to his contempt for the Germans. He is
ironical at the expense of the declamatory, rhetorical, complacent Frenchmen of whom Ramballe is an example, but he
appreciates their cheerfulness and bravery. Ramballe is a
naïvely vain and limited man, but he is not at all repugnant.
'They are also human beings,' says a Russian soldier, looking at
the French prisoner Morel. Even Davout spares Pierre's life
once human contact has been established between them; and it
is the Russian Dolokhov, not a Frenchman, who is responsible
after the death of Petya Rostov for the most brutal massacre
assumed to have taken place in the novel.

It is equally wrong to regard Petersburg high society in
general and the Kuragins in particular—vulgar, unprincipled
and unprepossessing as they are—as the incarnation of all that
is *anti-popular* and *un-Russian*. Anatole Kuragin, blackguard
though he may be, is just as much a Russian as Pierre. He dies
fighting for his country with just as much or just as little
patriotism as the average private soldier. Hélène does not
cease to be Russian because she is vain and debauched, and is
never seen in the company of the lower classes.

Much of the difficulty of accepting some current Soviet
interpretations of *War and Peace* as the apotheosis of the
narod is due to the imprecise meaning and use of the Russian
word. Tolstoy's wife used a word from the same root as
narod when she asserted that 'the idea of the people' had been
dear to her husband in *War and Peace*, just as 'the idea of the
family' was dear to him in *Anna Karenina*.[1] How are we to
interpret this claim? If we equate *narod* with the peasantry, we
can say with some certainty what Tolstoy's attitude to them
was when he *began* to write his novel. His school experiment
at Yasnaya Polyana had ended in disillusion. He had devoted
himself to the education of his peasants, lived among them, done
all he could to help them. But he had not succeeded. In a letter
of 1863, the year after he gave up teaching, he said: 'I must
confess that my view of life, the people [*narod*] and society is

---

[1] *Dnevniki S. A. Tolstoi 1860–1891* (Moscow 1928), p. 37.

now quite different from what it was when we last met. One can be sorry for them [the people], but it is hard to understand how I could have loved them so much.'[1] It was no doubt this reaction that led him to write in a discarded preface to *War and Peace* that 'the lives of officials, merchants, theological students and peasants do not interest me and are only half comprehensible to me';[2] and although he introduced into his novel men and women from the lowest orders of society, and although they are treated sympathetically in their brief appearances, it is a patent distortion of emphasis to imply that they constitute the focal point of the novel, or are its 'collective hero'.

The word *narod*, however, can have a much wider sense than that of 'the common people'. It can also be translated as 'nation'. Much of the implausibility of some Soviet interpretations of *War and Peace* would be removed if it were always made clear in what sense the word was being used. One can argue with conviction that Tolstoy's interest in 'the people' was not centred narrowly on the *muzhik*, whether as an object of affection or of dislike. It broadened out during the writing of *War and Peace* until it reached the point where 'the people' came to be identified with 'the nation'—with all the men and women who consciously or unconsciously manifested the *spirit* of the Russian people, all the soldiers, conscripts and partisans, who embodied the *spirit* of the Russian army. One can argue convincingly that, on Tolstoy's evidence in his novel, selfish interests predominated in peace-time Russia, class divisions were pronounced, anti-national sentiments prevailed: but that under the impetus of an enemy invasion and a defensive war for the motherland the discordant elements drew together, and a greater national unity was achieved than ever before. The gulf between the 'two nations', the gentry and the peasantry, and between the patriotic and unpatriotic elements of the gentry was greatly narrowed. The national heroism of 1812 was a truly *popular* phenomenon, popular in the widest and best sense of embracing all people, masters and men. Those

[1] J.E. LXI, 23. [2] J.E. XIII, 54.

leaders who instinctively understood the national spirit, allowed themselves to be led by it. Those who believed that they alone guided events came to grief.

This is a plausible point of view. But it is not, I think, the central idea of *War and Peace*. Goldenveizer quotes Tolstoy as saying: 'The most important thing in a work of art is that it should have a kind of focus—i.e. some place where all the rays meet or from which they issue. And this focus should not be capable of being completely explained in words. This, indeed, is the most important thing about a good work of art, that its basic content can in its entirety be expressed only by itself.' [1]

It is not easy to express in words the focal point of Tolstoy's novel. Broadly speaking it is the contrast between two opposite states: on the one hand selfishness, self-indulgence, self-importance, and the attendant evils of careerism, nepotism, vanity, affectation and the pursuit of purely private pleasures; on the other hand a turning outwards from the self, a groping towards something bigger, an endeavour to surmount individualism, a recognition that the cult of the self is an unworthy alternative to the service of one's neighbours, one's family, the community and the country at large. Most people, Tolstoy appears to be saying, are preoccupied most of the time with their own selfish cares. Some are incorrigible careerists like Boris Drubetskoy or Napoleon, place-seekers and intriguers. Some, such as Hélène or Anatole Kuragin, think only of their own pleasure and are not restrained by any scruples of conscience from gratifying it. They are superb animals—handsome, graceful, lithe—with the senses and the appetite of an animal, and a total lack of consideration for human beings. What is more, they are not at all disturbed by their selfishness and would no doubt be offended if it were suggested that they were anything but normal, decent people —not saints certainly, but no worse than their neighbours. To this category of people belong the statesmen and military leaders who believe that their work is important and devoted

[1] Goldenveizer, *Vblizi Tolstogo*, p. 68.

to the public cause, but who are really only implementing their selfish desires for fame, power and decorations.

Others again such as Natasha and Nicholas Rostov are fond of themselves and of the normal round of upper-class entertainment, the accepted and unquestioned way of life of the gentry. They are not troubled by profound thoughts; they are not moved to ask themselves difficult questions about the purpose of life in general or their own lives in particular. But although they may be a little vain, a little too complacent at times, they unquestionably create a favourable impression on the reader by virtue, among other things, of their simple, forthright characters, their ability to share in the universal pleasures and obligations of everyday life and their freedom from hypocrisy and intrigue.

Prince Andrew and Pierre are also endowed with their fair share of self-centredness and love of pleasure. But while they think about themselves a great deal, they are most emphatically not self-satisfied. Prince Andrew's acceptance of the virtues of social success, fame and military glory does not stand the test of time and he is brought to see the folly of his cherished ideals. Pierre is beset with doubts and torments, endlessly searching for a way of life which will have some purpose beyond the mere satisfaction of his instincts and desires. They are both seekers, spiritually restless, changing and evolving, not content to accept for long what is generally accepted. In a much smaller way, the sympathetic Captain Tushin is also a man of independent mind, a nonconformist, a 'Tolstoyan' character. It is not *necessary* to be a seeker in order to earn Tolstoy's commendation; but all seekers are commended by him.

If the focal point of *War and Peace* is the problem of the sublimation of the self, Tolstoy believed it could be answered as he was trying to answer it, and as Pierre and Natasha, Nicholas and Princess Mary, answer it, at least temporarily, in the closing chapters of their story. This solution is the sober acceptance of family responsibility at the sacrifice to some extent of the uninhibited individual personality, work which brings its own reward, and the pursuit of simple pleasures accessible to all; the recognition that it is right and natural that the sparkling, vivacious Natasha should become a somewhat staid and lustreless mother of children, and that her husband and her brother and her brother's wife should arrive at a seemingly happy state of active and fruitful domesticity.

This is the stage which Tolstoy happened to have reached (or would have liked to believe he had reached) in his own journey through life. But it is not quite the conventional ending where 'all live happily ever after'. The inference is plain that Pierre and Nicholas will drift apart. Pierre's clandestine activities will take him into the Decembrist camp, where Nicholas can never follow him. Significantly enough, it is Prince Andrew's son, Nicholas Bolkonsky, who is given the last word in the novel. He is portrayed as a true son of his father, and as such he is bound to side with 'Uncle Pierre' against Nicholas Rostov. Tolstoy's two greatest heroes, Andrew and Pierre, merge together in the young boy's thoughts at the very end of *War and Peace* in a humorous passage which points the way forward and shows the same astonishingly convincing grasp of the workings of a juvenile mind which Tolstoy had shown earlier in the best chapters of *Childhood*:

Meanwhile a lamp was burning as usual downstairs in young Nicholas Bolkonsky's bedroom (the boy was afraid of the dark and they could not cure him of this failing). Dessalles (the boy's tutor) slept propped up on four pillows—and his Roman nose emitted regular snoring sounds. Little Nicholas, who had just woken up in a cold sweat, was sitting up in bed staring in front of him with wide-open eyes. He had been woken by a terrible dream. He had dreamt that Uncle Pierre and himself were marching at the head of a huge army wearing helmets like the ones illustrated in his edition of Plutarch. The army was made up of slanting white lines that filled the air like the cobwebs which float about in autumn and which Dessalles called *le fil de la Vierge*. In front was Glory, which was just like these threads, only rather thicker. He and Pierre were happily wafted along nearer and nearer to their goal. Suddenly the threads which moved them began to slacken and become entangled. It was difficult to move. And Uncle Nicholas stood in front of them in a stern and threatening attitude.

'Did you do this?' he said pointing to some broken sealing-wax and pens. 'I loved you, but I take orders from Arakcheev [Alexander's Minister of War, with a reputation for harshness and brutality], and I will kill the first person to advance.' Little Nicholas looked round at Pierre, but Pierre was not there any more. Pierre was his father, Prince Andrew, and his father had no shape or form, but he was there all the same, and when little Nicholas saw him he grew faint with love: he felt himself powerless, shapeless and limp. His father caressed and pitied him. But Uncle Nicholas moved nearer and nearer towards them. Terror seized young Nicholas, and he woke up.

'My father,' he thought. (Though there were two good portraits of Prince Andrew in the house, the young Nicholas had never imagined him in human form.) 'My father was with me and caressed me. He approved of me, and he approved of Uncle Pierre. I'll do whatever he tells me. Mucius Scaevola burnt his hand. Why shouldn't something similar happen to me? I know they want me to study. And I will study. But some day I'll have finished, and then I'll *do* something. I only pray God that what happened to Plutarch's men will happen to me, and I'll do the same. I'll do even better. Everyone will know me and love me and admire me.' And suddenly he felt his breast heaving with sobs and he began to cry.

'Êtes-vous indisposé?' he heard Dessalles' voice asking.

'Non,' answered Nicholas and lay back on his pillow. 'He is good and kind, and I love him,' he thought of Dessalles. 'But Uncle Pierre! Oh what a wonderful man he is! And my father? Yes my father! I'll do something which even *he* would be pleased with...'[1]

With this unselfconscious tribute to the avuncular Pierre and his friend, cast in a favourite form which recalls Tolstoy's theory of dreams in *A History of Yesterday*, the novel peters out into three dots. Pierre—*alias* Tolstoy— is left in possession of the field.

The thesis of the superiority of service to the group over the purely selfish cultivation of the individual personality, which is central to the family scenes in *War and Peace*, is further

---

[1] Epilogue, 1, 16.

illustrated by Tolstoy's treatment of the historical characters, where the 'group' is not the family but the country. The thesis is expressed, however, in the historically dubious form of a contrast between a general who passively submits to events in the knowledge that they are too big and too important for him to control and an Emperor who believes that he is clever enough and powerful enough to impose his personality on the course of history. An examination of the rôle assigned to Kutuzov and Napoleon in *War and Peace* leads inevitably to a consideration of Tolstoy's views on history and historiography.

The immediate pretext for the formulation of these views was the French invasion of Russia. What force caused this mass movement of men from West to East and back again? What rôle did Napoleon, Alexander and their generals and advisers play? What was the *cause* of the invasion of 1812? Certainly not Napoleon, Tolstoy argues. He enjoyed neither physical nor moral power. He was no stronger and no better than anyone else. Nor can he be said, in Rousseauesque terms, to represent the transfer of the collective will of the people. And yet it appears that he had only to issue a decree and a whole army entered Russia. But—the argument goes—no command can be viewed in isolation, but only as one of a series of mutually interconnected commands. The commander of an army never deals with the beginning of an event. He always finds himself in the middle of a series of happenings in which he is himself taking part with thousands of other men, and the commands he gives are conditioned and determined by those events. An event is not *caused* by a command which precedes it. Power lies not in the issuing of a command, but in the *relations* between a commander and those he commands —in their relations, and not in the person of the leader or of any individual soldier.

In the text of the novel Tolstoy contends that Napoleon's orders before the battle of Borodino had no influence on its outcome. For one thing, the original orders were never carried out. For another thing, the promise that orders would be given in accordance with the enemy's movements once the

battle had begun was never kept. Napolcon was so far away
that he could not have known the course the battle was taking;
and not one of his orders during it was executed. 'The French
soldiers went to kill and be killed at the battle of Borodino,
not because of Napoleon's orders, but *by their own volition*...
Had Napoleon forbidden them to fight the Russians they
would have killed him and have proceeded to fight the
Russians *because it was inevitable*.' Here one comes to the crux of
Tolstoy's problem. The soldiers 'acted of their own volition'.
They fought 'because it was inevitable'. In an earlier part of
the novel Tolstoy had distinguished between the two sides of
the life of every man—his individual life where he has a certain
degree of freedom and his 'elemental, swarm-life' where he
inevitably obeys laws laid down for him. 'Man lives consciously for himself, but is an unconscious instrument in the
attainment of the historic, universal aims of humanity.' The
higher a man stands on the social ladder the less he is free. A
king, to quote Hegel, is history's slave.

Here and elsewhere Tolstoy assumes that although man is to
some extent free in his individual life, the area of freedom he
enjoys is severely limited. Thomas Hardy, whose *Dynasts* has
often been (unfavourably) compared with *War and Peace*, and
whose annotated copy of Tolstoy's novel reveals the influence
it had on Hardy's thinking, especially his attitude to Kutuzov,
held a very similar view. 'The will of man', he said, 'is neither
wholly free nor wholly unfree. When swayed by the Universal
Will, he is not individually free, but whenever it happens that
all the rest of the Great Will is in equilibrium, the minute
portion called one person's will is free.'[1] Tolstoy said that man
can choose to raise or lower his arm, and nobody but himself is
affected. But such actions are of little significance. In any case,
even when he acts alone, he is the product of his environment,
and his choice is far less free than he would like to think. But
for most of the time he is involved with other people, and the
number of conditioning factors is multiplied enormously.

[1] Quoted by J. Wain in his introduction to *The Dynasts* (Harmondsworth
Middlesex 1967).

His *reason* ought to tell him that he is not really free, but his *consciousness* contradicts his reason. It is necessary for a man to have the illusion of freedom to go on living, and it is not difficult for him to have it since there are so many unknowns, so many unknowables. The extent of our awareness of our freedom or of necessity depends in Tolstoy's view on three factors: how much we are involved with others; how great a time-lag there is between an action and our judgment of it; and the relation of one action to a chain of actions—to what comes before and what comes after. We are more free or less free in our own consciousness according to how much we know of our degree of dependence on factors beyond our immediate control. But ultimately, if our reason could reconstruct all these factors, it would be seen that we were the inevitable prisoners of historical laws. 'Every act' of Napoleon's or Alexander's, Tolstoy says, 'which appears to them an act of their own will, is in a historical sense involuntary, related to the whole course of history, and predestined from eternity'. For Tolstoy, as for Hardy's Spirits contemplating and commenting on the events of 1805–15, Napoleon is: 'In the elemental ages' chart, the meanest insect on the obscurest leaf.'

Napoleon, then, was not the cause of the invasion of Russia. Nothing was—or alternatively, everything was: such seems to be Tolstoy's unhelpful conclusion. This is not to say that he denies that events have causes; only that historians look for causes in the wrong places—or the wrong people. He himself was not afraid to offer specific causes for the destruction of the French army in 1812. The two he selected were the harshness of the Russian winter and the fury aroused in the Russian people by the burning of their towns and villages. But his point is that these 'causes' were not the consequence of voluntary acts by generals or statesmen, and were not foreseen by the people taking part in the events. Neither the French nor the Russians acted as if they understood the importance of the Russian winter. The Russians continued to resist while the French continued to press on. As for the retreat from Moscow and the partisan activity of the Russians—this was a spontaneous movement, not the result of a deliberate plan to lure the enemy to its destruction. Kutuzov was no more a genius than Napoleon.

What, to Tolstoy, was of supreme importance in the history of warfare was what he termed 'the spirit of the army', or more simply morale. It is made up of an infinite number of unknowable states and actions of faceless individuals. The task of the historian—and what a task it is!—is to try to integrate all the infinitesimally small differentials of history. He can never hope to know them all, but by recognising their infinite number and variety, he will cut down to size the so-called 'great men' of history and explode the myth of king-centred historiography.

The most confusing and seemingly contradictory aspects of Tolstoy's view of history are his ex-cathedra pronouncements on causality and predestination. 'There is, and can be, no cause of a historical event except the one cause of all causes,' he writes in one chapter, apparently unaware of the specific causes he adduces for the destruction of the French army. Elsewhere he says that the course of human history has been predestined for all time, which can only mean that man is powerless to alter it, 'spirit of the army' or no 'spirit of the army'. There is no cause except the first cause, 'but there are laws directing events, and some of these laws are known to us while we are conscious of others we cannot comprehend. The discovery of these laws is only possible when we have quite abandoned the attempt to find the cause in the will of some one man.' The laws of history are iron laws, and there is a hopelessness about the final words of *War and Peace*: 'It is necessary to renounce a freedom that does not exist and recognise a dependence [i.e. on historical laws] of which we are not conscious.' Equally chilling are the concluding lines of Tolstoy's article 'A Few Words about *War and Peace*': 'The activity of these people [i.e. the leaders of 1812] interested me only as an illustration of the law of predestination, and of that psychological law which compels a man who acts under the greatest compulsion to supply in his imagination a whole series of retrospective reflections to prove his freedom to himself.'

So much for the statement of the case. Before we try to assess it, it may be of interest to touch on some aspects of a general nature which have attracted the attention of Tolstoyan scholars.

Literary critics have on the whole resented Tolstoy's incursions into philosophy, first because they are allegedly out of place in a work of fiction, and secondly because they appear to be contradicted by the actions and behaviour of the fictional characters themselves. Common sense seems to favour the first view, and the case against them on artistic grounds is strong, although for my own part, since the ideas expressed are interesting and important, and since they are relevant to and arise directly out of the novel, I am prepared to accept them in the context for which they were designed. A more serious objection to the 'philosophy of history' of *War and Peace* is the charge that it does not square with the fictional narrative, and this I do not accept. The fact that so many of Tolstoy's characters act with apparent freedom, exult in the spontaneous, creative forces of life, choose their friends, their loves, their pleasures and their duties, act impulsively or accomplish deeds of heroism, does not at all refute his theories. The life of these people can be rich, many-sided, apparently self-determined— and yet the consciousness of freedom which permeates it can still be illusory. One can argue perfectly plausibly that Pierre's decision to marry Hélène is not a 'free' one; that fate brings Pierre and Natasha together; that chance unites Princess Mary and Nicholas; that Sonya is doomed to become an old maid. Although they regard their actions as free and, if they did not, would perhaps lose the will to go on living, their behaviour is not in any way inconsistent with the philosophy of the novel, which ascribes a pitifully small area of free will to man, but an infinitely large area of consciousness of freedom. Freedom, it has been said,[1] for the characters of *War and Peace* means going gladly into life's imprisonment. Everything happens as it has to happen, but also as everybody wants it to happen.

[1] J. Bayley, *Tolstoy and the Novel* (London 1966), p. 21.

The literary critic raises problems of relevancy and consistency; the historian of ideas is concerned with questions of provenance. Where did Tolstoy's ideas come from? How original are they? There are certain names which constantly recur in discussions of ideological 'influences' on *War and Peace*. A not very convincing case has been made out for Proudhon,[1] whom Tolstoy visited in Brussels in 1861 when Proudhon was finishing his own *La Guerre et la Paix: recherches sur le principe et la constitution du droit des gens*. With rather more plausibility, attention has been drawn to Tolstoy's circle of Slavophil or near Slavophil friends of a conservative or medievalist outlook —Pogodin, Yur'ev, Samarin and Urusov. Some sections of Pogodin's *Historical Aphorisms*, his correspondence with Tolstoy, his preoccupation with problems of cause and effect, freedom and necessity, his comparisons with phenomena from the world of physics, mechanics and mathematics, his use of the term 'differential of history', all point to an obvious affinity between the two men. Urusov's eccentric book on the campaigns of 1812–13, based on an attempt to discover the laws of war with the aid of mathematical analysis, certainly proved of immense interest to Tolstoy, in particular Urusov's positive (and untypical) attitude to Kutuzov, and his technical language which found an undoubted reflection in the similes and metaphors of the theoretical passages in *War and Peace*. Some ideas and expressions from Hegel's *Introduction to the Philosophy of History* and from Herzen's memoirs may have found their way into Tolstoy's novel. Of more importance in the history of ideas is Tolstoy's relation to de Maistre, which has been the subject of investigation by Boris Eykhenbaum in the Soviet Union and Sir Isaiah Berlin in Britain. Berlin makes it clear that the positive beliefs of the reactionary Catholic Savoyard diplomat were utterly alien to the Russian novelist; but that on the negative side both men shared the view that those who think that they control events, whether generals or statesmen, are the greatest fools; that there were no grounds for believing in human goodness and reason or the value and inevitability of

1 B. M. Eykhenbaum, *Lev Tolstoi, kniga vtoraya, 60-e gody*, Pt. IV, Chs. 1 and 2.

human progress by rational and scientific means to happiness and virtue. 'Both men', writes Berlin, 'looked for a harmonious universe and found war and disorder'; both 'offered to throw away the terrible weapons of criticism...in favour of the single great vision'.[1] As cynics and sceptics Tolstoy and de Maistre had much in common—and indeed it would not be difficult to show that many of Tolstoy's prejudices were shared not only by de Maistre and the Russian conservatives already mentioned, but also by other more distinguished eighteenth- and nineteenth-century European thinkers. But it would be absurd to think of Tolstoy as a great eclectic borrower or derivative writer. All authors are inevitably influenced by what they read, and originality of thought does not mean freedom from outside influence, but a new combination of ideas which in a new relationship express a new meaning. Tolstoy clearly found inspiration in de Maistre, Hegel, Rousseau, Proudhon even, as he found inspiration of a different sort in, say, Stendhal, Dickens, Thackeray and Sterne. He seized avidly at any confirmation of his ideas in other people's work and was happy to borrow their examples. Many of the negative sides of his work, his criticisms, prejudices, intolerance, are shared by one or other of the men he read and admired (admired, that is, for the force of their destructive criticism, not their positive philosophies). His central negative thesis, that individuals cannot consciously and rationally understand and guide the course of events, was hardly an original one. But his central positive thesis, that the 'great' men are not those who think they are guiding the course of events, but men like the simple, intuitively wise Kutuzov who passively surrenders when he knows he is powerless to control; that the national 'heroes' are not the generals and statesmen but the numerous unobtrusive individuals, noblemen or peasants, Rostovs, Tushins or Karataevs, who by their simplicity, their absence of affectation and hypocrisy, and their innate natural goodness are true representatives of the Russian nation; and that the process of understanding history begins not with the exposition of 'great'

[1] I. Berlin, *The Hedgehog and the Fox*, p. 80.

men's deeds, but with the integration of an infinitely large number of infinitely small actions—this is Tolstoy's original contribution to the historical novel.

To the psychologist it is a matter of interest why Tolstoy *needed* an answer to the question 'What is History?'—why he wanted an all-embracing solution, a system into which every part fits, and not piecemeal or patched-up solutions to problems as they crop up. Berlin, with the aid of a felicitous quotation from Archilochus, divides the great thinkers into foxes and hedgehogs. The foxes pursue many ends, often unrelated and contradictory, with no moral or aesthetic principle to connect them. They enjoy a vast variety of experience and think on many levels without wishing to draw all the threads together into one harmonious pattern. The hedgehogs try to fit the facts into an unchanging, all-embracing system, which provides unity at the expense of complexity. Bernard Shaw once drew a similar distinction between thinkers concerned with 'diversities' and those like Tolstoy who were concerned with 'unities'.[1] Berlin's contention is that Tolstoy was by nature a fox who believed in being a hedgehog. He wanted historical laws, which ruled out chance and genius, even though these laws must remain incomprehensible to us. He wanted a purpose in history, although he recognised that it must be beyond our understanding. And he wanted the historian to integrate. All the evidence of his eyes and senses contradicted what he wanted to believe. There was no sign of order, purpose, harmony, laws or progress in his experience of contemporary history or his reading of the past. Perhaps for that very reason he wanted to believe all the more that they *must be* there, but that the professional historians had led everyone astray by their false emphasis and their wrong questions. Psychologists and philosophers who study Tolstoy's life and works are bound to recognise the primacy of *should* over *is*, and *should* implies a moral injunction which, if everyone heeded, would result in a conformity, a pattern of behaviour which Tolstoy sought so earnestly in the years after *War and*

[1] *Prefaces* (London 1934), p. 162.

Peace. His philosophy of history, though not prescriptive or ethically centred, stems from the same psychological need for laws, a system, a pattern, a calculus, which made him ask the sort of questions he did about art and religion also, and provide the answers he felt obliged to provide.

It has never been fashionable to take Tolstoy's views of history seriously. At an elementary factual level, his slipshod handling of figures left him open to charges of carelessness, quite unbecoming in a man who is himself accusing the historians of factual inaccuracies. He says that the French lost one quarter of their army at Borodino, and in the same paragraph that they lost 20,000 out of 120,000 men. He says that the Russians lost 50,000 and the French 20,000, but puts their combined losses on another page at 80,000. These errors do not alter the gist of his argument, and are in themselves trivial, though indicative.

Much more serious is the accusation that he deliberately falsified the features of the historical Kutuzov to make him more suited to the part required of him. Kutuzov is stripped in the novel of his more unprepossessing characteristics (some of which appear in the drafts but not in the final version) and his lechery and sloth are played down. Conversely, some of his well-authenticated positive qualities of generalship—his initiative and his conscious acts of leadership—are ignored. It has been convincingly argued[1] that, despite what Tolstoy said, Kutuzov deliberately chose the site for the battle of Borodino and that it was a good site; that he took strong measures during the battle which Tolstoy chose to ignore; that Uvarov's action at Borodino, which was taken on Kutuzov's orders, checked Napoleon and prevented him from bringing up reserves—and so on. On the other hand, it is contended, Tolstoy turned a blind eye to Kutuzov's blunders. He failed to mention that Kutuzov forgot about 300 cannon he had at Borodino, which, had he brought them into action, would have altered the course of the battle. In order to show him as a man of fixed and

---

[1] See V. Shklovsky, 'M. I. Kutuzov i Platon Karataev v romane *Voina i mir*', *Znamya*, v (1948), pp. 137–45.

consistent views on the conduct of the war in 1812 he actually removed a short passage from the published version of the novel which implied the contrary.

One does not need to be a patriotic French historian to produce similar examples of Tolstoy's somewhat cavalier treatment of Napoleon. Do these distortions, then, make nonsense of all his historical thinking? Is his position as absurd as it seems?

On the subject of 'great men', it is hard to refute the view expressed by E. H. Carr[1] when he says: 'The great man is always representative either of existing forces or of forces which he helps to create by way of challenge to existing authority. But the higher degree of creativity may perhaps be assigned to those great men who, like Cromwell or Lenin, helped to mould the forces which carried them to greatness, rather than to those who, like Napoleon or Bismarck, rode to greatness on the back of already existing forces.' We have no need to dispense with great men and their influence, as long as we recognise that they too are moulded and influenced to a greater or lesser degree by the situations they inherit. In order to stress the latter point, Tolstoy framed his argument in an unpalatably exaggerated form, but it stemmed from his belief in the primacy of the 'forces' over the individual representative of power, and this belief is neither ludicrous nor untenable in the twentieth century.

Tolstoy postulates a first cause, which is not in itself unreasonable. He denies that man knows the ultimate aim and purpose of existence, and in this he does not lack support. He assumes that there are certain historical laws in operation, but since he does not define or illustrate them, the attack against him is not concentrated on this point. He does not deny that events have causes (as, for example, the French retreat from Moscow), but he does deny that man can consciously produce the result he wishes of an action, and when dealing with man in the context of society, it is hard to ignore this belief or to prove that B happened because A willed it, if B is an event of

---

[1] E. H. Carr, *What is History?* (Harmondsworth Middlesex 1965), p. 54.

any importance and involves many people. In the extreme form in which he puts it he contends—relying on the evidence of the past—that man cannot shape his future as he would like it to be; but from this not implausible reading of history he makes the unwarranted assumption that the course of history is therefore predetermined from the beginning. Since he was not a fatalist by temperament, and since he believed in the power to influence people to change their lives, to become different people, to exercise their will to abstain from some practices and embrace others, he had to rescue himself from the dilemma by falling back on the argument that we think we are free, we act as if we are free, and it is only this consciousness of freedom that makes life possible for us.

Why did he need to drag in predestination? Why did he not say that although you cannot know the outcome of your actions for certain when they involve other people, some outcomes are more probable than others in the light of past experience; that some people do exercise more influence than others; or that the 'spirit of the leader' can be infectious, just as the 'spirit of the army' can? Because he was revolting against a tradition of historical writing which needed to be resisted and still needs resisting. The fact that he overplayed his hand does not mean that the game was not worth the candle—and it would have been a better game still had he not taken the unnecessary step to predestination. Nothing is inevitable in history, but some things are extremely likely. There is still much to learn from Tolstoy's errors, which are a healthy corrective to the menace of human arrogance, dictator-worship and power politics. The very exaggerated and extreme nature of his conclusions makes one question the safe and unadventurous assumptions with which one unthinkingly goes through life, and it provides the sort of shock to habit and complacency which one often finds in great art and nowhere more so than in the great Russian novels of the nineteenth century.

6

'ANNA KARENINA'

The years immediately following the publication of *War and Peace* were years of deep and extensive reading and a rediscovered vocation to teach children and to write for them. Tolstoy now began to study in earnest the language and literature of classical Greece, particularly Homer, Xenophon and Herodotus. He re-read the plays of Molière, Goethe and Shakespeare and the classics of the Russian stage. He applied himself to Schopenhauer, Kant and Pascal with enthusiastic dedication. Despite a temporary revulsion from fiction, especially his own (he vowed he would never write any more 'long-winded rubbish like *War and Peace*'), he returned to work on *The Decembrists* and began a historical novel on the life and times of Peter the Great—only to abandon it as a result, no doubt, of his antipathy towards its hero. Significantly enough, his list of books which made the deepest impression on him during the years 1863 to 1878 included not only the *Iliad*, the *Odyssey*, the *Anabasis* and the Russian *byliny*, but also *Les Misérables* and the novels of Trollope, George Eliot and Mrs Ward. 'The best books of all are English,' he said in 1877. 'Whenever I take some English books home with me, I always find they contain something new and fresh.'[1] His main efforts, however, in 1871 and 1872 were concentrated on writing his *Primer* for peasant children, which is of far wider scope than its title might suggest. Not only did Tolstoy write many stories himself, whose narrative interest, brevity and simplicity were calculated to make a direct moral appeal; he also translated and adapted fables and folktales from Greek, Jewish, Oriental and Arabic sources, compiled a section on arithmetic and provided passages for reading from the natural sciences, the Russian chronicles and the Lives of the Saints. Among his own compositions for his primer were *A Captive*

[1] L. N. Tolstoi, *Pamyatniki tvorchestva i zhizni* (Moscow 1923), vyp. III, p. 34.

in the Caucasus and *God Sees the Truth but Waits*, which he was later to value more highly than all the rest of his fiction. But absorbing as his new work was, and contemptuous as he professed to be of his past success as a novelist, it was only a matter of time before circumstances conspired to turn his attention once again from the school-room to the world outside. In 1873 he was busy at work on what he insisted on calling his first novel—*Anna Karenina*.

The story of the writing of *Anna* is complicated and confused, and the lack of adequate dating makes an accurate chronological reconstruction of the plans and draft versions of the novel extremely difficult, if not impossible. The problem has been exhaustively treated in the U.S.S.R.,[1] and in the absence of any new material it is unlikely that the tentative solutions at present offered by Soviet textologists can be improved upon. To consider all the draft versions from the point of view of Tolstoy's technique as a novelist would be a lengthy and specialised undertaking. Here we must be content to mention only those changes in direction and emphasis which seem relevant to the ideas Tolstoy wished to express, or believed himself to have expressed, in his novel.

The first reference to *Anna Karenina* is to be found in his wife's diary for February 1870:

Yesterday evening he told me he had envisaged a certain type of woman, married, of high society, who had gone astray. He said his object was to make this woman merely pitiable, not guilty, and that as soon as he had envisaged this type, all the other characters and the men he had previously envisaged fell into place and arranged themselves round her.[2]

The starting point for the novel was to be adultery. 'Novels,' as Rose Macaulay says, 'have always been about sex, or rather sexes. There's nothing new in that; it's the oldest story in the world.[3] But Tolstoy's views about sex and the sanctity of

---

[1] See especially V. A. Zhdanov, *Tvorcheskaya istoriya 'Anny Kareninoi'* (Moscow 1957).
[2] *Dnevniki S. A. Tolstoi 1860–1891*, p. 32.   [3] *Told by an Idiot.*

marriage and the family were sufficiently clearly formulated by this time for one to be a little surprised by his intention to make his adulteress-heroine the object of pity, not blame. So firmly did he appear to believe in the virtue of family life that he even went so far in one of his letters, albeit under the immediate impact of Schopenhauer, as to justify prostitution if it served the higher cause: 'Imagine London without its 80,000 Magdalenes. What would become of its families?... Given the present complicated forms of life I think this class of woman is necessary for the family's sake.'[1] Tolstoy's other interests diverted him from the subject of sex for some time, until he was painfully reminded of it by the suicide of his neighbour's mistress, Anna Pirogova, who, on learning of her lover's attachment to another woman, sent him a note which he did not receive in time and threw herself under a train. Tolstoy saw her mangled body at the post-mortem. His wife recalled her as 'dark-haired, not beautiful, but very pleasant', in words strangely reminiscent of the description of Anna Karenina in one of the early drafts of the novel.

The following year Tolstoy began to write his book with the suicide of an adulteress as its *terminus a quo*. This fact should be remembered when he is accused of 'killing off' Anna, or driving his heroine to destruction. Had there been no suicide, there would have been no novel. The immediate stimulus to write was a re-reading of Pushkin's short stories, and in particular an unfinished fragment which began: 'The guests arrived at the country house.' 'That is the way to write,' he said. 'Pushkin gets straight down to business. Other people would start to describe the guests or the rooms, but he plunges into action right away.'[2] The opening lines of Pushkin's story served Tolstoy as a model for what was originally the opening scene of his own novel (now Part 2, Chapter 6)—the arrival of the guests at Princess Betsy's house. But it was more than a mere cue to plunge *in medias res*. The first draft of the scene in *Anna*

[1] J.E. LXI, 233.
[2] F. I. Bulgakov, *Graf L. N. Tolstoi i kritika ego proizvedenii* (St Petersburg 1899), p. 86.

reads like a variation on Pushkin's fragment, where the guests are gathered round the samovar discussing the fickle conduct of a certain young lady in whom 'there is much good, and far less evil than people think. But her passions will destroy her.' Curiously enough, the next fragment in the particular edition of Pushkin which Tolstoy happened to be reading at the time (it opens with the words 'In the corner of a little square'...) takes as its subject an unfaithful wife. Her revulsion towards her husband, her jealousy, suspicion and fear of her lover's coldness, his resentment at his isolation from society and his own fear of losing his independence all foreshadow in a remarkable manner the future relationships of Anna, Karenin and Vronsky.

Another book which Tolstoy was reading at the time was Dumas fils' recently published *L'Homme-femme*, which discussed the question whether to forgive an unfaithful wife—or kill her! He wrote about it enthusiastically to his sister-in-law, saying, 'One would never have expected a Frenchman to have such a lofty understanding of marriage or of the relationships in general between a man and a woman.'[1] Dumas' book saw the struggle between the male and the female as the basic conflict in life. Woman was the weaker creature, always likely to be unfaithful. Her salvation lay in the family. The husband should exercise a moral influence over his wife, educate her and forgive her whenever possible. But in the last resort he must play the rôle of judge and executioner; he must kill an unfaithful and unregenerate wife. In one of the early drafts of *Anna* the book figures in a discussion between the future Levin and a student. This particular passage did not reach the final version, but Dumas' conclusions and the need to reach his own opinion about them clearly disturbed Tolstoy, and indeed in one draft of the novel he actually toyed with the Frenchman's solution of the problem to the extent of making the future Karenin load his pistol and set off to murder the unfaithful Anna.

With Schopenhauer, Pushkin and Dumas fresh in his mind,

[1] J.E. LXII, 11.

Tolstoy set to work on his chosen theme with great alacrity. In a very short time he had written a full draft and expressed the hope that the novel itself would be completed in a fortnight. This was in 1873. In the event it was not finished until 1877, after long periods of dissatisfaction, depression and even revulsion, although the first sections began to appear in serial form in *The Russian Messenger* in 1875. What is now believed to have been the earliest version of *Anna* is a rough draft of the whole novel, which Tolstoy, contrary to his usual practice, mapped out from beginning to end in some thirty pages of texts and notes.[1] It began with Anna's liaison already under way. The scene opens at a soirée. The Stavroviches (the future Karenins) are the subject of discussion. The original choice of name, incidentally, is interesting for its similarity to that of Stavrogin in Dostoevsky's *Devils*, the last part of which had been published in *The Russian Messenger* the previous year, for the word 'devil' is used of Anna more than once at this early stage, and even in the final version Kitty observes a 'diabolical' streak in her. In the course of conversation at the soirée, the opinion is expressed that Stavrovich's wife will come to grief. When she eventually arrives 'she is more *décolletée* than all the others'. There is 'something bold and provocative in her clothing and her rapid way of walking'. She talks to diplomats in a loud, uninhibited voice about things which are not mentioned in salons. Reference is made to her mocking eyes and 'diabolical' face. Her husband on the other hand is gentle and shy. Her lover calls him wise and kind. He offers the other cheek and is ready to forgive. A divorce follows and Anna marries her lover. But although they are drawn to society like moths to a light, society will not receive them. Despite her two children Anna is lonely. 'All that was left was animal relationships and the luxuries of life.' Her unhappy and pathetic husband offers her the comforts of religion, but to no avail. The ending is appropriately laconic: 'She left home. A day later her body was found near the rails. Balashev [the original Vronsky] went to Tashkent, leaving the children with his

[1] J.E. xx, 23 ff.

sister. Mikhail Mikhailovich [the original Karenin] remained in the service.'

At this stage there is no mention of Kitty and Levin, and only a passing reference to the future Oblonsky and his wife. Numerous successive drafts introduce the contrasting families and take the action back well before the beginning of the liaison. Broadly speaking the main changes, apart from the introduction of some new scenes and the suppression of others, concern the original trio, Anna, Karenin and Vronsky. At first unattractive, vulgar, coquettish, stout and even ugly, Anna becomes progressively more beautiful, graceful and charming. (It has been suggested that in some important details she comes to resemble the portrait of Hetty Sorrel in *Adam Bede*[1] but perhaps the similarity is not so much in external appearances, as in the inability of the two women to stand alone and face their situation unaided.) Karenin on the other hand forfeits some of the sympathy he had at first aroused at his wife's expense, as a kindly, rather dreamy, magnanimous gentleman, a 'scholarly eccentric', trying with sincere Christian fortitude to endure a disaster which had overtaken him through no fault of his own. As the work of revision proceeded, Tolstoy imparted to him the now familiar characteristics of a cold, ironical, self-important bureaucrat. Similarly, Vronsky's image changes somewhat for the worse. If at first he is conceived of as endowed with exceptional intelligence and poetic gifts, indifferent to wealth and social position, and even for a time sincere in his desire to marry Kitty, Tolstoy goes to some pains at a later stage (by suggesting, for example, the coldness and at times hostility between him and Anna's son, or by emphasising his contempt for his social inferiors—'he looked at people as though they were things') to make him less immediately attractive.

These changes in characterisation are apt to be forgotten in discussions about the meaning of the epigraph to *Anna*, which has perhaps attracted more critical attention than it really

[1] See W. Gareth Jones, 'George Eliot's *Adam Bede* and Tolstoy's Conception of *Anna Karenina*', *Modern Language Review*, LXI (1966).

deserves. Tolstoy originally borrowed it from Schopenhauer, and it appeared in an early draft in the unbiblical form 'Mine is the Vengeance', an obviously literal translation of the German original 'Mein ist die Rache'. Tolstoy mistakenly thought it came from Solomon. What is now believed to have been the fifth version of the early chapters was headed by the same epigraph, although the first chapter was itself introduced by another thematic statement: 'For some, marriage is the most difficult and important thing in life; for others it is a trivial diversion.' Ultimately the familiar and definitive epigraph—'Vengeance is mine, I will repay'—assumed the form in which it was first used in Deuteronomy and by St Paul, and unfortunately rendered in an early German translation as 'Vengeance is mine. I play the ace!' What did Tolstoy mean by this?

One possibility is that he understood the words to emphasise the person, rather than the thing. Vengeance is *mine*, saith the Lord. It is the prerogative of God, not men. If this is so, he was no doubt influenced by his reading of *The World as Will and Idea* in which Schopenhauer advanced the argument that it would be the height of presumption for a man to act as a moral judge over his fellow men and to exact retribution for a wrong done to him, quoting the passage from Deuteronomy in support of his contention that it is the Lord who will repay. The Christian idea that there is an eternal justice beyond man's control, which Schopenhauer refers to in the context of the same passage, certainly commanded Tolstoy's respect. He was later to develop it by his vehement opposition to secular courts of law and by the prominence he gave to Christ's words: 'Judge not.' His later beliefs were clearly present in his thoughts on at least three occasions when he tried to explain what his intention was in choosing the epigraph he did. First he endorsed the interpretation proposed by the critic Gromeka[1] that there can be no absolute freedom in sexual love, but that there are laws which man is free to accept or reject, and on his choice depends his happiness or unhappiness. The family

[1] *Russkaya mysl'*, II (1883), p. 265.

cannot be broken up without causing unhappiness and a new happiness cannot be built on its ruins. Gromeka's apologia for the family as the only satisfactory basis for love, coupled with his condemnation of extra-marital sexual indulgence certainly had Tolstoy's approval at this stage of his life. But it is hardly an explanation of the epigraph, whether or not it explains (as Tolstoy said it did) 'what he unconsciously put into his work'.

Secondly he made it clear to his son-in-law, Sukhotin, in 1907[1] that he disagreed with Veresaev's interpretation that Anna came to grief because she would not surrender herself entirely to her new life and love, but worried about her position in society and became a jealous mistress; because she would not heed the promptings of her own heart, but did violence to her deepest and inmost feelings—for which offence 'the natural laws of life' wrought their vengeance. In rejecting this reading Tolstoy said: 'I chose this epigraph simply in order to express the idea that the wrong which a person does leads to all the bitter consequences which stem, not from other people but from God, and which Anna Karenina experienced too.'[2] This is an unambiguous declaration of intent (although it came thirty years after the novel was completed), but it takes no account of the fact that if Anna's conduct was wrong, so too was that of Oblonsky and Princess Betsy, who suffered no bitter consequences. On yet another occasion he recorded his opinion about the meaning of the epigraph when, in reply to a letter from two schoolgirls who put the question to him and offered their own answer 'that a person who has violated moral laws will be punished', he wrote back, 'You are right.'[3] But this too was nearly thirty years after the event.

It would be wrong to attach too much importance to these retrospective pronouncements, and one is tempted to agree that Tolstoy originally meant no more by his epigraph than a

[1] B. M. Eykhenbaum, *Lev Tolstoi, semidesyatye gody* (Leningrad 1960), p. 196.

[2] B. M. Eykhenbaum, *Lev Tolstoi, semidesyatye gody*, p. 197 (quoting V. Veresaev, *Vospominaniya*, Moscow 1940), p. 166.

[3] F. V. Buslaev, *Korrespondenty L. N. Tolstogo* (Moscow 1940), p. 166.

simple statement of belief, following Schopenhauer, that it is not for men and women to cast the first stone—a point which is made explicitly on more than one occasion in the novel. 'It's for God to judge them, not us,' says the Princess Varvara to Dolly;[1] 'it's not for us to judge'—Koznyshev echoes her words after Anna's death.[2] More important, however, is the fact that Tolstoy chose his text with *only* the Anna–Vronsky–Karenin plot in mind, at a time when Anna was a worse and Karenin a better person, and that it remained unchanged while the conception of the characters altered. There is no doubt that the rational side of him strongly disapproved of adultery, and his devotion to the 'idea of the family' in *Anna*, in his wife's words, is amply documented. It seems to be the case that Tolstoy intended to pronounce Anna guilty, but refused to tolerate her condemnation by other mortals. As the novel progressed and as Anna changed for the better, the gap between intention and realisation grew wider, and we are not asked to condemn her, as we might have been if the first draft, for which the epigraph was written, had been the last. The novel as we have it passes no explicit judgment on Anna. For this reason critical reactions to her predicament (as opposed to what may have been Tolstoy's original *intentions* about her fate) have differed widely from writer to writer and from generation to generation. There have always been those who have argued that whatever the extenuating circumstances Anna was wrong to commit adultery, and that the consequences for her, *being the sort of person she was*, would inevitably be tragic. In Britain Matthew Arnold was the first to set the moral tone, and while stressing the undoubted superiority of Anna over Madame Bovary, recorded his predictable Victorian belief that 'an English mind will be startled by Anna's suffering herself to be so overwhelmed and irretrievably carried away by her passion, by her almost at once regarding it as something which it was hopeless to fight against'.[3] This point of view, which draws support from Anna's undoubted moral deterioration

---

[1] *Anna Karenina*, 6, 20.   [2] *Anna Karenina*, 8, 4.
[3] M. Arnold, *Essays in Criticism* (London 1888), p. 269.

and almost hysterical possessiveness, is less commonly voiced today, and Tolstoy's alleged 'punishment' of Anna is inevitably contrasted with his treatment of Princess Betsy and Oblonsky, whose easy infidelities lead to no tragic consequences for themselves. Absolute standards of morality are less interesting than relative standards of justice. But Tolstoy's experience of life told him that some people suffer while others who behave in the same way do not. What interests him is not absolute categories of justice (the same punishment for the same offence), but individual people and their own sense of what is right and wrong. Anna has a conscience and she suffers for it. Betsy has no conscience, or is not shown to have, and she neither feels that adultery is wrong nor experiences unhappiness because of it. It is not for men to judge between them, for men did not implant that conscience. God has the right, so the epigraph may be taken to imply. But why should you suffer if you have a conscience and disregard it, but be happy if you have none, if the responsibility for the conscience or the lack of it does not rest with you alone? Tolstoy does not have to answer this question, but it is an essential part of his purpose that Anna should be a morally superior person to Betsy or Oblonsky, and should be capable of experiencing shame, horror and remorse.

It is fashionable nowadays to transfer the blame from Anna to society, and to attribute her tragedy to outmoded social conventions and antiquated divorce laws. D. H. Lawrence linked Anna's name with Tess of the D'Urbervilles as being at war with society, not God. 'And the judgement of men killed them, not the judgement of their own souls or the judgement of Eternal God.'[1] Or, in the very similar words of a Soviet critic, 'It was people, not God, who threw Anna under the train.'[2] One can make out a plausible case for this point of view, without reference to the novel, although Tolstoy would not have agreed with it and had certainly no intention of

[1] *Study of Thomas Hardy*, quoted in Davie, *Russian Literature and Modern English Fiction*, p. 141.
[2] V. Shklovsky, *Lev Tolstoi* (Moscow 1963), p. 475.

giving it any prominence. There is no evidence that Tolstoy himself believed, or expected his readers to infer, that, had Anna obtained a divorce and been received back into society, all her troubles would have been over, or that she would have felt no shame, jealousy or alienation. It is Tolstoy's strength as an artist that he does not attempt to shift the blame from the shoulders of the individual to the impersonal forces of the law. If he had shown Anna, duly divorced from her husband, living happily with Vronsky and bringing up a new family while seeing Seriozha at legally prescribed intervals, his novel would have been immeasurably weaker as a novel, whatever its contribution may have been to the literature of divorce law reform.

But there is a sense in which society *was* for Tolstoy the villain of the piece—and not simply because the divorce laws were unjust or because Russia of the 1870s happened to be a bourgeois, capitalist society with semi-feudal agrarian roots, and not, let us say, a society which rewarded men according to their work, or according to their needs. As he grew older the whole concept of organised society, the whole apparatus of state organisation—legal, military, administrative and executive—became increasingly distasteful to him. Of course he had not arrived at the stage of utopian anarchism when he was writing *Anna Karenina*. And yet it is already possible to sense in the novel a rooted dissatisfaction with society in the widest sense of the word, an aversion to materialism and a groping towards spiritual values, which is hinted at, almost as an afterthought, in Levin's monologues in the final chapters. One could argue that a feeling of claustrophobia pervades the novel, a sense that there is no *institutional* way out, that the only hope for man is a discovery of his spiritual self, beside which the actual form of social organisation is an irrelevancy. To some extent Levin, for all his blundering egoism, is a liberating force, and his searching individualism, irritating as it can be, adds a new dimension to the story, much as the war in *War and Peace* releases the characters from their constricting social bonds.

Yet another approach to Anna's tragedy is to see it as the result of leaving one inadequate man for another, and failing to find in Vronsky a lover equal to her demands and her deserts. This line of argument[1] stresses Vronsky's inability to satisfy 'a woman grown to passion and demanding it as the continuing centre of her life'. Anna, once awakened, must live her feelings right through; with Karenin she could live on a 'limited commitment'. She becomes a wife and mother without having been a girl in love. Vronsky brings out the girl in love, but by this time she is a guilty wife and mother. She has to give herself wholly...even her death is a revengeful move to make Vronsky love her more. By this argument Anna's tragedy is the inadequacy of her lover—and, needless to say, Tolstoy would not have been impressed by it. If adequacy means the total subordination of one's life to a woman's obsessive passion, no man can be deemed adequate. Anna, at a very early stage, comes to believe that she has certain claims on life, certain legitimate needs and the right to satisfy them. She is like a hungry person, she says, who has been given a piece of bread, and she stubbornly clings to the belief that she is entitled to it. As it turns out, the bread does not nourish, but poisons her, and we can only speculate whether she was mistaken in thinking she could not have survived without it or in believing that it was hers by right. As a starving creature, Anna at first gratefully accepts her piece of bread, but her appetite grows beyond her power to control it. She becomes a parasite, exploiting her lover. In the last resort it could be said that Anna's plight is the tragedy of living by and off another person, the tragedy of exploitation.

None of these approaches is wholly satisfactory, nor yet completely wide of the mark. There can be no 'impartial' attitude to Anna's conduct. One can try to say what Tolstoy thought about it, and if we agree with him we can contrive to draw the same 'message' from his novel. But if our conclusions are different from his intentions and different from one another's, this fact has little to do with the literary merits

[1] R. Williams, 'Lawrence and Tolstoy', *Critical Quarterly*, I, No. 3.

of the book except in so far as the greatest works of art seem to share the property of also being the most controversial. The literary merits of a thought-provoking novel must lie in the posing of the problems, not their solutions, as Chekhov realised when he wrote: 'Not a single problem is solved in *Anna Karenina*, but it satisfies completely because all the problems are correctly stated.'[1] If we leave aside for the moment the topical social issues and confine ourselves to the more universal problem of marriage and the family, we can appreciate what Chekhov meant.

One aspect of this central problem is illustrated by the theme of the unhappy family, the Karenins. Here the effect is achieved by balancing as nearly as possible the moral dignity and charm of Anna's character against her offence, and Karenin's bureaucratic coldness against his rectitude. The family background of the protagonists is important. Little or nothing is known about Anna's home life except that she was brought up and married off by an aunt. Karenin lost his parents when he was young, and was brought up by an uncle. Vronsky could not remember his father; his mother was involved in numerous liaisons. In all cases parental influence was minimal. There is no evidence of a happy and united home life. While this is not the fault of the younger generation, there is for some readers the implication in the statement of the theme that Anna and Vronsky were wrong to recreate a situation in which they themselves as children had been the innocent victims—the lack of a stable home environment.

It has been argued that Anna's marriage was not really a marriage, since it was not of her own making. Tolstoy, in stating the problem of the unhappy family, does not use this argument at all. She *is* married, and perhaps it was not such an unpleasant experience as she later persuaded herself to believe. Nothing is seen or known of her married life until Vronsky appears on the scene except for her reflections on returning from Moscow to Petersburg: 'Thank goodness, tomorrow I'll see Seriozha and Aleksei Aleksandrovich and my life—my

---

[1] Letter to Suvorin, 27 October 1888.

nice, everyday life—will go on as before.'[1] As a married woman she has to bear the terrible responsibility of choosing between a lover and a son. The choice made, she is shown to be unable to love her daughter by Vronsky as she loves Karenin's son. Now she is the victim of her own actions, and the inference is there to draw that if you behave as Anna does, you not only risk losing your legitimate son; you may also find that your illegitimate child can never be a substitute. For some readers the tragedy of Anna is the tragedy of a mother cut off from the son she loves, and not of a wife separated from a cold husband or a mistress jealous of an inadequate lover.

From time to time one senses the temptation on Tolstoy's part to weight the statement of his theme against his heroine, especially in the emphasis he places on Anna's growing moral deterioration. When Karenin sums up his objections to his wife's conduct under four headings: the flouting of public opinion, the violation of the religious sanctity of marriage, the unfortunate consequences for her son, and the unfortunate consequences for herself,[2] the order is significant. With Tolstoy it is reversed. He shows the ripening of jealousy and rancour. Anna is ready to tell Dolly that in her place she would forgive Oblonsky's infidelity, even if it should occur again. But when she herself is the victim, even the suspicion of Vronsky's cooling ardour is enough to make her incapable of forgiveness. She becomes more and more selfish. She becomes increasingly the slave of her passions (the 'animal relationships' of an early draft). She is determined to punish Vronsky. She resorts to contraception and drugs. She is the first of Tolstoy's heroines to smoke! In these different ways Tolstoy is suggesting that her choice was the wrong one for her. But if his rational prejudices steer him in one direction, his heart is quick to correct him. It is not merely Anna's physical attractiveness, her charm as a woman, which has to be offset against her fall from grace. It is her dignity, her compassion, the vitality, warmth and sincerity of her character, and the enormity of her suffering which tip the scales back again and leave the problem so

---

[1] *Anna Karenina*, 1, 29.   [2] *Anna Karenina*, 2, 8.

delicately poised in the balance. In comparing Anna Karenina, Effi Briest and Madame Bovary, one critic described Anna as the only wholly adult character of the three, and happily contrasted Fontane's tolerant compassion and Flaubert's detached psychological knowledge with Tolstoy's genuine love of his heroine.[1] Loving Anna, he fought against his rational urge to condemn her for breaking the rules; so too did he resist his reason when it told him that Karenin was right to keep them. Karenin has his redeeming features, but his heart is cold. It is his head which predominates, as symbolised by his surname (if we are to believe his son, who claimed that it was derived from the Homeric Greek κάρηνον (karēnon)), his constant ratiocinations, or simply his obtruding ears.

It is impossible to believe that Tolstoy's answer to the problem of marriage and the family as demonstrated through Anna and her husband was that divine retribution inevitably overtakes the adulterer; or that Anna could ever have found happiness with Karenin. Perhaps Tolstoy himself believed that a loveless marriage for Anna was the better of two evils, and it is possible to draw this inference from the novel to provide a 'solution', albeit an unhappy one. But so finely is the balance held that it is equally possible to draw many other inferences. Professor Poggioli can say with plausibility that Tolstoy sided with the person against the group (but not as Anna's destiny shows, against a morality standing higher than both the person and the group).[2] And yet the final word must be that 'we are not asked to accept anything definitive about passion'.[3] The charge of moral bullying cannot be laid at the author's door.

For those who obey the rules, the problem of family happiness should be easier. Kitty and Levin have their ups and downs, their periods of boredom and disillusionment, but at first sight the omens are auspicious. Not that Levin and his wife

[1] J. P. M. Stern, 'Effi Briest, Madame Bovary and Anna Karenina', *Modern Language Review*, LII (1957).
[2] R. Poggioli, *The Phoenix and the Spider*, p. 103.
[3] J. Bayley, *Tolstoy and the Novel*, p. 228.

provide a true contrast to Anna and her husband, for their marriage was a 'free' one, and we only see it in its early stages. Even so there is no smooth path for Levin, for the tormenting questions of faith and the meaning of life drive him to the edge of despair before the shadowy outline of a way back emerges. But that is another story. Happiness does not necessarily follow from obeying the rules of marriage, and if life is meaningless, so too must family life be. Although Tolstoy's head told him that life within the family is preferable to life outside it, his experience of living as reflected in Levin also told him that by itself it is not enough. Hence Mirsky's sombre comment: 'The novel dies like a cry of anguish in the desert air.'[1] Again there is no solution, only the prospect of a continuing struggle: but a prospect which, for all Mirsky's gloom, is a little brighter than the view from Anna's blind alley.

There is an interesting contrast in the novel between the major characters, whose conduct seems to be tried (but not condemned) by the author's standards of right and wrong, and some of the minor figures, to whom consistent ethical judgments do not apply, but only Tolstoy's personal likes and dislikes. Oblonsky and Princess Betsy are both unfaithful, but they are not only treated differently from Anna, they are treated differently from one another. Oblonsky emerges as a sympathetic and quite unregenerate charmer, a roué, but a genial and sincere one, and the subject of the author's kindly indulgence. On the other hand, Tolstoy never conceals his contempt for Betsy, who adds a surface layer of respectability to her immorality. There is little logic here, but much truth. D. H. Lawrence believed that Tolstoy had a marvellous sensuous understanding, but little clarity of mind.[2] I would say that Tolstoy had a clearer mind than Lawrence, but that the problems he dealt with defy the greatest minds and, despite social revolutions and divorce law reforms, are no nearer solution now than they ever have been.

[1] D. S. Mirsky, *A History of Russian Literature* (London 1949), p. 262.
[2] *Study of Thomas Hardy*, quoted by D. Davie, *Russian Literature and Modern English Fiction*, p. 144.

The problem of family happiness is inextricably bound up for Levin with that of the meaning of life and death. This is a man's subject. The Kittys, Annas and Natashas are not troubled by it. Pierre was, but thought he had found an answer. The problem is stated in *Anna Karenina* both on the philosophical and the physical plane. In physical terms it seems insoluble. In one of the grimmest passages in Tolstoy's fiction Levin watches his brother die. What are his reactions and the reactions of those closest to him? What clue does his death give to the meaning of life? He dies reluctantly, even angrily, without any comprehension of why he had existed or should cease to exist. The utter futility, the crude physical horror, even obscenity, of the scene are almost intolerable. The culminating chapter 'Death', the only chapter in the novel to be honoured with a title, is crucial to the statement of the case on a material plane. Rather lamely Levin concludes that in spite of death he feels the need to live and love, and a facile transition from Nicholas' death to Kitty's pregnancy, from inexplicable death to inexplicable life, from darkness to light, moves the story on from despair to hope—in marked contrast to Anna's solitary end with its rapid movement from light to darkness as life's candle is extinguished:

'He is gone,' said the priest and was about to leave; but suddenly the dying man's clammy moustache moved and a clear sharp sound from deep down in his chest was distinctly audible in the silence of the room: 'Not quite...soon.'

And a moment later his face brightened, a smile played under his moustache and the women who had come in began carefully laying out the body.

The sight of his brother and the nearness of death revived in Levin that feeling of horror at the unfathomable nature of death—and at the same time its nearness and inevitability—which had gripped him that autumn evening when his brother had come to see him. That feeling was even stronger now than before; still less than before did he feel capable of understanding the meaning of death, and still more terrible did its inevitability seem. But now, thanks to the nearness of his wife, this feeling did not reduce him to despair. In spite of death he felt the need to live and love. He felt that love was saving him from despair and that this love was growing stronger and purer under the menace of despair.

The one mystery of death, still unfathomed, had scarcely been enacted before his eyes than another equally unfathomed mystery succeeded it, calling him back to life and love.

The doctor confirmed his suppositions about Kitty. She was not ill but pregnant.[1]

And suddenly she remembered the man run over on the day she had first met Vronsky, and she knew what she had to do. With a quick, light tread she walked down the steps from the water-tank to the rails and stopped near the train that was passing right in front of her. She looked underneath the carriages at the screws and couplings and the big iron wheels of the first carriage as it slowly rolled by, and tried to gauge with her eye the middle point between the front and back wheels and the moment it would be opposite her.

'There,' she said to herself, looking at the shadow of the carriage and the mixture of sand and coal-dust which covered the sleepers—'there, right in the middle, and I'll punish him and be rid of myself and everyone.'

She tried to fall under the middle of the first carriage as it drew level with her. But the red handbag which she had begun to take off her arm delayed her and it was too late: the middle of the carriage had moved on. She had to wait for the next one. A feeling similar to that which she used to get when entering the water for a bathe gripped her and she crossed herself. The familiar gesture of the sign of the cross called to mind a whole series of childhood and girlhood memories, and suddenly the darkness that had covered everything for her was torn apart and for an instant life, with all its past joy and gladness, rose up before her. But she did not take her eyes off the wheels of the second carriage. And just at the moment when the middle of the carriage was opposite her, she flung down her red handbag, tucked her head into her shoulders, fell under the carriage on her hands and dropped onto her knees lightly, as though about to get up again at once. And at the same time she was horrified at what she was doing. 'Where am I? What am I doing? Why?' She tried to get up, to fling herself aside: but something huge and merciless struck her on the head and began to drag her along on her back. 'Lord, forgive me all!' she said, feeling it was impossible

<hr />

[1] *Anna Karenina*, 5, 20.

to struggle. A peasant was working on the rails, muttering something to himself. And the candle by which she had read the book, full of troubles, deceit, sorrow and evil, flared up with a brighter light than ever, illuminated all that had been in darkness, flickered, began to grow dim, and went out for ever.[1]

In metaphysical terms the problem is presented partly through Levin's dialogues with so-called clever men from which he learns nothing at all, partly through his own monologues which provide him with a precarious *modus vivendi*. In a savagely ironical passage in the opening chapters of the book the 'simple and natural' Levin interrupts a parody of an academic discussion on being and consciousness with the blunt question what happens after death. The dice are heavily loaded against the intellectuals, who ostensibly have no thoughts of their own, but fall back on quoting or disagreeing with a motley crew of fictitious German and Russian philosophers with such crudely suggestive names as Käse, Wurst and Pripasov ('Cheese', 'Sausage' and 'Provisions'). Tolstoy has no patience with the professional practitioners of wisdom, because the problems do not touch them closely. Levin at least is personally involved and a solution is of more than academic interest. Part 8 of *Anna* anticipates *A Confession* which in turn leads on to the *Criticism of Dogmatic Theology*, the *Translation and Harmony of the Gospels* and the later religious writings. Levin does manage to reason himself into a sort of spiritual equilibrium where reason is not all-important and where he can argue that just as astronomers have based theories on the movement of stars round a stationary earth which appears to the observer to be true, but which he knows to be false, so his own conclusions on good and evil may be true if they are verified by the experience of his own soul, despite the impossibility of giving them a rational explanation. Levin insists that some of these conclusions he had imbibed with his mother's milk, and his instinctive knowledge of what is right and wrong had saved him from falsehood, theft and murder. Tolstoy on the other hand, who presumably had imbibed much the same beliefs

---

[1] *Anna Karenina*, 7, 31.

from the same source, was apparently not prevented, as he tells us in *A Confession*, from committing the same offences.

And yet it is essentially true, and an important feature of Tolstoy's art as a novelist, that Levin, like Pierre and Olenin before him, should be shown to have reached the same stage in his battle with life as Tolstoy himself had reached at the time of writing. Levin's arguments offer no solution to Tolstoy, and are at best a holding operation. They can work just as long as the problem is swallowed up in the actual business of living.

Since the background of *Anna Karenina* is a contemporary one and since there is by the nature of things a strong sociological bias to Soviet literary criticism, it is not surprising that so much discussion of the novel in the Soviet Union, Party and non-Party, has turned on its reflection of Russian life in the 1870s in the light of Lenin's articles on Tolstoy and his belief that he 'mirrored' in his works the contradictions of the peasantry as a class which helped to account for the failure of the Russian Revolution of 1905.[1] Of vital importance to the Marxist critic is the exploration of the relationships between landowner and peasant as reflected in pre-revolutionary Russian literature, and the subject looms particularly large in Soviet scholarship today. One critic, writing of Tolstoy's fiction before 1880, called the Tolstoyan hero a landowner endeavouring to become a man while remaining a landowner; to which end he sought a rapprochement with the peasantry whom he considered to be *real* men.[2] In the words of another Tolstoyan scholar: 'The way of life of the landowners and peasants after the reforms and the changes and economic stratifications which had occurred in it found their most vivid and artistically convincing reflection in *Anna Karenina*.[3] From this aspect the novel is scrutinised for what it can reveal about the consequences of the Emancipation, the era of the reforms, the *zemstva* (elected local assemblies), the new law courts and the various liberal institutions which characterised the reign of

[1] V. I. Lenin, *Lev Tolstoi, kak zerkalo russkoi revolyutsii* (Moscow 1908).
[2] B. I. Bursov, *Lev Tolstoi i russkii roman* (Moscow–Leningrad 1963), p. 46.
[3] N. K. Gudzy, *Lev Tolstoi* (Moscow 1960), p. 101.

Alexander II. The most crucial problem of all in a vast agricultural country was the ownership and exploitation of the land, and the relationships between those who owned it and those who worked it (if they were not the same). One aspect of the problem in *Anna* is the decay of the big landed estates, neglect, absenteeism, as a result of which the gentry were becoming impoverished, and their stewards were usurping power and lining their own pockets. Levin does not hide his disgust at the way in which the gentry allow themselves to be cheated, their idleness and their failure to accept the responsibilities conferred on them by the ownership of land. On the other hand the peasantry—by nature hard workers—are not being rationally exploited. They do not understand the advantages of new machinery. They do not respond to the reforms of the more enlightened members of the gentry. Levin, like Tolstoy, felt that the key to Russia's economic future lay with the peasantry; hence his concern to understand them, their environment and their conditions of work, and his attempts to draw them into profit-sharing cooperatives. The practical sides of the problem are illustrated by Tolstoy in narrative passages describing representatives of the various classes at work: the poor peasantry toiling in the fields; the well-to-do kulaks in embryo exemplified by the family with whom Levin stops for a meal on his journey to Sviazhky's,[1] whose prosperity is based on the collective labour of the small family group; the prosperous merchants buying up the land for commercial purposes; and the landlords themselves, whether idle like Oblonsky, diligent but misunderstood like Levin, or 'progressive' like Vronsky on his model farm. The theoretical sides of the problem are presented mainly through dialogue, especially Levin's conversations with his half-brother and Sviazhky, when he is no longer observing other people, but talking, listening or thinking—never monopolising the conversation, often silent himself, his thoughts described by the author or expressed against the background of a dialogue. No solution is offered, but the implication is felt that

[1] *Anna Karenina*, 3, 25.

agriculture, which should be the basis of the country's economic prosperity, is shamefully lagging behind, and that the landowners, instead of devoting their attention to the land, are being sidetracked into *zemstvo* activities and county council elections, or are simply frittering their time away in idle talk. The peasant was for Tolstoy the focal point of the economy. For the Marxist critic he is 'the poet of the peasant revolution that lasted from 1861 to 1905',[1] not consciously understanding, but faithfully reproducing the revolutionary process in its vital stages.

If the agricultural issues tend to dominate, it is not to the exclusion of other social issues of the 70s which are frequently touched upon, albeit perfunctorily, in drawing-room conversation or after-dinner talk, but in sufficient detail to inform the reader of the most pressing matters of concern to educated Russian society of the day: conscription and military service, classical education, the divorce laws, women's education, spiritualism, the Serbian rising. Needless to say it does not give a fully representative social picture of the period, for Tolstoy is not concerned with the growth of industrialisation, urban poverty and squalor or the revolutionary movement ('nihilism' only figures in a suppressed draft version) within the context of the upper-middle-class society in which his characters move, ranging as it does from the *haut monde* to the Petersburg bureaucracy and the military circles—all treated with varying degrees of disapprobation—but necessarily excluding the rising manufacturing classes and the urban proletariat. But there is sufficient social background for one to understand, if not to agree with its implied emphasis, the opinion of a Soviet critic that *Anna Karenina* is a social novel, complicated by profound psychological problems.

The difficulties of the social approach are the difficulties inherent in the challenging but confused problem of the relations between society and art, given that literature cannot help drawing its material from life, but also that the artist is engaged in an act of fiction, and therefore at liberty to select,

[1] G. Lukács, *Studies in European Realism* (London 1950), p. 145.

distort and suppress. Is Tolstoy's picture of Russian life in the 1870s 'accurate'? By what criteria can one decide? How can there be such a thing as an accurate, truthful, scientifically verifiable and meaningful portrait of an age? Tolstoy regarded himself as an exponent of 'realism' with all its implications of the faithful representation of contemporary 'reality'. But he also regarded himself as an artist, not a historian or journalist. As a serious artist he was bound to ask himself what his art consisted of, and what relation it bore to the society which inspired it and for which it was intended.

Tolstoy liked to think out his problems on the pages of his fiction and it is not surprising that he should have introduced the disturbing question of the meaning and purpose of art into his novel. 'The characters in a work of art were for Tolstoy', it has been said, 'essentially a means of communicating his own thoughts about life to the reader as accurately and vividly as possible and at the same time helping himself to express them in concrete form.'[1] Substituting 'art' for 'life', this is probably the main justification for the appearance of the painter Mikhailov in *Anna Karenina* (modelled apparently on Kramskoy, who painted Tolstoy's portrait). The episode in Mikhailov's studio, in the words of a recent critic,[2] is not only significant in its timing, coming as it does when Anna and Vronsky have 'stopped living' their life of involuntary emotional stress 'and so have *leisure* for art'; it also reveals Tolstoy's 'distrust for art which is not an involuntary and necessary part of life of the individual and society. Italy is an aesthetic *enclave*; it symbolises the status of art as a fashionable upper-class amusement'. The episode can be taken to illustrate the viewpoints of three men, each having some claim to pronounce an opinion about art (in this case painting). Vronsky is the dilettante, the gifted amateur, with good taste and a certain imitative skill. He has talent, but he is inspired not directly by life, but indirectly by its embodiment in art. He is the sort of man whom Tolstoy is later to condemn in *What is Art?* as an exponent of feelings which are derivative and therefore

[1] N. K. Gudzy, *Lev Tolstoi*, p. 109.   [2] J. Bayley, *Tolstoy and the Novel*, p. 234.

insincere. Golenishchev, the writer, fulfils the rôle of critic, a profession which ranked particularly low in Tolstoy's esteem, and was to be a target for much subsequent invective. When Golenishchev voices his opinion about Mikhailov's master-piece, *Christ before Pilate*, he talks about the central characters but fails to notice the figure of John in the background which the painter himself believes to be beyond perfection. On the other hand he enthuses over the 'pretty' picture of two boys fishing which the artist has forgotten about—and does so because of its exquisite charm. The tendency to equate art with the charming, the pleasurable, the superficially attractive, was bitterly resisted by Tolstoy as we shall see later; at this stage, however, and within the framework of the novel, he was content to think aloud without steering the reader in one direction or the other. Mikhailov, the one creative artist of the three, is shown, significantly enough, *doing* the job, not talking about it. He is relatively poor and uneducated. He is prone to rapidly alternating moods of ecstasy and despair. Like Tolstoy he has a gift for detail and analysis, the faculty for drawing inspiration from the insignificant things of life, storing up in his memory every feature of a face, and using, for example, the expression of a tobacconist who sells him cigars to give life to the figure of a man seized with a paroxysm of anger. Like Tolstoy he is fitful, easily dissatisfied, suddenly elated, just as suddenly depressed. Like Tolstoy he wants to get at the character behind the conventional façade, to strip off the surface layers and reveal the essence of his subject. Mikhailov cannot understand the word 'technique' bandied about by Vronsky and Golenishchev. He knows that no amount of skill can make a bad subject good; and if a subject is good, and the artist sees it clearly and sincerely, he does not need 'technique' or the expertise inculcated by the art schools, for all 'the care and attention required to bring the idea to birth and produce it'. Needless to say his beliefs that 'talent' cannot paint a bad picture; that the *art* of painting does not exist and that a child or a cook who had shared the artist's vision would have been able to 'peel off the outer husk' of what he saw, do not command any more respect than Lenin's idea that his cook could run the government; but they form a necessary bridge between *Anna Karenina* and *What is Art?*

The Mikhailov episode poses the perennial problems: who is the best judge of a work of art, the artist or the critic; what rôle does technique play; how important is subject-matter; what is the relation of art to the eye of the beholder. The three visitors know which picture they prefer—the one which makes the most immediate impact—but the artist does not. Both caused him agonies and ecstasies—and both will be forgotten. The economy and lucidity of this condensed statement of some of the fundamental issues of art are in themselves proof of Tolstoy's remarkable artistic powers. He desperately needed an answer to his questions; but another twenty years were to elapse before hypothesis crystallised into dogma.

Chekhov was right to praise Tolstoy for the way in which he stated his problems, for his technical powers of exposition. Tolstoy might despise technique as a *substitute* for talent, but he knew that talent could not blossom without care and attention. When we think of his technique as a novelist, we are not concerned with technical virtuosity or the mechanical ability to work to rules, but with the method of approach adopted to the problems of structure, composition and characterisation which confront every novelist, however rare his genius and however original his inspiration. 'We must grant the artist his subject, his idea, his *donnée*,' said Henry James; 'our criticism is applied only to what he makes of it.'[1] We must study how the thing is done. Not that this can be done in isolation as a formalistic exercise, for what a man says and the way he says it cannot be entirely separated from the sort of man he is and the beliefs he holds. Sartre once said that 'the technique of a novel always refers us back to the meta-physics of the novelist'.[2] Matthew Arnold and D. H. Lawrence, when they write about *Anna Karenina*, tell us as much about

---

[1] Quoted in *Myth and Method*, ed. J. E. Miller (University of Nebraska 1960), p. 17.
[2] Essay on Faulkner, quoted by G. Steiner, *Tolstoy or Dostoevsky*, p. 6.

themselves as they do about the novel they are criticising. Even the Formalists and the New Critics cannot escape the conditioning factors of birth, race, country, class, education or political and religious beliefs. Chekhov said that he wished to be a free artist and nothing more, but his ambition was as unattainable as that of the man who wishes to be a 'free critic'. Nevertheless it is possible to maintain that a given novel has technical merits or shortcomings, or that in certain technical respects it is similar to or dissimilar from other members of its species. If we read through a representative selection of criticism devoted to *Anna Karenina* we shall find a surprisingly large number of reproaches levelled against Tolstoy's competence as a novelist. Not all of them come from foreigners, whose reliance on inadequate translations inevitably invalidates some of their remarks on style. When Edmund Gosse[1] criticises Tolstoy's style as negligent and confused, or commits glaring errors of fact in the course of his article, we pay no attention to him. Nor can one set any store by his strictures on the 'tedious and interminable length at which certain episodes are treated' or the opinion that 'there are some country scenes in *Anna Karenina* in which the author seems to have gone to sleep'. Nevertheless he makes at least two points which can be taken seriously: that Tolstoy suffered from 'lapses of memory' (to which we shall return later), and that there is a 'hiatus' in the progress of Anna's mind between her first meeting with Vronsky and her infatuation with him. There have been many unfavourable comments on Tolstoy's early handling of Anna's character and its development up to the moment of her adultery. Her relief at the prospect of returning to her 'nice, everyday life' might suggest either that her married life was not the torture she later imagined it to have been, or that she had learned to lie and deceive at an early age in a manner ill befitting her true nature. Tolstoy has been criticised also for starting Anna's fictional life with her crises and for not suitably preparing the ground;[2] for the

---

[1] Edmund Gosse, *Critical Kit-kats* (London 1896).
[2] P. Lubbock, *The Craft of Fiction* (London 1965), Ch. 16.

excessively hasty development of her liaison which telescopes
the drama of a year's struggle into a single sentence. He has
been reproached for his limitations as a psychologist, for his
penchant for the fairy-tale solution with its magical trans-
formations, his inability to convey mental chaos and disorder,
and the undue 'literalness' of his genius:

What is not altogether of this earth, what is to be found on either
hand of normality—the subconscious or the mystical—seemed to
Tolstoy unreal or subversive. When it forced itself upon his art,
he tended to neutralise it through abstraction and generality.

Or again:

There is something disturbing about the effortless manner in which
Tolstoy addresses himself to the notion of the soul. He enters too
lucidly into the consciousness of his creations and his own voice
pierces through their lips. The fairy-tale conceit 'from that day on
he was a new man' [and here one thinks of Levin's spiritual trans-
formation] plays too broad and uncritical a rôle in Tolstoyan
psychology. We are required to grant a good deal regarding the
simplicity and openness of mental processes. On the whole, we do
grant it because Tolstoy enclosed his characters with such massive-
ness of circumstance and elaborated their lives for us with such
patient warmth that we believe all he says of them.

But there are effects and depths of insight to which these splendidly
rounded creations do not lend themselves. Generally, they are
effects of drama. The dramatic arises out of the margin of opaque-
ness between a writer and his personages, out of their potential for
the unexpected. In the full dramatic character lurks the unforeseen
possibility, the gift for disorder. Tolstoy was omniscient at a price;
the ultimate tension of unreason and the spontaneity of chaos
eluded his grasp.[1]

The character of Vronsky has been held up as a failure—
'Tolstoy's *one* failure'.[2] In his own country Turgenev,
Saltykov–Shchedrin and Chernyshevsky all had unflattering
things to say about the lack of profound psychological analysis
in the novel, as the first parts began to appear in serial form. 'I

[1] G. Steiner, *Tolstoy or Dostoevsky*, pp. 275–6.
[2] P. Lubbock, *The Craft of Fiction*, p. 248.

don't like *Anna Karenina*,' Turgenev wrote in 1875,[1] 'although there are some truly great pages in it (the races, the mowing, the hunting). But it's all sour, it reeks of Moscow, incense, old maids, Slavophilism, the nobility etc...' And, again, 'The second part is simply trivial and boring.' With much more justification, he called Levin an egoist to the marrow of his bones. A contemporary critic actually spoke of the colourlessness and vagueness of the character of Anna herself.[2] As for the structure of the novel, it has often been suggested in a subjective way that Tolstoy included scenes which a more fastidious artist would have omitted: the scene in Mikhailov's studio, the chapters on the elections, much of Part 8 which follows Anna's suicide, the Varenka and Sergei episode, the description of Levin's wedding. Elsewhere[3] I have tried to show that Tolstoy, who prided himself on the structure of his novel, was sometimes careless and lost his sense of the passage of time; that Kitty and Levin spend a year longer on their journey than Anna and Vronsky, while Dolly's story is at least six years out of step; that ages are muddled, that distances do not tally and that the day on which the novel begins is both a Thursday and a Friday. The lack of consistency and coordination, while perhaps not surprising in a work of this length, is apt to be disturbing. It could have been avoided if he had written two novels instead of one, as some readers would like him to have done. As a final reproach, much has been said against Tolstoy's alleged tendentiousness, his string-pulling and manipulation of the characters in the interests of his overriding purpose, whether in attributing to him, as Lawrence did, 'a perverse pleasure in making the later Vronsky abject and pitiable',[4] or a vindictive satisfaction in turning Anna into the helpless victim of divine retribution. This body of negative criticism of Tolstoy's competence at his profession is impressively large. How valid is it, and if it is valid, what is there

---

[1] Letter to Polonsky, 13 May 1875.

[2] P. I. Weinberg, 'Russkaya zhurnalistika', *Pchela* (1876), No. 1.

[3] 'The Passage of Time in *Anna Karenina*', *Slavonic and East European Review*, (January 1967).

[4] Quoted by D. Davie, *Russian Literature and Modern English Fiction*, p. 151.

to say of Tolstoy's craftsmanship in *Anna* if we believe it to be a supremely fashioned work of art and not merely, in Arnold's phrase, a 'piece of life' its author had seen?

To isolate problems of form is to imply a form-and-content dichotomy which Tolstoy seemed to resist when he said that he could not have expressed what he did in *Anna Karenina* except in the way in which he actually did express it. To have altered the form would have been to alter the content. The fact that this is true, however, does not mean that it is not possible to examine the form which he finally decided, after many trials and errors, was the most appropriate for his purpose.

The first problem he faced was where to begin, and in what order and in what manner to introduce his characters. The original plan for the novel to open in a salon with the liaison between Anna and Vronsky already under way was soon dropped in favour of the decision to move the action back in time and to allow the curtain to rise on Oblonsky and Dolly. This had some obvious advantages. First, Oblonsky was connected by ties of friendship or marriage with nearly all the other characters, and every important person with the exception of Anna's husband is first mentioned in his presence or introduced through him. For this reason he was admirably suited to connect the two central plots hingeing respectively on Anna and Vronsky and Kitty and Levin. Secondly, his own situation as an adulterer foreshadows that of his sister (with whom there is a strong family likeness) and who is also to prove unfaithful to her marriage vows. Thirdly, his predicament allows Anna to be introduced as a mediator and to stress the irony of her position as one whose own marriage is to break down as an indirect result of trying to mend somebody else's.

Tolstoy took pains to ensure that his men and women should first appear in a situation and in a manner which would immediately tell us something typical and fundamental about their true personality and way of life. Oblonsky is weathering a matrimonial crisis. There have been others before, no doubt, and there will certainly be others again. His wife is sorting out the children's clothes, worrying about their minor ailments, pale, thin, apprehensive, on the point of leaving her husband but knowing at heart that she never can or will. The unconventional, slightly eccentric Levin comes bursting onto the scene at a run, evading the doorkeeper who has just ejected him. Kitty, nervous and unsure of herself, is skating unsteadily on the ice. Vronsky, the well-bred man of the world, is immediately seen in his rôle of handsome cavalier. Anna's entry is unusual in that it is so long delayed and is not treated with the same detail as that of the others. The surroundings are unpropitious. Her meeting with Vronsky is the only chance one. The note of fate, of ill omens and premonitions, is struck at the very start. As is usual with Tolstoy, the first entry is significant, but the previous history of the character is unimportant and reduced in the case of Anna to the barest minimum. Physical description is used sparingly and we are not overwhelmed with an indigestible mass of detail. In describing Anna's appearance, Tolstoy emphasises the features which are an outward and visible reflection of an inner state—the expression in her eyes, her smile, the radiance which comes from within and is not a surface adornment. But the essence of Tolstoy's characterisation is not static description, but an oblique vision which sees the many facets of an individual from a variety of viewpoints, each of which is valid as far as it goes, but each of which is only a partial truth. The side of Vronsky which Oblonsky shows to Levin is not the side which Kitty sees; and what he represents for Kitty is very different from the image he presents to Anna. The characterisation of Anna herself is particularly important in this respect. She has little or no biography. Her conversation is uninteresting. But she sparks off different reactions in different people, the cumulative effect of which is to reveal much more of her nature than the author's narrative does. It is a masterly stroke of Tolstoy's to allow the mutual infatuation of Vronsky and Anna to be observed largely through the eyes of Kitty, the discarded rival for his affection. She imagines that their every word, when they dance together at the ball, is important, whereas in fact they have little or nothing to say to each other. It is not Anna's lips, but her eyes which talk. What her lips are *doing* matters more than what they are saying. The emphasis is on the vocabulary of light and fire, on the lips curved into a smile, on an expression repeated and underlined. What Kitty is made to sense is the fatal inevitability of what is taking place between them. Anna tries to restrain her joy, but it shows through 'in spite of herself'. Vronsky's look seems to say to Kitty, 'I only want to save myself, but I don't know how.' Anna's charm seems to her to be 'terrible and cruel'; there is something 'strange and diabolical' about her. Nobody but Kitty is aware of this underlying streak in Anna's nature, but, making due allowance for Kitty's natural resentment, the clue is dropped for us to pick up.

The first impressions of Tolstoy's characters are composed from many points of view. This aspect of his characterisation is very much a part of his technique as a novelist. So too is the manner in which he engineers change and development in the lives of his men and women, the emphasis always being not on what they become, but on the process of their becoming. Tolstoy has very few 'flat' characters. They nearly all have some dimensions. This does not mean that they all undergo change and development. Many novelists show a character in great detail, adding continually to it and revealing new sides in the course of their narrative. But these new aspects of the man or woman are in keeping with what we already know about them. They can easily be inferred. They do not give a new direction. Many of Turgenev's characters are more or less complete from the beginning. They are faced with a crisis, fail to surmount it, and go on being what they were before. In *Anna* Princess Betsy's set and the professional intelligentsia belong to this category. So does Oblonsky, who never goes beyond what he is in the first few chapters, which contain all the prerequisites for what he does later. Neither Kitty nor Dolly develops significantly. Kitty's is a natural growth to maturity. Her girlish naïveté gives way in the normal course of things to sober motherhood. Her early infatuation for Vronsky has been compared, in the purpose it serves, to Romeo's infatuation for Rosaline.[1] It gives her a yardstick by which to measure her later feelings for Levin as Vronsky is able to measure his for Anna. Marriage and motherhood show Kitty in a new light, but it is not an unexpected one. She is not a thinking woman, beset by doubts, which call for a radical alteration in her way of life. Karenin has his moments when he is shaken out of his rut, as when he turns the other cheek during Anna's illness or when he contemplates giving her a divorce. But at the crucial moment, his ways are too set, his beliefs and principles too unassailable to get the better of the bureaucrat in him. There is no real flexibility in his make-up. Vronsky on the other hand is more mobile. He seems to become a new man under the influence of his love for Anna, prepared to make almost any sacrifice if only she would marry him (married life had ceased to be the ludicrous and distasteful thing it had seemed before he met her), and if only she would allow him the degree of freedom to live and work which any husband might reasonably claim. Committed by birth and upbringing to the values and the way of life of a wealthy, conformist aristocracy, he renounces a brilliant career, spurns ambition, turns his back on society, tries to kill himself, and when this fails, devotes himself with exemplary patience and kindness to a woman becoming daily more unbalanced and difficult to live with. Of course some of his responses can be predicted by what he thinks people will approve of, or by what is the done thing in the given situation. He can be self-satisfied and egotistic, but he is less of an egotist than Levin. His opinions are much more conventional than Levin's and there is no spiritual dimension to his make-up, as there is with Levin or Pierre. But it is surely wrong to see him as the 'negative type' he has become in the estimation of some Soviet critics and producers. Indeed some people feel that Tolstoy, who had so much of Levin in him, had a subconscious admiration for those qualities in Vronsky which he himself lacked and which he professed to despise. Without indulging in such speculations, one can at least assert that Vronsky's

---

[1] G. Steiner, *Tolstoy or Dostoevsky*, p. 61.

evolution refutes Lubbock's claim that, as a character, he is a
failure. Vronsky's development is significant, but it is not as
far-reaching as that of Levin or Anna, the one groping painfully from agnosticism to faith, the other the progressive
victim of neuroticism and despair. Levin's thoughts and Anna's
feelings are alike unorthodox by the standards of the society in
which they live. Neither his thoughts nor her feelings give
them any rest. They are vital, dynamic, responsive people in a
constant state of flux. Tolstoy is at his best in creating such
characters and exposing them to life's crises. His psychological
intuition is apparent in almost every chapter. When Levin and
Oblonsky dine together, Tolstoy observes, in a phrase which
Chekhov would have admired, that for all their bonhomie
'each was thinking only of his own affairs and was not concerned with the other'.[1] 'I know that you are fond of me,' says
Levin to him, 'and that's why I'm terribly fond of you.'[2]
Again, Levin is credited with a feeling of particular pleasure
that Kitty, 'who had made him suffer so much should be
suffering herself', having chosen to ask Oblonsky about her
health not when the ground had been suitably prepared but on
the spur of the moment during the climax of their snipe-
shooting expedition.[3] His brother's derogatory opinions about
the new *zemstva* and other public institutions are distasteful
to Levin—although he fully agrees with them—'coming from
his brother's lips'.[4] His own state of mind is admirably conveyed by such apparently commonplace remarks as, 'Levin
both liked and did not like the peasants, just as he liked and
did not like men in general,'[5] and, even more to the point,
apropos of an argument between himself and his half-brother
Koznyshev: 'Of course I'm right and he's right.'[6] Whether it
is Levin's self-consciousness in expressing borrowed opinions
or his spontaneous acknowledgement that what he is doing for
the peasants he is doing for his own good, not theirs,[7] there is

[1] *Anna Karenina*, 1, 11.
[2] *Anna Karenina*, 1, 10.
[3] *Anna Karenina*, 2, 16.
[4] *Anna Karenina*, 1, 25.
[5] *Anna Karenina*, 3, 1.
[6] *Anna Karenina*, 3, 6.
[7] *Anna Karenina*, 3, 30.

something simple, direct but yet profound in Tolstoy's psychological observations. He is particularly good when handling the relation between Vronsky and Anna, after Vronsky has been needlessly summoned home from the elections by his jealous mistress:

'Well, how is Annie?' he asked timidly from downstairs, looking at Anna as she ran to meet him.

He was sitting on a chair, and a footman was pulling off his warm boots.

'All right, she's better.'

'And you?' he said, shaking himself.

She took his hand in both of hers and drew it to her waist never taking her eyes off him.

'Well, I'm very glad,' he said, coldly scanning her, her hair and her dress which he knew she had put on for him. *He admired it all, but how many times had he admired it before?* And his face assumed that stern and rigid expression she dreaded so much.

'Well, I'm very glad. And are you well?' he said wiping his wet beard with his handkerchief and kissing her hand.

'Never mind,' she thought, 'as long as he's here. When he's here he can't and daren't stop loving me.'

They spent a gay and happy evening with Princess Varvara, who complained to him that Anna had been taking morphia in his absence.

'What could I do? I couldn't sleep...My thoughts wouldn't let me. When he's here I never take it. Hardly ever.' He told her about the elections and *Anna was able by her questions to lead him on to talk about what made him happy—his own success.*[1]

Anna is mistress of the situation, and can charm away Vronsky's understandable anger at being duped, by an appeal to his old weakness which—changed man that he is—he has never conquered.

One of the outstanding examples of Tolstoy's simple and truthful grasp of the workings of the human mind is the account he gives of Dolly's thoughts on her journey to and from Vronsky's estate, and the shifting moods of justification,

[1] *Anna Karenina*, 6, 32. My italics.

envy, gratitude, anxiety, embarrassment and relief to be going home. As she travels out she thinks:

'And they attack Anna. What for? Am I any better? At least I have a husband I love. Not as I would like to love him, still I do love him, while Anna never loved hers. How is she to blame? She wants to live. God put that wish into our hearts. Very likely I should have done the same. I still don't know whether I did right in listening to her that terrible time when she came to Moscow. I ought to have left my husband then and started a new life. I might have loved truly and been truly loved. Are things any better now? I don't respect him. He's necessary to me,' she thought about her husband, 'and I put up with him. Is that better? At that time I could still have been admired, I still had my good looks.' Darya Aleksandrovna pursued her thoughts, and would have liked to look at herself in the mirror. She had a little travelling-mirror in her handbag and would have liked to take it out; but looking at the backs of the coachman and the clerk who was jogging up and down, she felt she would be ashamed if either of them turned round, and she did not take out the mirror.

But without looking at her mirror she felt that even now it was not too late, and she thought of Sergei Ivanovich who was particularly nice to her, and of Stiva's friend, the good-natured Turovtsyn, who had helped her nurse her children through the scarlet fever and was in love with her. And there was someone else, quite a young man, who, as her husband had told her jokingly, found her more beautiful than her sisters. And the most passionate and impossible romances rose before Darya Aleksandrovna's imagination. 'Anna did quite right, and I shall never reproach her for it. She is happy, she makes another person happy and she is not crushed like me but probably as bright, clever and impressionable as she always was,' thought Darya Aleksandrovna, and a roguish smile curved her lips, for as she thought about Anna's romance, she constructed on parallel lines an almost identical romance with an imaginary composite figure who was in love with her. Like Anna, she confessed everything to her husband. And Stephen Arkadich's astonishment and bewilderment at this avowal made her smile.

Such were her day-dreams as she reached the turn off the main road that led to Vozdvizhenskoe.[1]

[1] *Anna Karenina*, 6, 16.

But life at Vozdvizhenskoe was not all Dolly had imagined it to be:

During the game of croquet Darya Aleksandrovna was not enjoying herself. She did not like the bantering tone kept up between Anna and Vasenka Veslovsky or the general unnaturalness of grown-ups playing a children's game without any children. But so as not to upset the others and to pass the time away somehow she joined in the game again after a rest and pretended she was enjoying it. All that day it seemed as though she was acting in a theatre with actors better than herself and that her bad acting was spoiling the whole performance.

She had come with the intention of staying two days if all went well. But in the evening she decided during the game to leave next day. The maternal cares and worries which she had so hated on the way now appeared to her, after a day without them, in quite a different light and tempted her back.

When Darya Aleksandrovna, after evening tea and a row by night in the boat, went by herself to her room, took off her dress and sat down to arrange her thin hair for the night, she felt a great sense of relief.

It was even unpleasant for her to think that Anna would presently be coming to see her. She wanted to be alone with her thoughts.[1]

These few chapters devoted to Dolly's visit and the conflicting impressions it makes on her are surely among the finest passages in the whole of Tolstoy.

A recent perceptive study of the novel[2] has drawn attention to some of the small but true psychological touches so typical of Tolstoy's characterisation—the fact that Levin's spirits rise in fine weather despite his feelings of anguish over Kitty, the fact that grief is never so totally absorbing that there is no room for the pleasures of work and play, the fact that it is 'the uneventful moment, not the spotlit crisis of choice, which determines the future' for Anna. In the same general context much use has been made of the metaphor of removing the covers, as Mikhailov the painter 'removed the wrappings, as it were, that partially obscured the form of his picture', the

[1] *Anna Karenina*, 6, 22.
[2] Barbara Hardy, *The Appropriate Form* (London 1964), pp. 174 ff.

outer shell of custom, convention, propriety which conceals and protects the inner essence of a man or woman. Stendhal expressed much the same idea in diagram form in a letter illustrating man's nature in terms of the surface and the submerged rocks at sea. Professor Green, in drawing attention to this, adds that only in the novel could he (Stendhal) adequately perform the process of stripping away the layers formed by habit.[1]

Yet habit, too, is an important aspect of characterisation. Habitual gestures, movements of the hands, the eyes, the lips are given special prominence in Tolstoy, and not only in the case of people like Karenin who are creatures of habit. Karenin can hardly be blamed for his protruding ears any more than can his spiritual brother Casaubon for his unprepossessing appearance—'doubtless an excellent man who would go to heaven', writes George Eliot, 'but the corners of his mouth were so unpleasant'.[2] But the cracking of his knuckles is intended to be as suggestive a property of the man as Anna's repeated habit of slipping her wedding ring on and off her finger must surely have symbolic overtones. It is the nervous gestures of the people we meet which we notice, and the novelist needs them as identification marks; at the same time it is his privilege to be able to reconstruct the life behind the gesture as we try to do, with less omniscience, in the case of our own friends and acquaintances.

We saw above that Tolstoy has been reproached for his handling of spiritual crises in the lives of his major characters, especially Levin and Pierre. There is some justification in the charge, but I think that it fails to give sufficient weight to the fact that spiritual and moral transformation can be an irrational, unpredictable and momentary phenomenon. The power of the moment, the flash of awareness, the sudden making—and breaking—of resolutions are things which many of us have experienced in our own lives. Religious conversion can be a precipitate act, although the preliminary processes may have gone on for a long time. Surely there is room in the vast

---

[1] F. C. Green, *Stendhal* (Cambridge 1939), p. 217.   [2] *Middlemarch*.

world of Tolstoy's novels for a record of an instant of illumination, a casual word or experience which defies reason, but which, while it lasts, can count for more than many years of intellectual toil. However ephemeral Levin's discovery of faith may have proved to be, and however unorthodox its cause, it does not deserve to be relegated to the world of the fairy-tale or the nursery.

In real life no person lives in isolation. He always has an environment, though he may be at odds with it. Lukács once observed that in Tolstoy's novels it is usually only fools and rogues who are in harmony with their milieu, and that it is an axiom that men and women of any value must inevitably be disappointed in life.[1] But the relationship between man and society, inimical or otherwise, is of vital concern to Tolstoy, and is one of the important 'links' and 'connections' which he referred to in the context of the architecture of his novel when he said: 'In almost everything I have written, I have been guided by the need to gather together thoughts which were interconnected...; but every thought expressed separately in words loses its meaning and is terribly impoverished when taken by itself out of the connection in which it occurs'.[2] More explicitly with reference to *Anna Karenina*, he wrote in the reply to the criticism that there is no architecture in the novel: 'On the contrary I am proud of the architecture—the arches have been constructed in such a way that it is impossible to see where the keystone is. And that is what I was striving for most of all. The structural link (*svyaz'*) is not the plot or the relationship of the characters (friendship), but an inner link.'[3] Just as it is wrong to see the story of Anna and Vronsky in isolation from the other parallel and contrasting themes, so too would it be mistaken to isolate dreams from their organic connections with events in the dreamer's waking life, or faith from its practical relationship to the problems of daily living. Everything is related to everything else in Tolstoy's scheme of things.

[1] G. Lukács, *Studies in European Realism*, p. 190.
[2] J.E. LXII, 269.   [3] J.E. LXII, 377.

From a structural point of view, of course, the most obvious example of interrelationship is the close knitting together of the three main stories which illustrate the central theme of life inside and outside the family. This is a powerful argument against those who maintain that Tolstoy should have written two novels, not one. It is not a case of injecting a family novel into a tragic drama of passion and suicide. Kitty and Levin, Anna and Vronsky, are the obverse and reverse sides of what is fundamentally the same problem. A Soviet critic, in an awkward but comprehensible phrase, refers to the interaction of the two central plots as being based on 'the simultaneity of action of contrasting thematic lines'.[1] The scene switches constantly from one 'line' to the other; what is happening to one pair is simultaneously contrasted with what is happening to the other. Levin is unsuccessful in his love for Kitty; Vronsky succeeds with both Kitty and Anna. Kitty is ill as a result of her unhappy emotional experiences; Anna flourishes in her first love for Vronsky. As Kitty's life takes a turn for the better, Anna's takes a turn for the worse. Levin lives happily in the country; Anna and Karenin live miserably in the town. Levin acquires a wife and leaves for the country for 'a new and happy life'; Anna loses a husband and goes abroad, but cannot build 'a new and happy life' there. Levin acquires a son; Anna loses one. Levin's family life in the country goes on; Anna's life outside the family comes to an abrupt end. The scheme could easily be extended, and while the stories are strictly speaking out of step because of Tolstoy's carelessness over the passage of time, the structural plan is clear and fairly faithfully adhered to. As in *War and Peace*, Tolstoy varies the pattern from time to time. Levin's visit to Koznyshev, which preceded his visit to Oblonsky, is described after it. The scene at the horse-races is followed by Vronsky's visit to Anna on the afternoon before them. Rather surprisingly, Levin does not meet Anna until the next to last part of the novel, shortly before her death.

But if, broadly speaking, the parallel and contrasting fates of

[1] V. A. Zhdanov, *Tvorcheskaya istoriya 'Anny Kareninoi'*, p. 208.

the main group of characters provide the skeleton framework, there is a marked difference between the dramatic nature of the Anna and Vronsky story and the undramatic nature of Levin's and Kitty's. It has been aptly said that a sense of impending tragedy pervades *Anna Karenina*. From the 'bad omen' when the guard is run over at the railway station on the first meeting between Anna and Vronsky to Anna's suicide at another railway station, there are constant reminders of fate, of irrational coincidences and correspondences, of an inevitability which is as inexorable as the decree of fate in classical Greek drama. Anna does not struggle, says Merezhkovsky; she is a contemplative victim swallowed up by the elements. The dramatic nature of her story is enhanced by the use—some would say too overt use—of symbols. More than one critic has commented on the loose wedding-ring which slips on and off Anna's finger, or the apparent responsibility of Vronsky for the death of Frou-Frou, his mare, and the destruction of his mistress—a parallel which is more pointed in a draft version where the sight of Anna at a jump causes Vronsky to falter and lose the race as he is later to lose his career because of her, and inadvertently to break his beloved mare's back as he will inadvertently be the cause of Anna's death. In one early version Anna was called Tatyana and the mare Tanya (the diminutive of Tatyana). The name Frou-Frou may well owe its origin to the nickname of the heroine of a French play of that title, popular at the time in Moscow, who abandons her husband and son and goes off with her lover. The parallel could hardly have been missed by the contemporary reading public.

But perhaps the scene which stands out most vividly as one to which Tolstoy attached obvious symbolic importance is the description of the snowstorm which rages throughout the meeting of Vronsky and Anna on their train journey back to Petersburg. This is one of the great scenes in Tolstoy. The irony of the situation is at once made apparent, for Anna is thinking with relief of her return home to her 'nice life' after leaving Moscow a day early to avoid meeting Vronsky. During their chance meeting on the train, few words are exchanged, and those formal and banal. Words can be false, but gestures and mannerisms are less easy to counterfeit, and these we are allowed to see. Tolstoy has to convey the confusion and turmoil in Anna's mind created by this fateful meeting, and against a kaleidoscopic background, a rapid series of impressions of people opening and shutting doors, a platform creaking, someone's stooping shadow, the rapid movement of muffled figures and the sound of a hammer upon iron, the storm rages in all its fury. It symbolises the storm in Anna's mind—the wind was so strong that it seemed nobody could stand up against it—but it is a *snow*-storm, and has the further suggestion of a life-giving, exhilarating force. The struggle is seen on Anna's face. She is both frightened and happy. Everything is disconnected. She cannot concentrate. Nature emphasises her mood:

The terrible storm tore and whistled between the carriage wheels, along the telegraph poles, round the corner of the station. Carriages, poles, people, everything in sight was covered on one side with snow, and the snow was getting thicker and thicker. For a moment the storm would abate, but then it would swoop down with such gusts that it seemed impossible to stand up against it. Meanwhile people ran along talking cheerfully and continually opening and shutting the big doors, their footsteps scraping along the boards of the platform. The stooping shadow of a man glided past beneath her feet and she could hear the sound of a hammer against iron. 'Give me the telegram,' shouted an angry voice from the stormy darkness on the other side. 'This way! Number 28!' cried several different voices and muffled figures ran by, covered in snow. Two gentlemen with lighted cigarettes in their mouths walked past her. She drew another deep breath of air and had just put her hand out of her muff to take hold of the rail and get back into the carriage, when another man nearby in an army greatcoat stepped between her and the flickering light of the lamp-post. She looked round and immediately recognised Vronsky's face. He saluted and bowed to her, and asked whether she wanted anything and whether he could be of service to her. She gazed at him for quite a while without answering, and in spite of the shadow in which he stood, she saw, or fancied she saw, both the expression on his face and in his eyes. It was the same expression of respectful admiration which had so affected her the night before. More than once she had told herself during the past few days, and again only a moment ago, that Vronsky was for her only one of hundreds of identical young men one meets everywhere, and that she would never let herself as much as think of him; but now, the very moment she met him, she was seized by a feeling of joyful pride. She did not need to ask why he was there. She knew as certainly as if he had told her that he was there to be where she was.

'I didn't know you were travelling. Why are you travelling?' she said, lowering her hand which was just about to grasp the rail. And her face shone with uncontrollable joy and animation.

'Why am I travelling?' he repeated, looking straight into her eyes. 'You know I'm travelling to be where you are,' he said. 'I can't do otherwise.'

And at that moment the wind, as though surmounting all obstacles, scattered the snow from the carriage roofs and clanged a sheet of iron it had torn away, while up in front the hoarse whistle of the locomotive gave a mournful and gloomy hoot. The sheer horror of the storm now seemed to her more beautiful than ever. He had said the very thing which her soul longed for, though her reason feared it. She made no reply and he saw the struggle in her face.[1]

The details of the storm, which are intensely vivid, are not there for their own sake. They are not like Hardy's Egdon Heath, an entity in its own right, which is far more powerful than man. They are a link between animate and inanimate phenomena, an essential part of Tolstoy's technique of characterisation. The railway setting provides an obtrusive and dramatic leitmotif— an understandable one, since Anna's prototype met her death on the rails, and Tolstoy was well known for his hostility to this new sign of progress and desecration of the countryside— the railway engine, rushing headlong to its destination at the cost of death or disaster. References to railways pervade the novel, and play a big part in knitting together the themes of love and death and providing dramatic cohesion. Whether it is Anna's first meeting with Vronsky at Moscow station, the

[1] *Anna Karenina*, I, 30.

death of the guard, her return to Petersburg on the same train as Vronsky, the meeting between Vronsky and her husband at Petersburg station, Oblonsky's children playing trains and the passengers falling off the roof, Levin declaring on a railway platform that it is time he were dead, the provincial hotel where Levin's brother dies, with its 'modern, self-satisfied railway-induced sense of bustle', Anna's dream and her suicide, or Vronsky's glum departure by train for the Serbian Wars—the railway is an ever-present protagonist with a tragic rôle to play. An interesting comparison has been made between *Anna Karenina* and *Dombey and Son*,[1] which Tolstoy had probably read in Russian in *The Contemporary* (although there is no actual record of his having done so before 1878). Karenin and Dombey have marked similarities in their attitude to family life and to their wives. The first person to visit Dombey after Edith had left him was his sister; in an early draft of *Anna* it was Karenin's sister—in the final version it is Lydia Ivanovna, whose place she takes—who first came to console him. In both novels the crisis is precipitated by a riding accident. Florence Dombey's dream of trying to reconcile her feelings for her father and her stepmother and showing that she loves them both recalls Anna's dream that she was the wife of both Vronsky and Karenin and shares her love between them. More significantly, both Anna and Carker are killed beneath a train.

It would be wrong to press the comparison too far, or to make extravagant claims for Tolstoy's 'railway symbolism'. The game of hunt-the-symbol is better played with other authors, and it has been well said that critical techniques evolved in response to an age of extreme experiment may, precisely because they work admirably with Joyce or Gide, work less well with Fielding or Balzac. The point remains that the Anna and Vronsky story is of an altogether different degree of intensity and complexity from the rest of the book. This is certainly connected to some extent with Tolstoy's belief that he was writing a *novel* for the first time in his life—he had

[1] M. H. Futtrell, *Dickens and Three Russian Novelists: Gogol, Dostoevsky and Tolstoy* (Ph.D. thesis), (London 1955).

refused to call *War and Peace* a novel, it will be remembered; that novel-writing is an art; that art has conventions; and that he too must pay regard to the practice of other novelists. As a result *Anna Karenina* is more 'like a novel' than anything else he wrote, and the Anna–Vronsky story is his most 'novelistic' plot. Perhaps Mr Bayley overstates his case when he says that Tolstoy allowed himself to become *too* obsessed with significance and metaphors, and that his art suffered from being too consciously professional.[1] It is a fact that these significances—the extinguished candle in Anna's death scene is another one—do strike one at times as being artificially contrived. And yet the picking up of threads, the recurrence of motifs, the final return to initial associations (Anna's red handbag, the guard run over, the peasant on the rails in the same scene)—the closing of the circle as it were—not only help to create the symmetrical architecture of which Tolstoy was proud, but also, and more important, the claustrophobic atmosphere so essential to the expression of the theme.

By contrast, the saga of Kitty and Levin, in which the crises are surmounted or else swallowed up by life, is relatively undramatic and more frankly educative. Their structural function has been neatly aphorised as a lightning rod upon which the energies of Tolstoy's didacticism were discharged, relieving the weight of it on the parallel plot.[2] That this is true in so far as it concerns the theme of family happiness in no way invalidates the opinion that Levin 'liberates the book so that it can grow to Tolstoyan size; he saves it from the classic—and diminished—novel pattern of Flaubert and James'.[3] The function of the third couple, Dolly and Oblonsky, is quite simply to steer a middle course, and to combine the theme of adultery with that of the continuation of married life with all its ups and downs.

It is difficult to accept Lionel Trilling's claim that Tolstoy dispenses with manipulative techniques, distortion, plot, etc.,

---

[1] J. Bayley, *Tolstoy and the Novel*, p. 191.
[2] G. Steiner, *Tolstoy or Dostoevsky*, p. 283.
[3] J. Bayley, *Tolstoy and the Novel*, p. 202.

or the guarded assertion by Philip Rahv that 'in a sense there
are no plots in Tolstoy'.[1] Barbara Hardy says that there is
no plot in *Anna Karenina* in the sense of elaborate scheming and
intricate intrigue, but complicates the issue by adding that
'Destiny is the plot'.[2] To my mind there are not only plots
(although not of a tight, melodramatic or Dickensian nature),
but they are singularly well organised and constructed.

Like a good detective story writer, Tolstoy drops hints about
the likely future outcome of a situation and leaves clues for the
observant to pick up. The warnings and forebodings which
Anna senses early on, and Kitty's recognition of a streak in
Anna's nature which the others do not see are obvious examples.
The early conversation between Kitty and Levin before he is
refused, when Kitty says 'I have confidence in you' and when
he replies to her question: 'Surely you must feel dull in the
country in winter, don't you?' with the words 'No, not a bit,
I'm very busy', foreshadows their situation much later on in
the novel. Oblonsky assures Levin that Dolly has second sight
and that *she* believes that Kitty will marry Levin. Even before
Kitty is rejected by Vronsky, Tolstoy gently prepares the
ground—'But something uneasy clouded her thoughts about
Vronsky'—while her father's prognostications about 'the
conceited popinjay who is only amusing himself' turn out
to be only too justified. The device of anticipation, though
hardly original, is evidence of careful planning.

I have tried to answer some of the charges levelled against
Tolstoy's novel of psychological and structural weaknesses
which seem to me to have been very much exaggerated and to
be dwarfed by his very obvious power of human understanding, his masterly characterisation and his technical prowess.
The reproaches made against Tolstoy's language and style
seem equally unfounded. No one would wish to deny his love
of repetition, his addiction to certain clusters of words (e.g.
'to experience a feeling similar to that which...'), his fondness

[1] L. Trilling, *The Opposing Self* (London 1955), who quotes Rahv's essay of
1951.
[2] B. Hardy, *The Appropriate Form*, p. 187.

for schematic classification and some of the tricks of classical rhetoric. Clumsiness and awkwardness there occasionally is, but sometimes less than in the language of the critic who upbraids him. There are certain positive features of Tolstoy's prose style which even an indifferent translation should not obscure: its fundamental directness, lucidity and absence of any obtrusive affectation, the vivid imagery of his relatively few, but memorable, similes and metaphors, or the rôle played by vocabulary in characterisation (for example the concentration on fire and heat in the portrayal of Anna). But no translation, however careful, can preserve the inviolability of what, in a different context, has been referred to as 'these words in this order',[1] or, to quote Tolstoy himself, 'the only possible order for the only possible words'. No translation has been able to convey the rhythm and balance over which Tolstoy laboured diligently and long, the syntactical differences between the author's narrative and the speech of his characters or the peculiar linguistic flavour imparted to the words of Karenin or Ryabinin or Veslovsky, which characterises and individualises, so that the manner of their saying a thing is as significant as the content of what they say. The careful choice of the right idiom and tone of voice not only expresses obvious differences between the speech of the upper class, the bourgeoisie and the peasantry, but also—and here we broach the charge of tendentiousness—the author's subjective appreciation or depreciation of the men and women of his own class. Of course Tolstoy weights the scales against Vronsky by making him speak only French to Anna (Levin would never have done this). Of course he is unfair in the sense that clever people are taken down a peg or two by having stupid arguments attributed to them—not only the intellectuals whose verbose abstract ratiocinations are contrasted with the simple and laconic vocabulary of Kitty and Levin, but even the intuitively wise Levin himself, who is made to argue that a peasant who can read and write makes a far worse labourer, or that there is no

[1] D. Lodge, *Language of Fiction* (quoting J. M. Cameron), (London 1966), p. 33.

need to have courts of law since *he* is not going to cut anybody's throat. Similarly Sviazhky suffers in his arguments with Levin by being made to shy away from Levin's questions although they are not at all difficult for him to answer. Some people consider Vronsky's handsome, manly image to be somewhat demeaned by his incipient baldness and his toothache. Anna's later addiction to smoking and contraception is a token of Tolstoy's especial displeasure. Such 'interference' cannot be denied, but it is not the heavy hand of authorial pronouncement but the subtle intrusion of the author's personality—and in the last resort the novel is great because of that personality. If we did not feel the mind and thought of Tolstoy working behind his characters, no amount of classical detachment could compensate for our impoverishment. A writer's genius, said Malraux, resides less in what is said or how it is said than in the strength of the personality which lies beneath. Tolstoy could have converted the humblest subject into a literary masterpiece 'because he had the talent of a Tolstoy, but primarily because he was Lev Nikolaevich. The force of Christ's answer when faced with the woman taken in adultery is not due to the talent of the evangelists.'[1]

In *Anna Karenina* Tolstoy demonstrated his immense range of knowledge of human nature, his breadth of sympathy and understanding and an anger tempered by charity. His extraordinary powers of observation, his vivid and detailed depiction of contemporary life with hardly a trace of sordidness or naturalism, allied to a seriousness of purpose and a deep concern with the fundamental issues of life in society, make his novel one of the truly great works of European literature.

[1] Quoted by E. W. Knight, *Literature Considered as Philosophy* (London 1957), p. 133.

7

'CONFESSION' AND 'RESURRECTION'

Tolstoy's spiritual crisis is traditionally ascribed to the later half of the 1870s. At the height of his fame and creative power, a wealthy and successful man with a large and growing family, he became the victim of growing moodiness and depression, and sought in earnest for an answer to the meaning and purpose of life in a religious faith which could prescribe rules of behaviour without requiring him to engage in practices, or subscribe to beliefs, which his reason found repugnant. What was unusual about his conversion, said his friend and disciple, Aylmer Maude, was that 'it came so late in life and so gradually, and that the intellect played so great a part in it'.[1] And yet the seeds of rebellion against the accepted values of his class, in the name of a faith which was personal and nonconformist, had been sown a long time before. Their growth can be traced through Tolstoy's fiction, from *Childhood* to *Anna Karenina*, in the doubts and fears and searchings of the various Tolstoyan heroes. From his letters of the early 1870s and his wife's reactions to his thoughts and behaviour, one can glean his growing preoccupation with problems of life and death. His renewed pedagogical experiments were an attempt to relate education to the needs of living. His encounters with dissenting religious sects in Bashkiria, especially the Molokans, reawakened his interest in religion as a way of life and not an adherence to ritual forms. At the same time he was deeply immersed in the study of Schopenhauer. Moreover, his own illness and the deaths of two of his children exacerbated his increasing morbidity. Before long he was making his first pilgrimage to the Optin monastery to seek comfort and inspiration from its elders and monks. The study of Tolstoy's life in the decade following the publication of *War and Peace* is a necessary prelude to an understanding of the crisis which culminated in 1879; but it is his own *Confession*, begun in the

[1] A. Maude, *Life of Tolstoy*, I, 384.

same year, which is the best introduction to the spiritual struggle he was to wage for the remaining thirty years of his life and which was to have such profound repercussions on his art.

The last part of *Anna Karenina* leads logically into Tolstoy's *Confession*, which in turn is the prelude to his numerous religious treatises expounding his beliefs, his revised version of the Sermon on the Mount and his attempt to express in artistic form in his last full-scale novel, *Resurrection*, the true message of the Gospels as he understands them, stripped of their theological excrescences and purged of their supernatural mystique. Tolstoy, like the German theologians of the nineteenth century and their twentieth-century disciples, was at first concerned to rationalise from the life and teachings of Jesus, the man, a satisfying prescription for human behaviour and the establishment of the kingdom of heaven on earth as summed up in the five laws which were to form the climax to *Resurrection*, enjoining men not to kill, not to commit adultery, not to bind themselves by oaths, not to demand an eye for an eye and not to hate, but to love their enemies. Christianity, however, was only one field of exploration, and it was not long before he extended his researches eastwards. His reading embraced the Vedas, the Upanishads, Confucius, Mencius and Lao Tzu. He came to believe that the most important task of his life was to synthesise the wisdom of East and West, and his hostility to material progress, his political quietism, and his vegetarianism were all nurtured by his oriental studies. This is not the place to expound or criticise his well-known and uncompromising ideals. But before turning to *Resurrection* we may pause for a moment on the *Confession*, which is the clearest, most relentless and most devastating statement we have of its author's spiritual pilgrimage. None of the great confessional literature from St Augustine to Rousseau can match Tolstoy's short work for power, eloquence, concise if not always logical thought, and the ability to convey with colloquial simplicity the grandeur and nobility of biblical language. Step by step he recounts his early loss of faith, his disillusionment in its various

TOLSTOY

surrogates—self-perfection, literary fame, the nineteenth-century belief in progress—and his growing despair, halted only temporarily by marriage and family responsibilities which could not conceal the fact that he had no answer to the question of the purpose of life when faced with the prospect of inevitable death:

One can only live when intoxicated with life; when one is sober it is impossible not to see that it is all a mere fraud, and a stupid fraud! There is actually nothing amusing or witty about it, it is simply cruel and stupid.

There is an Eastern fable, told long ago, about a traveller caught in open country by a wild beast. To escape from the beast the traveller jumps into a dry well, but at the bottom of the well he sees a dragon with its jaws open to devour him. And the unfortunate man, not daring to climb out lest he be destroyed by the wild beast, and not daring to jump to the bottom of the well lest he be devoured by the dragon, seizes hold of a branch of a wild bush growing in a crack in the well and clings to it. His arms grow weaker and he feels he will soon have to abandon himself to the destruction which awaits him above or below; but he still clings on and as he clings on he looks round and sees that two mice, one black and one white, are steadily circling round the branch of the bush he is hanging on and gnawing at it. Soon it will snap and break off, and he will fall into the dragon's jaws. The traveller sees this and knows that he will inevitably perish; but while he hangs there he looks round and finds some drops of honey on the leaves of the bush, reaches them with his tongue and licks them. So I too clung to the branches of life, knowing that the dragon of death was inevitably waiting for me, ready to tear me to pieces, and I could not understand why this agony had befallen me. And I tried to lick the honey which had previously consoled me, but the honey no longer gave me pleasure, while the white and black mice—day and night—gnawed at the branch I was clinging to. I saw the dragon clearly, and the honey was no longer sweet. I only saw the unescapable dragon and the mice, and I could not tear my gaze away from them. And this is not a fable, but the real, irrefutable truth comprehensible to all.

The deception of the joys of life which used to allay my fear of the dragon now no longer deceived me. No matter how often I

was told: 'You cannot understand the meaning of life, so do not
think about it, but live,' I could no longer do it because I had done
it for too long. I could not now help seeing day and night running
round and bringing me nearer to death. That is all I could see,
because only that is the truth. All the rest is lies.

The two drops of honey which diverted my eyes from the cruel
truth longer than any others—the love of my family and of writing,
which I called art—were no longer sweet to me.[1]

If life was meaningless, so too was art, literature and the family.
For an answer to his problems and to save himself from suicide,
he turned first to the philosophers, then to the educated people
of his own class and finally to the uneducated masses who for
the most part were believers. Their faith made it possible
for them to go on living—but it was inseparable from Orthodox ritual and dogma which he, from a rational point of view,
found repugnant. Besides, there were the vexed questions of
comparative religion and the Church's attitude to war.
Tolstoy concludes that the Church's teaching must contain a
mixture of truth and falsehood and that he must endeavour to
separate the one from the other. He accepts that some things
will always remain inexplicable, but adds, 'I want everything
that is inexplicable to be so, not because the demands my mind
makes are wrong, but because I can see the limits of my mind.'[2]

Having looked back over his past life, a life without faith,
and found it evil, he looks forward to the good life of the
believer—if only he can once believe. There is no doubt that
his confession was torn from his soul in a moment of acute
despair. As he said when writing it: 'This is not a work of
art, and it is not for publication.' And yet he did publish it (not
in Russia, where it was banned in 1882, but in Geneva in 1884),
and it is precisely because it is a work of art and not a tract that
it still retains its appeal today. For if one applies to it the criteria
of hard logic and common sense (as Tolstoy liked to do when
he was leading for the prosecution and not the defence), its
arguments leave much to be desired. When Tolstoy tries to
show the inability of philosophers to answer his questions, he

---

[1] *Confession*, Ch. 4.   [2] J.E. LXII, 504.

cites only those philosophers and religious thinkers whose views support his case that life is meaningless and that death is better than life. As has been said in another context, he is prepared to try to understand everything scientifically, except the mind of those with whom he disagrees. While blaming metaphysics for drawing conclusions based on the study of a mere fraction of mankind, he is himself guilty of generalising from the particular and confining philosophy to the selected thoughts of a few untypical, but like-minded exponents. Again, he says on one occasion, 'I would rather lose my life than my reason', and on another that 'only faith which is unreasonable makes life possible'. His numerous generalisations supported by 'for the most part' or 'almost all' (believers for the most part are stupid, cruel and immoral...unbelievers for the most part are intelligent, upright and moral...almost all writers are immoral and worthless...) and his oversimplifications of the sort 'All that people truly believe in must be the truth', his exaggeration of his own vices or his idealisation of the faith of the common people: all belong as much to the realm of his art as to life. Indeed, at the time of writing his *Confession* and accusing himself of lying, theft, adultery, drunkenness, violence and even murder, he was telling his friend Strakhov: 'Write your biography. I keep meaning to do the same. Only one must aim to make all one's readers feel disgusted with one's life.'[1] While it is hard to deny Tolstoy's sincerity, it is equally hard to deny his artifice. Concealed by the colloquial language, the omitted pronouns, the seemingly casual 'and', 'but', 'thus', 'and so', lie the carefully constructed runs of threes, the sets of nouns and verbs, sometimes five or six in number with no conjunctions, the rhetorical appoggia-turas and the conscious literary exploitation of the parable, the long simile or the dream.

Turgenev, while impressed by what he thought was Tolsoy's sincerity and conviction, if not his art, criticised the book because it led to the most gloomy negation of human life; 'a sort of nihilism' he terms it, thinking perhaps of Bazarov in

[1] J.E. LXII, 500.

his own *Fathers and Sons*. His remark is open to more than one interpretation. Tolstoy, like Bazarov, was contemptuous of authority and its hallowed principles. Both men tended towards puritanism, both had more than a touch of self-righteousness and contempt for human weakness. Both were to reject art, though for different reasons; both give the impression of being uncompromisingly honest with themselves; both get away with one-sided, weighted arguments because of their stark simplicity and apparent sincerity. But if Bazarov, the rationalist and materialist, believes in science, knowledge and the primacy of the mind, Tolstoy uses his immense powers of reason and his vast knowledge to exalt faith above science and rationalism. If Bazarov was a nihilist because he only wanted to destroy ('to clear the site'), Tolstoy was emphatically not so, because he was groping towards a positive faith which could give him the strength to lead a moral life, the sanction for which was to be at least in part the precepts and example of Christ.

If we regard nihilism in a wider context than that of Bazarov, we shall find more justice in Turgenev's remark. On the one hand Turgenev feared that Tolstoy's peasant-oriented, Christ-based morality would mean the end of civilised life as he himself understood it—education, urbane manners, good food and drink and the company of civilised women; he rightly foresaw Tolstoy's renunciation of meat and alcohol, upper-class art, liberal institutions, 'good taste', and sex as pleasure, without which life indeed would have ceased to matter for him. On the other hand he may have sensed Tolstoy's leanings towards Buddhism and Nirvana, the axiom that death is better than life and that faith is only a temporary palliative by means of which to endure the short time before the inevitable passage into nothingness—the feeling Prince Andrew has before his death when he wonders whether God is the Great All or Nothing. And yet there is no hopelessness in Tolstoy's work, only an endless seeking which provides that quality of ambiguity and lack of finality so important to a work of art, but inappropriate in a propaganda treatise.

Much of Tolstoy's other writing on religion and the practical problems of pacifism, slum conditions, prostitution and vegetarianism belongs unmistakably to the literature of pamphleteering. This is not to say that its value is in any way diminished. But the assessment of it falls outside our scope and we can leave aside the merits and defects of his polemics against the Orthodox Church, his translations of the Gospels or the numerous articles in which he starts by knowing the answers and devotes all his powers to giving them the maximum force and the widest currency.

Ten years were to elapse between Tolstoy's first draft of the *Confession* and the opening chapters of *Resurrection*. Another ten years were to pass before *Resurrection* was published in 1899. The original stimulus for the novel was a story told him by his lawyer friend Koni which he had heard in the course of his professional duties. A young orphan girl who had been brought up by a wealthy lady had been seduced by a relation of her benefactor. When her pregnancy was discovered she was driven out of the house and abandoned by the man who had seduced her. She became a prostitute and was arrested on a charge of stealing money in a brothel. Among the members of the jury at her trial was her seducer. His conscience was aroused and he offered to marry the girl, but her early death from typhoid frustrated his purpose. Tolstoy's interest in his friend's story was not solely due to its artistic possibilities, as the following admission to his biographer Biryukov makes clear: 'When I was young I led a very evil life, and two incidents from it still particularly torment me... These were a liaison with a peasant girl from our village before I was married—there is an allusion to it in my story *The Devil*—and the second was the crime I perpetrated on Gasha, the maid who lived in my aunt's house. She was innocent. I seduced her, they drove her out of the house and she came to grief.'[1] No doubt Tolstoy exaggerated the consequences of his offence, for when he came to work up Koni's story and describe the seduction of Maslova by Prince Nekhlyudov, his wife re-

[1] P. I. Biryukov, *Biografiya L. N. Tolstogo* (Moscow 1922), III, 317.

corded her husband's affair with Gasha in her diary and gave it a less tragic ending: 'It also distresses me very much that Lev Nikolaevich, an old man of seventy, should be describing scenes of adultery between an officer and a maid with particular relish, like a gastronome savouring a tasty dish. I know—he himself told me in detail—that he is describing his liaison with his sister's maid at Pirogovo. I saw this Gasha afterwards, she's an old woman of seventy now. He himself pointed her out to me, to my chagrin and disgust.'[1] At all events the undoubted autobiographical attraction of the story did not mean that the writing of it came easily to Tolstoy. Indeed the novel might well not have been completed at all had it not been for the fact that in 1898 Tolstoy proposed to sell it with two other stories to provide money to help the Dukhobors—sectarian refugees from tsarist persecution—to resettle in Canada. With a fixed object in mind it was necessary to finish the task for better or worse. 'These stories', he said, speaking of *Resurrection, Father Sergei* and *The Devil*, 'are written in my old manner which I now disapprove of. If I go on revising them until I'm satisfied with them I'll never finish. Having promised them to a publisher I shall have to let them go as they are. The same thing happened with *The Cossacks*.'[2] And so *Resurrection*, begun in 1889–90 and continued in 1895–6, was resumed and finished in 1898–9. In Tolstoy's diaries and letters we find much evidence of the continual tussle between the demands made on him as a novelist and as a propagandist for art in the service of a higher cause. He felt the need to bring his present outlook on things to bear on all aspects of Russian life, to write an extended *What I Believe* covering the major social problems of the day, an encyclopaedic *profession de foi* which, while masquerading as a novel, would do the work of a tract. 'I began to think how nice it would be', he said in 1891, 'to write a novel *de longue haleine*, illuminating it with my present view of things and collecting all my ideas together in it.'[3] He wanted to begin with an invective against the whole legal

[1] *Dnevniki S. A. Tolstoi, 1897–1909* (Moscow 1932), p. 81.
[2] Letter to Chertkov, 14 July 1898.   [3] J.E. LII, 5.

system and its absurdity. He wanted, moreover, to contrast the 'two extremes of true love with its false middle,'[1] the youthful innocent love of Maslova and Nekhlyudov and their married love with extra-marital sexual relations and prostitution. But while his intentions were abundantly clear, he was disturbed by the effect they might have on the novelist's concern with problems of psychology, structure and composition. For he wanted Nekhlyudov to be a complex character and refers in the diaries to his 'duality', and yet he also wanted him 'to simplify his way of life', not unnaturally expressing the fear that 'cela n' empiète sur le drame'.[2] Marriage was to be the climax to his relations with the woman he had seduced, but how early should the climax come? A passage from his diary in the 1890s is revealing. 'Novels end with the hero and the heroine getting married. They ought to begin with this and end with their getting "unmarried", i.e. becoming free. Otherwise to describe people's lives in such a way as to break off the description with their marriage is just the same as describing a man's journey and breaking off the description at the point where the traveller falls into the hands of bandits'[3]— not a simile likely to have pleased his wife!

The beginning and ending of his own novel proved particularly troublesome to Tolstoy. Should he start from the positive side with the young Maslova? Or from the negative side with Nekhlyudov's seduction of an innocent girl? Or better still, with a court scene on which the whole fury of his satire could be discharged? In the event it is Maslova who opens the proceedings, but a Maslova already tainted by years of poverty and vice. The other opening gambits are employed in the first few chapters so that no ideas are wasted, and in this respect the beginning of the novel, troublesome as it was, proved far less difficult to write than the conclusion. In the final drafts, Maslova tries to dissuade Nekhlyudov from marrying her, but he insists. They marry in the prison chapel and go off together to settle in Siberia. Maslova helps in the garden, does the housework, reads, studies and helps her

[1] J.E. LIII, 35.   [2] J.E. LIII, 34.   [3] J.E. LII, 36.

husband. Nekhlyudov gets on with his writing. After a while the authorities move them on to the Amur district from where they eventually escape to London, where Nekhlyudov is able to propagate his ideas on the evil of private ownership of land. In the very different final version Maslova marries another prisoner, while Nekhlyudov reads the Gospels and prepares to live a new life. Tolstoy found this solution equally unsatisfactory and planned to write a sequel on Nekhlyudov's peasant life—but never did. Agrarian problems and Henry George's Single Tax were very much in Tolstoy's thoughts at this time, and indeed he feared that the land question loomed too large in *Resurrection* to the detriment of the central moral issue of guilt and expiation and the psychological exploration of Nekhlyudov's character. The difficulty of keeping so many objectives in view, and the constant and growing tension between propaganda and art inevitably left their mark. As his crisis receded, Tolstoy's views crystallised and hardened, and when he returned to *Resurrection* for the last time he no longer had the breadth of human sympathy, the vast apprehension of reality or the restless spirit of enquiry which animated *War and Peace*. Critical opinion is often shifting, but no serious critic would deny that Tolstoy's last novel is a vastly inferior work of art to the two great novels which preceded it.

The reader whose appetite for Tolstoy has been whetted on *War and Peace* will be struck more by what is missing in *Resurrection* than by what is there. Gone are the domesticity, the poetry of 'marriage and the hearth', the ballroom, the salon, the charm, vivacity and graciousness of the best representatives of upper-class society and with them the complement of aristocratic life—hunting, coursing, and the outdoor activities of the country gentleman. Psychologically speaking, there is a striking absence of motivation for character development. The author assures us that Maslova really loves Nekhlyudov, but we are not shown how she reached this conclusion and we are not convinced by what we are told. Nekhlyudov's conversion is the result of the author's *sic jubeo*—and perhaps there is no other way of showing the sudden moment of awakening to faith. But the precarious *détente* which Levin achieves after *his* conversion is both more complex and more credible than the uncompromising assuredness of Nekhlyudov's five commandments.

Missing too from *Resurrection* are the richness and variety of the parallel and contrasting themes of the earlier novels. Aldous Huxley, in the person of Philip Quarles, has some apt things to say about structural problems in music and the novel. 'The abrupt transitions', he writes apropos the novel, 'are easy enough. All you need is a sufficiency of characters and parallel, contrapuntal plots. While Jones is murdering a wife, Smith is wheeling the perambulator in the park. You alternate the themes. More interesting, the modulations and variations are also more difficult. A novelist modulates by repudiating situations and characters. He shows several people falling in love, or dying, or praying in different ways—dissimilars solving the same problem. Or vice versa, similar people confronted with dissimilar problems.'[1] In *Resurrection*, however, Tolstoy, while exploiting transition and antithesis, prefers to work with a single plot line and to impart unity to the novel by the central theme of guilt and expiation.

The new theme of expiation is in marked contrast with *Anna Karenina*, for Anna can never redeem her lapse; she is fighting a losing battle from the start. Indeed there are many new departures in *Resurrection*. Nekhlyudov is the first Tolstoyan hero to renounce his class. Maslova is the first heroine who is not an aristocrat. For the first time in his novels the representatives of 'the people' far outnumber those of the aristocracy. In subject matter, though not of course treatment, *Resurrection* has more affinity with Dostoevsky's fiction than with Tolstoy's earlier novels. The theme of humanity among convicts calls to mind *The House of the Dead*. Maslova's rejection of Nekhlyudov for fear of ruining *his* life echoes Nastasya's refusal to marry Myshkin in *The Idiot*. The motif of conscience overtaking the criminal and leading

[1] *Point Counter Point*, Ch. 22.

him through suffering to the threshold of a new life and the suggestion that 'from that day the hero became a new man' recalls *Crime and Punishment*. Tolstoy's theme of guilt and expiation weaves together two strands and fuses an individual and a class problem. The story of the fall and regeneration of two individuals is complicated by the fact that one is an aristocrat and the other is not. Only by turning his back on his own class and striving to know and do right by the lower classes can the burden of Nekhlyudov's class guilt be discharged. Tolstoy handles the theme of crime and punishment by showing the conflicting attitudes to both of the individual and the state. In the eyes of the state Nekhlyudov is innocent. His offence is not recognised as such. No state institution will punish him for doing what his own class, the upholders of the state, regard as normal for a young man in similar circumstances. The weight of authority is turned wholly against the woman—whether in the person of her guardian who turns her out of doors, or the court of law which is only concerned with what she has become, not how she was driven to become what she is. But in Nekhlyudov's own eyes, he alone is guilty, and he is faced with the problem: who has the right to decide— the individual or the state? The problem is posed in its most acute form by making him a party to the pronouncement of the judgment of the state on a crime of his own individual making.

Resurrection has been called the most synthetic of Tolstoy's novels.[1] In one sense this can be taken to refer to the synthesis of the individual and the class problem. In another sense it may mean the synthesis of its author's social, political and religious opinions, for it contains the essence of his mature views on most of the fundamental questions of life. The belief that all judgment is not only useless but immoral, that judges and juries are not only not infallible, but careless, indifferent, ill informed and unworthy by their own shortcomings to pronounce sentences on their fellow men; that men in authority

[1] Lednicki, 'Tolstoy through American eyes', *American Slavic and East European Review*, xxx (1947).

from the public prosecutor to the lowest officer are inevitably corrupted by the power they exercise and forget human considerations when acting in their official capacity; that the organised church has made a mockery of Christ's teaching and lent its authority to everything from the incantation over the bread and wine to the practice of war, capital punishment and all forms of legal constraint and violence; that people are convicted for being morally superior to their society; that taxation is robbery; that military service and the conditions of army life inevitably lead to depravity and the need to act against one's conscience; that educated society is for the most part selfish, venal and hypocritical; that sexual relations are frequently degrading and offensive to human dignity; and that only when evil men stop trying to reform evil men and all acknowledge their guilt before God, vowing not to kill, hate, swear, fornicate or exact retribution but learning to respect and love as Christ (not the church) enjoined them will there be any prospect of founding the kingdom of heaven on earth—all these beliefs are gathered together in one place, and expressed in *Resurrection* with an uncompromising and dogmatic vehemence.

In *Resurrection* it is the law which is the arch offender, and in attempting to achieve an artistic synthesis of his material Tolstoy knits together the three strands of Nekhlyudov, Maslova and the pursuit of justice. He divides his novel into three parts. Part 1 is the offence, the trial, the verdict and the discrediting of the law; its satire is directed against legal institutions. Part 2 is the attempt to use the law to right the law and its target is the bureaucracy. Part 3 purports to show that it *is* possible to change human beings; and ruthless satire gives way to an attempt to understand and live with the victims of state oppression.

The tripartite division of the novel provides a good structural foundation, but the building of the individual sections is uneven. It is the first part which has the most cohesion. A brief examination of Part 1 will show how Tolstoy tried to 'mount' his story, still using his favourite devices of juxtaposition and antithesis. The novel opens on what should be a joyful note.

It is spring. The trees are in leaf. The birds are singing. The sun is shining. But it is spring in a big city—a contradictory notion—where men have desecrated natural beauty, disfigured the land and learned to cheat and torment each other. This is the cue to introduce Maslova in jail and for the author to tell her story in narrative form without mentioning her seducer's name. Immediately afterwards, Nekhlyudov's life of luxury is contrasted with Maslova's squalid existence before the two come face to face in court. He recognises her; she does not recognise him. A vicious satire on the court and its proceedings juxtaposes those in authority and those in their power. Then Tolstoy turns the clock back ten years and 'in his old manner' writes the best chapters in the novel, prefaced by the simple statement: 'The relations between Nekhlyudov and Maslova had been as follows.' In a typically Tolstoyan climax, light and darkness are contrasted as the beautiful description of Easter, the snow, the church music, the bright clothes and the Easter greetings is followed abruptly by the sordid manoeuvres of seduction, the girl's resistance having been carefully eroded to the point where she becomes a not unwilling accomplice:

She tore herself away from him and returned to the maids' room. He heard the latch click. Then all grew quiet, the red light in the window disappeared, only the mist remained and the noise on the river.

Nekhlyudov went up to the window—nobody was to be seen. He knocked—there was no answer. Nekhlyudov went back into the house by the front door, but could not sleep. He took off his shoes and walked barefoot along the passage to her door, next to Matrena Pavlovna's room. At first he heard Matrena Pavlovna snoring peacefully and was about to go in when she suddenly began to cough and turned over on her creaky bed. He stopped dead and stood like that for five minutes or so. When all was quiet again and her peaceful snoring was again audible, he walked on, trying to step on the boards that did not creak, until he reached her door. Not a sound could be heard. She was obviously not asleep, or he would have heard her breathing. But as soon as he whispered 'Katyusha', she jumped up, came to the door and tried to persuade him—angrily it seemed to him—to go away.

'What are you doing? You mustn't! Your aunts will hear,' her lips said, but her whole being said, 'I am yours.'

And it was this only that Nekhlyudov understood.

'Open, just for a moment. I implore you.' He hardly knew what he was saying.

She said nothing; then he heard her hand feeling for the latch. The latch clicked, the door opened, and he went in.

He took hold of her just as she was in her coarse, stiff chemise, her arms bare, picked her up and carried her out.

'Oh, what are you doing?' she whispered.

But he paid no attention to her words, as he carried her off to his room.

'Oh, don't, let me go,' she said, and clung closer to him...

When she left him, silent and trembling, without a word, he went out into the porch and stood trying to understand the meaning of what had happened.

It was getting lighter outside. The cracking and tinkling and spluttering of the breaking ice on the river below grew louder, and now a gurgling sound could be heard as well. The mist had begun to settle down below and the waning moon came out from behind the mist, casting a gloomy light on something black and weird.

'What does it mean? Is it a great happiness or a great misfortune which has befallen me?' he asked himself. 'Everybody does it, everybody does it,' he said to himself and went to bed.[1]

A stroke of the pen, ten years pass and we are back in court to witness the miscarriage of justice—the account and circumstances of Maslova's trial, incidentally, having some striking similarities with the trial of Vera Kapitonovna, in Gorky's *The Three of Them*, which was written a year after *Resurrection* was published. The verdict pronounced, Nekhlyudov leaves for a sumptuous dinner at his prospective fiancée's; Maslova returns to her cell to hunger and humiliation. The scene shifts to the jail as Nekhlyudov tries to obtain permission to visit Maslova, and in yet another pointed juxtaposition of incompatibles the strains of a Liszt rhapsody 'so unsuitable to the place' float from the prison warden's house. As Maslova lies

---

[1] *Resurrection*, Pt. 1, Ch. 17.

awake in prison Tolstoy recalls through her thought processes the occasion when, already pregnant, she ran through the wind and rain to the railway station to catch a glimpse of Nekhlyudov passing through by train. Once again we have the familiar antithesis: Nekhlyudov laughing and joking inside the brightly lit carriage, Maslova standing weeping in the dark:

It was a dark, rainy, windy autumn night. One moment the rain would splash down in big warm drops, the next moment it would stop. Katyusha could hardly see the path across the field and it was pitch-dark in the wood so that although she knew the way well, she lost the track through the wood and reached the little station where the train stopped for three minutes, not as she had hoped, before it arrived, but only after the second bell. As she ran onto the platform Katyusha saw him at once in the window of a first-class carriage. The carriage was very brightly lit. Two officers on velvet-covered seats were sitting opposite each other in their shirt sleeves, playing cards. Candles were burning and dripping on a table by the window. He was wearing tight-fitting breeches and a white shirt, and was sitting on the arm of the seat, leaning against the back and laughing at something. As soon as she recognised him she knocked on the window with her frozen hand. But at that moment the third bell rang and the train slowly began to move; at first it moved backwards, but then the carriages began to jerk forwards one after another. One of the players stood up with the cards in his hand and looked out of the window. She knocked again and pressed her face to the glass. Then the carriage at which she was standing gave a jerk and started to move. She walked beside it, looking through the window. An officer tried to lower the window, but could not. Nekhlyudov got up, pushed him aside and began lowering it himself. The train picked up speed. She quickened her step to keep up with it, but it kept gaining speed and just at the moment the window was lowered the guard pushed her aside and jumped into the carriage. Katyusha dropped behind, but kept running along the wet boards of the platform. Then the platform came to an end and she could hardly save herself from falling as she ran down the steps on to the ground. She kept running, but the first-class carriage was a long way ahead. The second-class carriages passed her, then the third-class carriages, faster still, but she kept on running. When the last carriage with the tail-lamp had gone by she had already passed the water-tank and the wind raged round her, unsheltered as she was, tearing her shawl from her head and making her dress cling to her legs at one side. The wind carried her shawl away, but she still ran on.

'Aunty Mikhailovna!' cried a little girl who was trying to keep up with her. 'You've lost your shawl!'

'He's sitting in a velvet armchair in a brightly lit carriage, joking and drinking, while I'm standing out here weeping in the mud and the darkness and the wind and the rain,' Katyusha thought to herself as she stopped, threw back her head, seized it in her hands and sobbed aloud.[1]

Her thoughts: that people live only for their own pleasure and that all talk about God and righteousness is so much deception, lead straight into the most vicious of all Tolstoy's satires—the prison chapel service—the epitome of all that is inappropriate and unnatural. A paragraph or two will give the flavour of Tolstoy's bitterly ironical, polemical and blasphemous style which begins to predominate in his later writing:

The service began.

The service consisted of the following. The priest, having dressed himself in a particularly strange and very uncomfortable attire, was cutting up and arranging little pieces of bread on a saucer and then putting them into a cup of wine, uttering various names and prayers as he did so. Meanwhile the deacon, without a pause, first read, and then sang in turn with the convict choir, various Slavonic prayers, difficult enough to understand anyway, and still more so when read and sung fast. The content of the prayers mainly consisted of a desire for the well-being of the Emperor and his family. Prayers about this were said many times, both together with other prayers, and separately on one's knees. Apart from that the deacon read several verses from the Acts of the Apostles in such a strange, forced voice that it was impossible to understand anything, and then the priest read out very distinctly a passage from Mark's Gospel which told how Christ rose from the dead, and before flying up to heaven to sit on the right hand of his father, appeared to Mary Magdalene,

[1] *Resurrection*, Pt. I, Ch. 37.

from whom he drove out seven devils, and then to eleven of the disciples, and how he ordered them to preach the Gospel to all creation, declaring that he who did not believe would perish, but he who believed and was baptised would be saved and would, moreover, drive out devils and heal people from illness by laying hands on them, and talk in strange tongues and handle serpents and, if he should drink poison, would not die but remain unharmed.

The essence of the service consisted in the fact that the pieces of bread cut up by the priest and put in the wine were, by certain manipulations and prayers, supposed to turn into the body and blood of God...[1]

A few pages in this vein are followed, as a natural antidote, by the return of spring, the green grass and the trees in leaf. Chapter 41 echoes Chapter 1, and at last Nekhlyudov and Maslova meet again. The first part ends on a note of hope for her, as the second and third parts do for him. Out of the three strands—Nekhlyudov, Maslova and the apparatus of the law— Tolstoy has woven a pattern which is simple, plain and satisfying.

As the novel progresses, however, the structural synthesis is not maintained. The imbalance caused by the constant urge to denounce, the oversimplification, the crude irony and obstinate refusal to allow more than one point of view, the diminished sympathy and human understanding, all overshadow the occasional brilliant evocation of atmosphere, poignant scenes and wealth of realistic detail conveyed in direct and forceful language which are the hallmark of the mature Tolstoy. Most people will agree that 'the best qualities of *Resurrection* are not characteristic of the later Tolstoy; they are rather, in a minor degree, those of *Anna Karenina* and *War and Peace*'.[2] Unfortunately the urge to point a moral, discreet in the two earlier novels, becomes overt and offensive in *Resurrection*, which, in the last resort, is not a search, but an analysis of society in the light of revealed truth.

[1] *Resurrection*, Pt. 1, Ch. 39.
[2] D. S. Mirsky, *A History of Russian Literature*, p. 307.

8

THE LATER STORIES

'One usually thinks that most conservatives are old men and most innovators young men. This is not quite so. Most conservatives are young people who want to live, but who neither think nor have the time to think how one *should* live, and so choose as their model the life they have always known.' These controversial words from *The Devil* have an unmistakably autobiographical ring, for Tolstoy as an old man was not a little proud of his nonconformity. The themes of nearly all his late stories were chosen to enable him to express his iconoclastic attitude to the organisation of society, the administration of justice and the relation between the sexes. Those on the subject of sex have attracted the greatest publicity. Uncompromising, perverse and uncharitable, they share a common loathing of the sexual act, whether lawful or unlawful, committed or merely meditated. The premise of *The Kreutzer Sonata* is that carnal love is selfish and that unselfish love needs no physical consummation. Do people go to bed together, asks its 'hero' Pozdnyshev, because of their spiritual affinities or the ideals they have in common? The knowledge and recollection of his own sexual indulgence in the past dominate his thinking to the exclusion of all else. He assumes that his wife's musician friend has only one thought in mind, and as the text for *The Kreutzer Sonata* (and *The Devil*) reminds us: 'But I say unto you that everyone who looketh on a woman to lust after her hath committed adultery with her already in his heart.' Pozdnyshev murders his wife because he is tormented by jealousy. It follows for him that all husbands must be jealous, all wives unfaithful. His thoughts are controlled by the assumption that every possibility of evil must result in evil. The potential for good is simply discounted. Music is potentially evil because, like the presto in *The Kreutzer Sonata*, it may arouse feelings which cannot be satisfied by the music itself. Sexual passion is the root of all evil. Social conventions, low-cut dresses and the medical profession are accessories before the fact. By the second chapter of the story we already know Pozdnyshev's opinion of love and marriage and we know that he has murdered his wife. The narrator's rôle, apart from occasional interruptions, is negligible; he is not important enough to form a barrier between Pozdnyshev and the reader, or between the author and his hero.

In *The Kreutzer Sonata*, Tolstoy adopted Turgenev's method, putting a first-person narrative in the thin frame of a third-person setting. Just as, in many of Turgenev's novels, a party of gentlemen converse at dinner until one of them begins to recount an episode of his youth, which thereupon becomes the novel, so, in *The Kreutzer Sonata*, the general conversation in a railway-carriage resolves itself into a personal confession.[1]

Pozdnyshev completely dominates the scene with his powerful, polemical monologue, which by its very nature is unable to actualise the character of his wife and her suspected lover or to consider them from any point of view except his own. His wife has no opportunity to state her case. Her friend is treated with the same contempt which Tolstoy reserves for Napoleon, the bureaucrats and the intelligentsia: 'He had an unusually well-developed posterior like a woman's, or like a Hottentot's, so they say.' Of course Pozdnyshev is his own prosecutor, and one who shows no mercy. As he says to himself when he decides to go and see his dying wife, whom he has stabbed: 'Yes I expect she wants to repent...' He is given

the thankless task of acting as Tolstoy's agent in the story. He is required to express Tolstoy's views, but with a pathological violence and peculiarity supposedly his own. It is as if we knew that Shakespeare hated sex, but not so much as Hamlet does; and was disgusted with human beings, but not in quite so sensational a fashion as Timon. Tolstoy can neither release Pozdnyshev nor conceal himself behind him.[2]

Pozdnyshev's arguments are absurdly exaggerated and inconsistent and flavoured with Tolstoy's addiction to percentage

---

[1] D. Davie, *Russian Literature and Modern English Fiction*, p. 190.
[2] J. Bayley, *Tolstoy and the Novel*, p. 283.

generalisations—90% do this, 99% do that; music is responsible for 'most cases' of adultery in our society. The body is the ever-present villain, the animal the symbol of unbridled incontinence, for all that it compares favourably with the human species in refraining from intercourse during pregnancy and suckling.

Significantly enough, in the light of Tolstoy's own prejudices, the whole story takes place in a railway carriage. Pozdnyshev himself comments on the emotional upheaval caused by railways. He claims to be afraid of railway carriages. He acknowledges a temptation to lie down on the rails—all this with reference to another train journey he is describing on his way to catch his wife, as he hopes, *in flagrante delicto*, a train journey within a train journey, as it were, which provides a structural basis for the story. And structurally speaking, it is taut, powerful and gripping, despite its occasional inept dialogue and its motley material culled from Tolstoy's letters to Chertkov and the books and letters he received from the American Shakers. A sensitive and, on the whole, convincing attempt has recently been made to relate the structure of the story to Beethoven's sonata itself.[1] It is an approach which is capable of further exploration. Put briefly, the argument is that Tolstoy's story appeals mainly to the ear; that the human voice is the literary equivalent of the solo instruments; that one's attention in reading (or listening) is constantly being drawn to sounds; and that the 'confessional' form of the narrative is the nearest literary approach to the music of piano and violin, 'two voices that strive through the sonata to become one'. We are reminded that Beethoven's sonatas are characterised not only by intensity of dramatic feeling, but also by violent contrasts of moods and emotion. The structure of the story can plausibly be shown to correspond to general sonata form, and the Presto of the first movement—following an opening Adagio—which is so important for Pozdnyshev, is peculiarly important for the theme of the story as a whole.

[1] Dorothy Green, '*The Kreutzer Sonata*: Tolstoy and Beethoven', *Melbourne Slavonic Studies*, 1 (1967).

The author of the article observes that 'the violin is the dominating instrument, the inviting instrument' in the Presto; 'the piano changes key and sidesteps the issue. There is an extraordinary progressive ascending movement at the end, which strongly suggests a dragging away by force; there is a significant silence, a kind of consent, and a haunting passage which could suggest shame, and the movement ends with a burst of passion from both instruments, with the violin in control.' Like the sonata, Tolstoy's story falls naturally into three movements with a slow introduction. 'The subject of the first movement concerns the general notion of solicitation between the sexes and the particular instance of this in Pozdnyshev's own courtship, wedding and honeymoon. As in the sonata, there are false starts, the subject is introduced, dropped, hinted at...Pozdnyshev at first is dominant, the narrator parries the question he raises and Pozdnyshev finally becomes the narrator...The first movement of the sonata is disturbing, passionate and at times violent, and so is the story.' The second movement (Chapters 13–19) corresponds to Pozdnyshev's married life and his growing jealousy, with each of the two partners contending for power, 'or rather striving to be free from the dominance of the other'. The third movement introduces the musician, and its pivotal point is the Kreutzer Sonata itself, the final chapter (28) rounding it off like a coda, and returning us to the mood of the Adagio opening. In musical terms the analogies could be pressed further without doing violence to the thesis which, when retailed in this eclectic manner, does less than justice to an article which is stimulating and well argued. Tolstoy's well-known receptivity to music and his intuitive feeling for musical form lend point to the musical analogies already made in the context of the Sevastopol sketches and developed further with reference to the composition, tempo and progression of *The Kreutzer Sonata*.

Structural considerations apart, few other novelists could have made compelling reading out of sentiments and arguments which are irritating and manifestly unjust. Few other novelists could have given pathos and poignancy to the ending of a story whose limits appear to be laid down by the advice proffered in its opening chapter: 'Do not trust your horse in the field, or your wife in the house.'

The Devil, by contrast, is not a story of obsessive jealousy or marital discord. The tragedy, which Tolstoy resolves variously in two different endings (in one the man commits suicide, in the other he kills his wife), stems solely from the husband Irtenev's lapse before marriage—an affair described with typically Tolstoyan reticence, which eschews naturalistic detail and leaves everything to the imagination. Happily married, he fears that his self-control will fail him against his will and his better judgment. His wife is good, kind and loving, but she is not realised as a person. His former mistress, the potential threat to Irtenev's fidelity, is hardly less nebulous. Irtenev monopolises the story. The women are merely A and B, the necessary bases of the triangle of which he is the apex. Had *The Devil* been cast in the form of a first-person monologue this would have mattered less. But narrated as it is by an omniscient and ostensibly impartial author, its balance is inexcusably upset and it is distinctly inferior to *The Kreutzer Sonata*.

Father Sergei, the third of the major stories on the theme of sex was, like *The Devil* and *Resurrection*, completed by Tolstoy after years of neglect in order to raise funds for the Dukhobors. Its powerful and moving plot combines the motif of the Prince who renounces the world, the theme of the saint who is tempted and falls and the idea of the false (rationally motivated) conversion and the true conversion which springs from the heart. Prince Kasatsky, a handsome, successful and ambitious aristocrat, leaves the world to enter a monastery on discovering that his fiancée had been the Emperor's mistress. He struggles against pride and sexual desire, is tempted, resists and eventually succumbs, only to be spiritually reborn on witnessing the example of a woman who lives for other people, for whom good is something to be done, not to be seen to be done. This is how Tolstoy expressed the idea of his story in his diary:

'There is no peace of mind either for the man who lives a secular life in the world or for the man who lives a spiritual life on his own. Peace of mind only comes when man lives to serve God in the world.'[1] Spiritual pride is no less insidious than its secular variety.

The pattern of the story is provided by the parts played in the life of the Prince-monk by three different women: the first, whose determined assault he withstands by mortifying the flesh, the second who wins an easy and unpremeditated success, the third who is the passive intrument of his spiritual resurrection. There are many recognisably Tolstoyan touches: the description of a May evening, the trees in bloom, the nightingales singing, which plays the same anticipatory and contrasting role in Kasatsky's seduction as the Easter service does in the seduction of Maslova in *Resurrection*; the laconic entry on the sexual act; the moment of crisis issuing into reminiscences of childhood; the significant physical details ('the thin withered neck with prominent veins behind the ears'); and the occasional arresting metaphor ('He replaced his faith on its shaky pedestal, as one replaces an object of unstable equilibrium, and carefully stepped back from it so as not to knock and upset it'). Typical, too, is Tolstoy's habit of imparting unflattering physical attributes to a person antipathetic to his hero—the abbot of the monastery, for example, who has, almost predictably, a fat body, a protruding stomach, short plump hands and a bald head.

The fact that *Father Sergei* was never published in Tolstoy's lifetime, and not therefore finally revised, no doubt accounts for some of the minor narrative inconsistencies—whether in the colour of the Prince's hair which at first is grey but much later is 'still black', or in the charge of murder which he brings against himself, an unexpurgated allusion to a discarded episode. More serious is the feeling that Father Sergei is not basically a changed man. It is true that the motive for his conversion—a woman who takes little or no part in church life, regards her prayers as mechanical and claims to lack any

[1] J.E. XXXI, 264.

real religious feeling—is not unconvincing; and she is no less abruptly introduced than Karataev or Levin's peasant. 'The only thing is', she says, 'that I know how bad I am.' But Sergei is only allowed one brief appearance after his change of heart when, as a wandering pilgrim, he accepts alms from a French traveller and gives it away to a blind beggar and 'rejoiced particularly because he had despised the opinion of men'; when in fact he had behaved in a way which was entirely consistent with what would have been expected of him in the situation if he had *coveted* 'the opinion of men'. Tolstoy does not succeed in showing a new man in action, no doubt because human nature stubbornly resists the attempt to change it, no doubt also because Tolstoy himself was too much in the grip of egotism to create a character who had mastered it—if indeed any exist outside the pages of hagiography. Kasatsky cannot cease to be Kasatsky—he resumes his old name towards the end of the story—any more than Tolstoy, for all his novel theories and practices, could cease to be Tolstoy.

Vanity and sexual desire tormented Tolstoy almost to the end of his days—but not more insistently than the fear of death. Two of his finest stories of the later period are devoted to this theme. *The Death of Ivan Il'ich* is a harrowing account of the agonising end of an ordinary man who has achieved worldly success as a judge, but when faced with the dreadful inevitability of death, reviews his past and comes to the realisation that what he had valued then is of no significance now, that summoned before the highest court his case is a hopeless one, and that all he can do is, by dying, to rid his family of an unwanted encumbrance. In reaching this conclusion he loses his fear of death. An interesting parallel has been drawn between Tolstoy's story and Kafka's *The Trial*.[1] In the midst of ordinary and, to them, wholly satisfactory lives, Ivan Il'ich and Joseph K. are struck down by mysterious catastrophes. K. fails to win his case in an unknown court which tries him on an unspecified charge and he is executed. Ivan Il'ich fails to

[1] P. Rahv, *Image and Idea: The Death of Ivan Il'ich and Joseph K.* (New Directions Paperback, 1957).

recover from an 'unheard of' illness which the doctors cannot diagnose. The 'case' and the 'illness' are variations of the same device which allows the author to play God so as to confront an ordinary self-satisfied mortal with an extraordinary situation, rout his confidence and reason, and destroy him. Much closer to the text, however, is Maxim Gorky's use of Tolstoy's theme in his play *Yegor Bulychov and the Others*, in which the nearness of death compels the hero to look back over his apparently successful life, and to find it wanting.

Like several of Tolstoy's later stories, *The Death of Ivan Il'ich* incorporates the confessions of an ordinary commonplace individual, a man like many other men, who is overwhelmed by a crisis which shatters his whole outlook on life and forces him, however late in the day, to see the light—or at least a chink of it. Ivan Il'ich is a successful bureaucrat, a conformist, a creature of habit (could it be significant that his surname Golovin is, like Karenin's, derived from the word for a 'head' —the one in Russian, the other in Homeric Greek?). He excludes his own emotions, his own personal opinions, his individuality; he is characterless and featureless except in so far as he resembles other people in what he does and where he lives. His tragedy is—to be mortal. 'Why this torture?' he asks himself when gravely ill. And he answers: 'for no reason, It just is so.' By a supreme irony, he receives the same treatment from his doctor, when on trial for his life, as he himself had been accustomed to mete out to others in court. Before he dies, it has been said, 'he sees the inner light of Faith, renunciation and love'.[1] But faith in what? And whom does he love? And how can he help renouncing life when he is at death's door? The fear of imminent death may explain his reappraisal of the values he has lived by: but it must be cold comfort to believe that the only purpose in his life is to cease to be—and so cease to be a burden to other people. Tolstoy resists a facile 'religious' conclusion—the light he sees at the bottom of his imaginary sack is not God's love or immortality, but only a release from suffering. The 'positive hero', the healthy

[1] D. S. Mirsky, *A History of Russian Literature*, p. 305.

peasant lad who waits cheerfully on his dying master, is a shadowy stereotype. Life is stripped of all its poetry. We are offered only the sordid flesh, physical pain, exposed breasts, human excreta. We are told that Ivan Il'ich was once capable, cheerful, lively and agreeable, but we never see him in this happy state where at least the daily round of work is a compensation for the inevitable disappointments of life. The story begins with his death. After a flash-back to his early life, it proceeds with ever narrowing focus to his last excruciating moments. There are narrative touches of which Chekhov or Maupassant would have been proud. The scene at the onset of Ivan Ilich's illness, when he overtrumps his partner at cards, calls vividly to mind the passage in Chekhov's *Gusev* where the dying soldier gets his cards confused, calls hearts diamonds and muddles up the score. As a whole the story is so constructed technically that the chapters become increasingly shorter, with rare exceptions, as the climax approaches and the range of vision becomes more and more restricted (so much is it telescoped, in fact, that the passage of time is blurred and the characteristic Tolstoyan discrepancies of age appear as the years fly by). Characteristically Tolstoyan too are the description of the thoughts aroused in his colleagues and friends by Ivan Il'ich's death—the prospects of unexpected promotion, the sense of relief that it is someone else who has died—the polemic against the medical profession or the observance of the proprieties; and indeed the thoughts about death which are ascribed to Ivan Il'ich himself are phrased in much the same way as those of Prince Andrew in *War and Peace* when faced with the almost certain prospect of extinction.

The Death of Ivan Il'ich, which Bunin may have had in mind when he wrote *The Gentleman from San Francisco*, has a modern existentialist flavour. In Sartre's words, 'nothing can save man from himself, not even a valid proof of the existence of God'.[1] Man's situation is tragic and absurd—but not hopeless. For Ivan Ilich the ray of hope comes too late to compensate for what he comes to regard as the futility of his past existence.

[1] *L'Existentialisme est un Humanisme*, 1946.

Tolstoy's short tale *Master and Man* is also on the theme of an eleventh-hour act of 'unselfishness' in the face of death; it is, however, more conventional. A merchant and a peasant lose their way in a snowstorm. The merchant tries to escape and leaves the peasant to his fate. Chance brings him back to the place where the peasant is lying in the snow. On the impulse of the moment he throws himself on top of him, sheltering him with the warmth of his coat and body. When the two are found, the master is dead, but the peasant is still alive, saved by the seemingly unselfish act of an otherwise selfish man—in some respects the characters and relationships of the two men are a variation on the theme of Ivan Il'ich and his 'man' Gerasim.

In his diary Tolstoy expressed himself dissatisfied with the poverty of content of the story, but was pleased with its artistic form.[1] Perhaps this provided the impulse for formalistically inclined scholars to subject it to a 'close-reading' technique and to extract from it not only the recurring symbol of the circle and the repetition of the number three, but also symbolic overtones of Christ's passion.[2] Casual names and incidents are thus made to bear a heightened importance. There is of course no doubt that the merchant Brekhunov's name has a derogatory sound in Russian (*brekhun* means a 'braggart' or 'liar'). But when it is pointed out that he comes from the village of Kresty (the Crosses), and lives 'in the shadow of the cross'; that when he stops to rest at a house on his journey he sits down at the head of the table for what is his last supper; that he overtakes a sledge driven by one Simon; that he is guided on his way by a certain Peter who turns back and leaves him to his fate; that he thinks he hears a cock crow; that there are several allusions to wormwood; and finally that he lies down on his servant with arms spread out in cruciform fashion—one's reaction is one of incredulity tempered by a sneaking admiration for the critic's ingenuity. The crucial moment of the story

---

[1] J.E. LIII, 3.
[2] See 'Tolstoy's *Master and Man*—Symbolic Narrative', *Slavic and E. European Journal*, III (1963).

is the decision of an ordinary and by no means charitable man to perform an act which seems to be the embodiment of Christian charity. It is here that Tolstoy's innate sense of artistry comes to his aid, and while I do not share the view that *Master and Man* is on a higher artistic plane than the *Death of Ivan Il'ich*, I believe that Mr Bayley puts his finger on the essential point when he writes:

The motives of the merchant, his businesslike vigour and his desire to share his self-satisfaction with someone else, as if it were a bargain; the obvious calculation that in keeping Nikita (the peasant) warm he will be keeping himself warm too—all this makes the impulse to help the servant both moving and convincing. The moral of the story works without strain because the nature and personality of Brekhunov is fully established and he is allowed to remain true to it throughout.[1]

Most of Tolstoy's later fiction, whether published in his life-time or posthumously, whether on the themes already illus-trated or on such subjects as physical violence (*After the Ball*), guilt and repentance (*The False Coupon*) or prostitution (*Françoise*), are frankly edifying, admonitory and polemical. Their language is less varied and supple than that of the great novels. *Hadji Murat*, however, falls into a rather special category. Its ten principal drafts were written over the years 1896–1904, but no definitive version was completed by the author. It is worth emphasising that Tolstoy chose for his last major work a theme which took him back to his youth and to the fighting in the Caucasus in which he had himself been involved. Its subject matter and his treatment of it run directly counter to his professed belief in the doctrine of non-resistance, and his appeal to men to love their enemies and to turn the other cheek. He recognised this anomaly when he confessed to his daughter that he was ashamed of himself and was writing his story 'on the quiet'![2] For the historical Hadji Murat was one of the leaders of the mountain tribesmen who fought under Shamil to resist the Russian conquest of the

[1] J. Bayley, *Tolstoy and the Novel*, p. 95.   [2] J.E. LXXIV, 124.

Caucasus in the 1850s. Having deserted to the Russians to avenge himself on Shamil, he changes sides again out of concern for the safety of his family, and is killed after a most desperate and tenacious resistance. Tolstoy records in his preface how he was reminded of an old Caucasian story 'part of which I saw, part heard from eyewitnesses and part imagined to myself'. Taking as his starting-point the death of a hero, he expands his subject into a broad panorama of life in the Caucasus and European Russia, ranging from the primitive mountain villages to the court of the Emperor Nicholas I. Much of his material is borrowed wholly or in part from the many works of reference which he consulted assiduously: articles and memoirs in historical journals, the letters of the Russian colonel Prince Vorontsov, the reminiscences of Poltoratsky, an officer who also figures in Tolstoy's story, and various ethnographical treatises on the Caucasus. His respect for the surface 'facts' of history is shown by his diligent quest for the historical Hadji Murat. Did he have a noticeable limp? Did his house have a garden? Did he faithfully observe Muslim ritual? Did he speak any Russian? These questions, and many similar ones, he tried to answer accurately and conscientiously. As with his early Caucasian stories, he also drew on his own diary, which provided the rough basis of the first draft of *Hadji Murat*, entitled *The Thistle*, and supplied the metaphor of the sturdy and tenacious plant which survives the cart wheel and the plundering hands of man, and which is the symbol Tolstoy chose to frame his narrative:

I was going home through the fields. It was midsummer. The meadows were mown and they were just about to cut the rye.

There is a wonderful assortment of flowers at this time of the year: red, white and pink clover, fragrant and fluffy; pert, milk-white daisies with bright yellow centres and a musty, spicy smell; sweet-scented yellow charlock; tall, pink and white harebells; creeping vetch; prim scabious; yellow, red, pink and lilac; plantain with a suspicion of pink down and a faintly pleasant scent; cornflowers which are bright blue in the morning sun and pale blue with a rosy blush as they fade in the evening; and tender, almond-scented, drooping bindweed flowers.

I had picked a large bunch of different flowers and was on my way home when I noticed a magnificent purple thistle in full bloom in a ditch. It was the sort we call a 'Tartar', which the mowers are careful not to scythe; if they should accidentally cut it, they throw it out of the hay so as not to cut their hands on it. I thought I would pick this thistle and put it in the middle of my bunch. I clambered into the ditch, chased away a shaggy bumble-bee that had embedded itself in the heart of the flower and was blissfully dozing there, and tried to pick the flower. But it was very difficult; the stem pricked me on every side, even through the handkerchief which I had wrapped round my hand, and it was so terribly strong that I struggled with it for a good five minutes, breaking the fibres one by one. When I finally plucked the flower, the stalk was all tattered and even the flower did not seem so fresh and beautiful. Moreover, its coarse and rough appearance made it a poor match for the other flowers in the bunch. I regretted having foolishly spoilt a flower which looked fine where it was, and threw it away. 'But what energy and vitality', I thought, as I remembered the efforts I had made to pluck it. 'How desperately it defended its life and how dearly it sold it'.

The way home lay through a freshly ploughed, fallow field of rich, black earth. I walked up along a dusty path. The ploughed field, which was in private hands, was very large, and nothing was visible on either side or up the hill in front except the black, evenly furrowed, but still unharrowed earth. It had been well ploughed and not a single plant or blade of grass showed up—everything was black. 'What a cruel, destructive creature is man, how many living creatures and plants of every kind he has destroyed in order to support his life!' I thought, involuntarily looking for something alive in the midst of this dead, black field. Then I saw a clump of something to the right of the path in front of me. When I came closer, I saw it was another clump of 'Tartar' thistle, whose flower I had idly plucked and thrown away.

The 'Tartar' bush had three branches. One had been broken off and the part that was left stuck up like the stump of a severed arm. The other two each had a single flower. These flowers had once been red, but were now black. One stem was broken, and the top half dangled down with a dirty flower at the end; the other still pointed upwards, though coated with a film of black earth. It was obvious that the whole bush had been crushed by a wheel and had sprung up again, crooked but still standing. Part of its body, so to speak, had been shorn off, its bowels ripped out, an arm cut off, an eye gouged out. But it still stood there, refusing to surrender to man, who had destroyed all its brethren round about.

'What energy!' I thought. 'Man has conquered everything, destroying millions of blades of grass, but this fellow has still not surrendered.'

Then I remembered an old story of the Caucasus, part of which I saw, part heard from eyewitnesses and part imagined to myself. This story, as it has taken shape in my memory and imagination, is as follows.[1]

This vividly evocative and memorable passage is a good illustration of both the moral flavour and the metaphorical associations of the better stories of Tolstoy's last years. There is the same intimate knowledge of the countryside and the same power of minute observation which distinguished his earlier landscape descriptions; but there is also something obtrusive and too consciously 'literary' about the simile of the severed arm or the body metaphors. In *War and Peace* one seldom feels that here is a professional writer practising his art. In the passage above, good as it is, one can sense a certain striving for effect.

There is more than a hint of Tolstoy's early Caucasian stories in the chapters about the death of an ordinary Russian soldier, Avdeev, who is wounded in a Chechen attack, the report sent back to headquarters and the reception of the news by the soldier's family. In Avdeev himself there are overtones of Platon Karataev. The familiar Tolstoyan note of denunciation is clearly audible in *Hadji Murat*, nowhere more so than in the merciless attack on Nicholas I and his entourage; while the assault on 'the two despotisms, European and Asiatic', of Nicholas and Shamil (to quote Tolstoy) reinforces the opposition to autocracy and brutality so marked in the stories *After the Ball* and *What For?*, which are also set in the reign of Nicholas I.

While writing *Hadji Murat*, Tolstoy spoke of the need to

---

[1] *Hadji Murat*, Introduction.

convey in art the changing and contradictory aspects of human beings; change the context, and the same man appears in a different light. 'How good it would be', he said, 'to write a work of art which would clearly express the shifting nature of man; the fact that he is both villain and angel, wise man and fool, strong man and most helpless of creatures.'[1]

One recalls the passage from *Resurrection*:

One of the commonest and most widespread superstitions is that every man has certain definite qualities of his own: that a man is good, evil, wise, stupid, energetic, apathetic, and so on. People are not like that. We can say of a man that he is more often good than evil, more often wise than stupid, more often energetic than apathetic, or the reverse; but it would not be true if we were to say of one man that he is good or wise, and of another that he is evil or stupid. But we always classify people like this, and it is wrong. People are like rivers: the water in them is always the same, but every river is now narrow, now rapid, now broad, now slow, now clear, now cold, now muddy, now warm. So it is with people. Every person carries in him the seeds of every human quality, and sometimes he manifests some qualities and sometimes others, and it often happens that he appears unlike himself while still remaining one and the same person.[2]

In a somewhat similar vein Tolstoy emphasised the need to present his hero, Hadji Murat, in many different guises as warrior, family man, enemy and friend. 'There is an English toy called a "peepshow" (Tolstoy uses the English word), and under its glass, first one thing is shown and then another. That's the way to show Hadji Murat—as a husband, as a fanatic and so on...'[3] On yet another occasion Tolstoy noted in his diary: 'I dreamt about an old man—Chekhov has already anticipated me. The old man was particularly good because he was practically a saint, but at the same time he drank and swore. For the first time I clearly understood the force which characters acquire from having shadows boldly superimposed. I'll do this with Hadji Murat and Mar'ya Dmitrievna' [the mistress of an officer in the story].[4] Reading

[1] J.E. LIII, 187.   [2] *Resurrection*, Pt. I, Ch. 59.
[3] J.E. LIII, 188.   [4] J.E. LIV, 97.

through some of the draft versions of the story, one realises the considerable labour Tolstoy expended in making Hadji Murat a rounded character by applying chiaroscuro effects and by the 'peepshow' technique of using a rapid succession of different pictures. In a slightly different sense the expression 'peepshow technique' can be applied to the composition of the book as a whole, with its rapid glimpses not merely of Hadji Murat, but of a cross-section of Russian life from Petersburg to the Caucasus. These glimpses are not haphazard. There is a striking symmetry about the order and arrangement of the twenty-five chapters, which start with a description of nature, progress through the ranks of the Russian army to the provincial society life in miniature of the Caucasus, to the court aristocracy and finally to the Emperor himself, then back in the reverse direction through the officer class to the ordinary soldier who tells the story of Hadji Murat's heroic death; while a final coda recalls the crushed thistle in the ploughed field and the inanimate world of nature of the preface. A judiciously used and characteristic subject inversion enables one to see the dead man's severed head and to hear the reactions of witnesses before the events leading up to the death are themselves described. Unlike Tolstoy's greatest fiction, however, there is little scope in *Hadji Murat* for psychological complexity or the exploration of mental states and processes. Much is on the surface. There is much narrative action. The omniscient author only withdraws to the extent of allowing his hero to relate the story of his early life to Prince Vorontsov's *aide*. And yet there is no mistaking the Tolstoyan stamp. Eyes talk, dreams and reality coincide at the moment of awakening, the nightingales, silent during the firing, burst into song again after Hadji Murat's death to signify the ceaseless continuity of life. Even the inaccuracies of language and the misuse of gerunds ('having had a smoke, conversation started up again between the soldiers') betray the author.

Hadji Murat has been unjustly neglected by foreign readers, no doubt because of the infelicitous rendering of the colloquial speech of soldiers and tribesmen which mars the standard translations, and the lack of polish which a final revision for the press would have ensured. Crystal-clear, exciting and supremely well narrated, it has claims to belong to that category of universal literature which Tolstoy prized so highly in his treatise *What is Art?*; for although on the one hand it acknowledges the driving force of vengeance and ambition, and although it does nothing to further the cause of passive resistance, its pathos is grounded in what Tolstoy called 'those very simple, everyday feelings accessible to all'—the feelings of family solidarity and of compassion for human life.

9

ART, DRAMA AND THE PEOPLE

It is still a stimulating experience to read *What is Art?* for all
its infelicities of language, repetitiveness, irritating pontification
and patent absurdities. It is stimulating because it never ceases
to be thought-provoking. How could such an intelligent man
come to reject so much of the world's artistic heritage? How
could he renounce his own masterpieces, fearing, like Gogol,
that his art would merely aid the devil's cause? Was it that his
conclusions had been reached before the argument began, and
that his intelligence and ingenuity were devoted to trying to
match the two?

Herbert Read once quoted Ruskin as saying that a work of
art, in addition to looking well, must also speak well and act
well. 'People who emphasise the need of art to speak well', said
Read,

are usually moralists of some kind. Their greatest representative was
Tolstoy, but with a different morality in mind they have more
recently been represented by the socialist realists in Russia who
believe that the function of art is primarily to further the cause of
socialism. Art for such people is merely an effective way of saying
or illustrating some idea (a religious or political ideology), and the
importance of art therefore corresponds to the importance of its
message.[1]

Tolstoy believed that art should 'speak well', and that its
function is a moral one—to unite mankind. To pave the way
for his moral theory of art, he had to repudiate those theories
which relate its function to beauty or pleasure. He argued that
there has been no objective definition of beauty, for those who
have defined art as the manifestation of beauty have also
defined beauty as that which gives pleasure, and this is a
subjective definition since what pleases one man does not
necessarily please another. Therefore, to say that the aim of art is
beauty, is to say nothing. In this respect he is sharply at variance

[1] H. Read, *A Coat of Many Colours* (London 1947), p. 27.

with, for example, those who believe that there are 'laws' of beauty which are derived from nature—schooled as he was in the German tradition of aesthetics, he showed no little originality in rejecting the existence of a Beauty outside the eye of the beholder—or the advocates of art as a way of doing or making things in a rhythmical way and of beauty as bound up with, if not coextensive with rhythm.[1] Nor could he accept that the function of art is to give pleasure, although he recognised that pleasure is a legitimate by-product and that 'good art always pleases'.

His own definition of art is expressed in terms of what it does, not of the properties of what it produces (although the distinction between 'does' and 'should do' is always a tenuous one with him). 'To evoke in oneself a feeling once experienced, and having evoked it in oneself, to transmit that feeling by means of movements, lines, colours, sounds or forms expressed in words in such a way that others experience the same feeling —such is the activity of art.' Much of this definition is taken from Véron's *L'Esthétique*, with the important addition that 'others experience the *same* feeling'. While Véron is the immediate source for Tolstoy's formulation of the activity of art, he draws heavily on Schassler (*Kritische Geschichte der Aesthetik*) and Knight (*Philosophy of the Beautiful*) for his historical survey of aesthetic theories and their inadequacies. Needless to say, there is nothing new in the concept of art as the expression and communication of feeling, a concept popularised in England above all, perhaps, by Wordsworth. Tolstoy, however, has some qualifications to make. He admits that the artist can transmit not only feelings which he has experienced, but also ones which he has imagined. He also makes a highly controversial distinction between 'feelings', which are transmitted by art and 'thoughts' which are transmitted by words, by-passing the fact that both thoughts and feelings can in literary art only be expressed verbally. His definition is a wide one, for it embraces 'artistic activity' as well as what are traditionally

[1] See for example H. Read, *The Meaning of Art* (London 1951), and D. S. MacColl, *What is Art?* (Harmondsworth Middlesex 1940).

called the fine arts. More important, he contends that a person's attitude to art depends in the last analysis on his understanding of life, on what he considers to be good and evil, and on what religion, in the broadest sense, he professes. I say in the broadest sense, because Tolstoy emphatically does not mean by religion the doctrine of any established church, or indeed the Christian religion at all. But his concept does involve an ethical system, however loose, which is concerned with man's relations with other men, and with a God, however ill defined; a system which enables man, through the working of his conscience, to distinguish good from evil. In his *Introduction to the Works of Maupassant* he emphasises the need to refer back from the work of art to its author, and his outlook on life, for that will inevitably determine the moral qualities and values of his *œuvre*. 'When we read or contemplate a work of art by a new author, the basic question which always arises in the depth of our heart is: "Well, now, what sort of person are you? And how do you differ from all the people I know, and what new thing can you tell me about how to look at this life of ours?"'

Starting from such premises, Tolstoy looks back at the attitude to art and life held by the Greeks, the Jews, the early Church, the Middle Ages and the eighteenth-century aestheticians. He concludes that with the loss of 'religious perception' in his age, the content matter of art has become impoverished; it reaches a much smaller audience; it has become more affected and obscure; the feelings it transmits are no longer sincere (i.e. flowing from 'religious perception') but such as to appeal to the pride, sensuality and ennui of the ruling classes. Art has ceased to be art and has become a counterfeit of art—whether through loss of sincerity due to imitation and borrowing, the poaching of one art on the preserves of another (programme music), the desire to be 'striking' or 'effective' (to appeal to the external senses) or to interest only the mind (for example, by intricacies of plot). To a loss of religious perception must be added the growing professionalism of artists, the pernicious role of art criticism and the activity of schools of art (one cannot teach the transmission of feelings).

Tolstoy argues that true art can be distinguished from counterfeit art by its degree of 'infectiousness', the extent to which it conveys the artist's feelings and creates in the recipient a sense of union with him and with those infected by his art ('all art unites people'). This in turn depends on the individuality of the feelings transmitted, the clarity, and above all the sincerity with which the feelings were experienced in the first place. Those feelings which flow from a perception of the brotherhood of man and are therefore likely to unify, and those which are accessible to all men regardless of their education and intelligence should be the proper subject matter of art. From the art (literature) of the past and present Tolstoy singles out Schiller's *Die Räuber*, Hugo's *Les Pauvres Gens* and *Les Misérables*, Dickens's novels, especially *A Tale of Two Cities* and *A Christmas Carol*, *Uncle Tom's Cabin*, *Adam Bede* and Dostoevsky's *Memoirs from the House of the Dead* as examples of the highest art flowing from 'love of God and man'. Examples of good 'universal' art are more difficult to find, especially in the context of modern literature, but he mentions, with reservations, *The Pickwick Papers*, *David Copperfield*, *Don Quixote*, Molière's comedies and some of the stories of Pushkin, Gogol and Maupassant. All his own works he regards as bad art with the exception of the two stories *God sees the Truth but Waits* and *A Captive in the Caucasus*. The art of the future, he concludes, will transmit feelings which embody the highest religious perception of the age, not merely those accessible to the ruling classes.

So much for the synopsis of a treatise which is open to attack from many angles. Throughout it there is a constant ambivalence between pronouncements which appear to be statements of fact ('all art unites') and those which are unashamedly normative or prescriptive ('art should cause violence to be set aside'). We may applaud the latter, but dispute the value of the former on the ground that the links formed by art are often weaker than political or religious ties. Similarly, the sentence: 'Art, like speech, is a means of communication, and therefore of progress, i.e. of the movement of humanity forward towards perfection', combines an unimpeachable fact with an unwarranted hypothesis. The basic contention that one's appreciation of art depends on one's philosophy of life would seem to be contradicted by the fact that conservative and communist, Christian and atheist, pacifist and militarist, vegetarian and carnivor will all agree that *War and Peace* is an outstanding work of art, although their reasons may differ and the degree of their 'infection' cannot be measured. Tolstoy argues that art acts (he means 'should act') on people regardless of their education or state of development and relegates *War and Peace* to the category of bad art because it is 'upper class' and therefore of limited appeal; for upper-class art, he says, always remains incomprehensible to the masses. Fortunately he has been proved wrong by his own countrymen. He is equally wrong when he says that the feelings which allegedly constitute the chief subject-matter of late nineteenth-century art such as, for example, honour, patriotism and 'amorousness', evoke nothing but bewilderment, contempt and indignation among the working classes; or that the poetic, the realistic, the striking or the interesting have no connection with art. As for his communication theory, how is one to judge if the artist's feelings are sincere or if the identical feelings are experienced by his audience? In the course of his treatise he states that only *that* art is 'true' which imparts feelings not previously experienced. But not only is this not possible; it is not even desirable. 'Novelty is stimulating', it has been said, 'for we are all apt to be bored'; but 'familiarity is restful for we are all apt to be lazy'.[1] Both surprise and recognition have a place in art.

There are many points on which it is easy to agree with Tolstoy. It is clear that aestheticians have tended to take those works of art which are acknowledged to be good and have tried to frame a theory to match them. It is plausible to believe that there can be no objective definition of beauty; that beauty is not something which resides in an object; and that the concept 'beauty' does not include the concept 'goodness'. It

[1] E. F. Carritt, *An Introduction to Aesthetics* (London 1949), p. 28.

is obvious that the process of art does involve the process of communication of emotions. On the other hand it is just as easy to criticise Tolstoy for his imprecise terminology, his false analogies, his wishful thinking, or his 'realistic' and essentially novel-orientated approach to art. What is more important, however, to modern philosophers is that he wilfully confused the two subjects of ethics and aesthetics, of moral and aesthetic argument. 'One engages in moral argument', Professor Hampshire has written,

in order to arrive at a conclusion—what is to be done or ought to have been done; one had the practical problem to begin with, and the conclusion ('this is better than that') is always more important than the route by which one arrives at it; for one *must* decide one way or the other. But a picture or poem is not created as a challenge or puzzle, requiring the spectator to decide for or against. One engages in aesthetic discussion for the sake of what one might see on the way, and not for the sake of arriving at a conclusion, a final verdict for or against; if one has been brought to see what there is to be seen in the object, the purpose of discussion is achieved.

He concludes that 'everyone needs a morality to make exclusions in conduct; but neither an artist nor a critical spectator unavoidably needs an aesthetic'.[1] The same point is taken a stage further in another essay in the same collection: 'The alternatives have commonly been posed as if we had to say either that there is aesthetics or else that "it's all a matter of personal preference", but perhaps the truth is that there is no aesthetics and yet there are principles of literary criticism, principles of musical criticism, etc.'[2] Some contemporary aestheticians would maintain that this is a more fruitful approach to the problem of art than the Tolstoyan attempt to reduce everything to a single universally applicable formula. One can dispense with a theory of art, one can try to abjure with Wittgenstein the 'craving for generality' and confine

[1] 'Logic and Appreciation', in *Aesthetics and Language*, ed. W. Elton (Oxford 1954), p. 165.
[2] Passmore, 'The Dreariness of Aesthetics', in *Aesthetics and Language*, ed. W. Elton, p. 50.

one's observation to what is, not to what should be—what is, in one particular art or one aspect of it, regardless of whether it is there in another art or another aspect. By this view Tolstoy attempted the impossible, and his treatise provides no principles which can give us a clearer insight into any one particular work of 'art' (for want of a better name) which has stood the test of time. Aesthetics is less helpful than art criticism when it comes to understanding art. But if Art with a capital A is meaningless, how can individual works of art be meaningful? This is the question which tormented Tolstoy and he would not have been satisfied to have been told that it was not the right question to ask. That it is still being asked and that a solution to it is still being sought in terms as comprehensive, dogmatic and socially orientated as Tolstoy's, is evident from the writings of the exponents of Socialist Realism. For, like Tolstoy, they acknowledge that the power of art for good or evil is so great that it must be forced to serve society, not the pleasures of the ruling few. Where Tolstoy saw art as a quasi-religious activity whose object was to promote the brotherhood of man, Socialist Realism assigns to it the secular goal of the brotherhood of socialist man.

We have spoken so far of Tolstoy's general beliefs and prejudices in the realm of art. What of his particular antipathies —to Shakespeare, Wagner, the Symbolists? With the 'new art' of his own lifetime it was a matter of rationalising his own personal dislikes and generalising from his own particular case. 'I have no right', he said in *What is Art?*, 'to condemn the new art on the ground that I don't understand it.' But this is precisely what he does. He detested the Symbolists. The Symbolists were obscure. Therefore obscurity is bad art. He disliked Wagner. Wagner resorted to programme music. Therefore programme music is bad art. With Shakespeare, however, the matter is not so simple. Tolstoy was not alone in disliking Wagner or the Symbolists. But he was almost alone in belittling Shakespeare —although he might claim *some* kinship in this respect with Voltaire and Diderot, Robert Bridges or G. B. Shaw. In *Shakespeare and the Drama* the criticism is levelled mainly against *King Lear*—hence Orwell's[1] contention that Tolstoy saw in Lear, the man, a reflection of himself and his own bitter experience of life, his lack of humility and his act of renunciation which brought him no happiness. But the same criticisms could equally well have been applied to *Hamlet*, for Tolstoy's English edition of the play contains more than seventy marginal notes, nearly all of them unfavourable. He charged Shakespeare with faulty and implausible characterisation, unnatural relationships between the characters themselves, impossible situations, anachronisms, vulgarity, feeble puns, unnatural and affected language, the lack of a sense of proportion and the absence of 'religious convictions' or a positive outlook on life and the relations between man and his neighbour and between man and God. Undoubtedly there was in Tolstoy an iconoclastic urge—and the greater the target, the fiercer was his fire. Undoubtedly, too, his inadequate knowledge of English prevented him from feeling the immense subtlety and variety of Shakespeare's language. But his most serious failing was to approach Elizabethan drama with the critical apparatus of the nineteenth-century realistic novel, to look for the type of characterisation and the degree of lucidity which he admired in his own novels, for all his later ambivalent attitude towards them. It is interesting that when he *does* praise Shakespeare it is precisely for his use of exclamations, gestures and repetitions to convey states of mind and change of mood—for using in fact Tolstoy's own tools. Once again the belief that there are universal rules of art which should be as valid for one species as for another and the failure to recognise that not all art aspires to the condition of the novel as practised by its nineteenth-century practitioners led Tolstoy into the most monstrous errors.

There are good reasons for thinking that Tolstoy was not as sensitive to poetry as he was to music, and that the conventions of verse (if not its harmony and euphony) were as much an artificial impediment to him as the conventions of opera and the stage. But while he never felt the urge to write poetry, he

[1] 'Lear, Tolstoy and the Fool', in *Shooting an Elephant* (New York 1950).

trespassed widely on the field of drama. Including all the unfinished versions, fragments and projects which survive in draft form, it has been calculated that he wrote or began to write sixteen plays. Three are still regularly performed in Moscow. A fourth, with its last act unfinished, is still read though not produced. The three major plays are all contemporary in period, realistic, verging on the naturalistic, in form, and of a vehemently satirical social content which is the dramatic counterpart of his tractarian literature of the same period, ranging over the plight of the landless peasant, the evils of drink and violence, and the shortcomings of the aristocracy and the social institutions of the bourgeoisie. Outside Russia it is *The Power of Darkness*, written in its first form in 1886 in seventeen days but not performed there until 1895, which is most widely known. Its sombre and gruesome plot of greed, adultery, poisoning and infanticide set in the poverty and squalor of a peasant village made it an obvious butt for its author's own displeasure, for its naturalistic Zolaesque excesses belong to the kind which he expressly condemned in *What is Art?* At the same time the theme illustrated by its sub-title—'If a claw is caught the bird is lost'—and the climactic conversion of the chief sinner might seem to put it into the category of universal and religious art applauded in the same work. The story, with the exception of the poisoning scene, was taken almost literally from a court case in Tula. Tolstoy twice saw the defendant after the case had been brought to his notice and was well briefed with the unsavoury details. The story shows obvious traces of Ostrovsky's influence and it is no surprise to find that its most enthusiastic champions included Zola, Gorky, and Shaw. Steiner[1] observes that one must look to the plays of Synge to find anything comparable. Maeterlinck went so far as to say that it was the greatest of all plays—to which Tolstoy, when told, is said to have replied, 'Why doesn't he imitate it then?' Ibsen, while generally appreciative, ventures the criticism that 'the author has not fully mastered dramatic technique. The play has more conversations

[1] G. Steiner, *Tolstoy or Dostoevsky*, p. 128.

than dramatic scenes, and in many places the dialogue seems to me epic rather than dramatic.' On the negative side criticism has tended to focus on what is undramatic, on the lengthy tendentious exchanges on credit banks or the mechanical conversion of Nikita, on the naturalistic details, the Repin-style realism, the coarseness of speech; or the fact that the play reads better than it acts. Most Soviet critics, on the other hand, find ample illustration in it for their theses on pre-revolutionary rural life, the *mores* of the village, the pernicious power of money, or Lenin's picture of Tolstoy as the mirror of the peasant revolution in Russia. The play certainly allows scope for widely differing interpretations. The character of Nikita's father, Akim, 'a god-fearing peasant', may be played, as the author intended it to be, as a Karataev-like variation on the theme of the virtue of non-resistance to evil. In recent Soviet productions, however, the tendency has been to represent his moral influence as ineffectual and as playing no part in Nikita's conversion.

Maxim Gorky must certainly have had Akim in mind when he wrote *The Lower Depths*:

In Luka's [the central character's] facile moralising and inexhaustible flow of consoling words Gorky wished to reproduce what he saw as Tolstoy's fundamental lack of concern for people, which he concealed behind constant readiness to offer them moral advice... Luka is a kind of Dostoevskian double of Tolstoy; his vagrant life is a debased version of the great man's spiritual seeking, his gratuitous advice on how to live the *reductio ad absurdum* of Tolstoyan moral instruction. *The Power of Darkness* was first presented in the Moscow Arts Theatre on 5 September 1902, not long before the *première* of *The Lower Depths*. In Gorky's treatment of Luka, the Russian theatre-going public could not but see a polemic with the Tolstoyan rustic sage, Akim.[1]

Not only is Akim's a controversial role. Nikita's mother, Matrena, may also be played as a peasant Lady Macbeth, or as an ordinary, canny old woman, anxious to secure a comfortable life for her son, as Tolstoy himself suggested. What is interest-

[1] F. M. Borras, *Maxim Gorky the Writer* (Oxford 1967), p. 168.

ing, however, to the student of Tolstoy's plays is not so much
the later interpretations of them which seek to shift responsibility from the individual to society, but the approach made by
a great novelist to an art form which was not his own. Tolstoy's
clearest pronouncements on the difference between the novel
and the drama date from the very end of his life. In 1908 he
wrote:

The novel and the story are painter's work; the craftsman wields a
brush and applies touches of paint to the canvas. You have back-
grounds, shadows, merging shades of colour. But the drama is a
purely sculptural field. You need to work with a chisel, not to
apply touches but to carve reliefs.[1]

Clearly a play calls for more streamlining than a novel, for
finer lines, for stripping away, rather than laying on. But if the
sculptor is too much imitated by the dramatist, the danger is
that the end product will be statuesque; the frozen immobility
of a mask may hide the shifting complexity of a human being.
In the same year, Tolstoy commented again on the difference
between the two genres, which had been brought home to him
while writing *The Power of Darkness*:

Here [i.e. in a play] one must not, for example, pave the way for
the heroes' emotional experiences, one must not make them think
on the stage and recall things, or elucidate their character by
digression into the past. All this is dull, tedious and unnatural. The
public must be confronted with ready-made states of mind...
Such hewn-out characters and their mutual impacts touch and
move the spectator. But monologues and modulations of colours
and scenes only make the spectator sick...[2]

This assertion that the characters must be already formed, and
that there is no room for them to think anew or develop into
something different is an absurdly constricting one. Tolstoy
does admit that he violated his precepts by employing monologues, but regards it as a lapse. As for character development,
there is little to be found in his plays, and in a dramatic respect

---

[1] *Teatr i iskusstvo*, XXXIV (1908), p. 580.   [2] *Teatr i iskusstvo*, pp. 580–1.

he is the loser; for it is here that his great talent as an artist lay, and despite his pronouncements to the contrary, there is plenty of room for it on the stage.

The basis of the structure of *The Power of Darkness* is the moment of time, separated by intervals of six or nine months in each act. Numerous short scenes spotlight the principal moments of the tragedy (but the changes of scene and the number of characters are appropriately fewer than in his other plays in view of the need for greater dramatic intensity). It is impossible to agree with those critics who see each new stage in the play as revealing new features of character which have been acquired in the course of the action. There is dramatic tension—especially the conflict between the two women, Nikita's mistress and wife Anisya, and her stepdaughter, Akulina, who is seduced by Nikita and whose baby he helps to murder. The struggle between the two women to be mistress in Nikita's house is one of the play's great dramatic moments. For the rest, it is a series of set pieces, of which Shaw singled out for special praise the scene where a drunken old soldier gives Nikita the courage to go out and confess and 'lifts him above his cowardice and selfishness'.[1] There is much finely modelled statuary in the play, but it is the finished work and not the process which we see; not the progress to degeneracy but new degenerate acts by people who are already deeply tainted. 'Drama', said Tolstoy to Goldenveizer, 'instead of relating to us a man's whole life, should put him in such a position and tie such a knot that the man can reveal himself fully in the process of disentangling himself.'[2] The conclusion of the play, however, when Nikita sees the light, suggests that it is Tolstoy who is revealing himself, rather than his hero. Nevertheless, it is a moving experience to see *The Power of Darkness* acted on the Soviet stage, and if it has never enjoyed the same success in England, this is not due to the harrowing nature of the theme or the tendentiousness of the ending, but to the infelicitous rendering of the highly colloquial peasant speech, flavoured

---

[1] Quoted by A. Maude, 'Tolstoy as Dramatist', Preface to Tolstoy's *Plays* (Oxford 1923). [2] Goldenveizer, *Vblizi Tolstogo*, p. 114.

with recorded conversations and proverbs from Tolstoy's note-books, which has quite defeated the translator (though no doubt one could improve on the 'Oh my!' 'Deuce take 'em!' 'Here's a go!' 'Shan't!' of the Maude version).

The Fruits of Enlightenment is a light-hearted domestic comedy revolving around the foibles of the gentry and the land hunger of the peasantry. A vivacious lady's maid uses her wits and the occasion of a spiritualist seance to induce her gullible master to sell some land to the village commune on the peasants' terms and not his own. Among the playwrights he knew, Tolstoy had a special affection for Molière and Gogol, and it is not difficult to see where he drew his inspiration from in this case. The irreverence and the well-aimed satire of the play, as well as its social message, had a strong appeal for Bernard Shaw, who gave it an enthusiastic welcome in *The London Mercury*, calling it 'the first of the *Heartbreak Houses* and the most blighting'.[1]

The four acts all take place in the same wealthy landowner's town house, and they are all played out in the space of twenty-four hours. There is a large cast, roughly equally divided between upper and lower classes, an exceptionally long first act with a rapid succession of scenes, and a recognisably Tolstoyan penchant for antithesis, juxtaposition and contrasting character-types. Comic mispronunciation, idiosyncrasies of language and recurrent 'laugh-lines' in the speech of the peasants show the same concern for the rôle of the spoken word in drama as Tolstoy showed in a very different context in *The Power of Darkness*. The play grows out of speech mannerisms, worked into a number of set theatrical situations carrying marked polemical or satirical overtones. The satire in *The Fruits of Enlightenment* is double-edged; its sharper edge is directed against the trivial, idle and gullible gentry, but many a laugh is contrived at the expense of the comic peasants, the profligate, insolent butler or the dandified coachman. The play opens with the butler and the maid on stage. The scene is the entrance-hall of a luxurious town house in Moscow. Doors open off to the

[1] *London Mercury* (May 1921).

rooms of the master and his son. The owner of the house and his family shout from inside or appear from their rooms while their visitors pass to and fro before the servants' eyes. The effect is to create a picture of the life of the gentry as it appeared to their servants—a device which Gogol used in his *Servants' Quarters* from the unfinished play *Vladimir of the Third Class*, with which there are some striking similarities. Predictably and rightly, current Soviet productions emphasise the satire against upper-class life without turning the peasants into positive heroes, and the result is an extremely funny comedy of manners; not great theatre, but eminently theatrical.

The Live Corpse is less successful on the stage, despite its considerable box-office appeal, and poses more problems for the producer. Tolstoy said that the revolving stage prompted him to write the play; and certainly one feels, when confronted with the inordinate number of scene changes and sets and the uncomfortably large cast, that here is an author playing with a new toy. Produced posthumously, it was never properly completed by Tolstoy. Its theme is the intrusion of the law into the domestic relations between a husband and wife. The husband pretends to commit suicide in order to allow his wife to marry another man and himself to live with a gypsy. The plot misfires, the deception is discovered, the wife and her two husbands are prosecuted and Protasov, the 'hero', finally shoots himself to free them all from the clutches of the law. There is a certain complexity about the character of Protasov, retiring, self-pitying, abject, but capable of vehement social protest, and the producer has to strike a balance between the passive and the active sides of his personality. On the Soviet stage *The Live Corpse* has moments which are genuinely moving, powerful and thought-provoking, but taken as a whole it cannot compare, on either the tragic or the comic level, with the two earlier plays, and, for all its plot interest, it is decidedly jerky and bitty.

The only other dramatic work of any significance is *The Light Shineth in Darkness*, to which Tolstoy returned on and off over a period of twenty years or more, but which he never completed; the fifth act only exists in the barest outline as a page of notes. It is not now produced, and is of biographical rather than dramatic interest, for all Bernard Shaw's perverse assertion that it was Tolstoy's masterpiece. In it Tolstoy seems to be mocking all his most cherished ideas and to be pointing to the disastrous results which are likely to follow from becoming a 'Tolstoyan' (if only of an inferior variety!), while at the same time showing how difficult it is for a man to act as he thinks right when his wife and family do not share his ideas and when his whole domestic environment is hostile to them.

'Nicholas Ivanovich Saryntsev destroys his own life and the lives of those who love him best by seeking to realise a programme of Tolstoyan Christianity and anarchy. Nor is he portrayed as a martyred saint. With pitiless veracity Tolstoy shows the man's blindness, his egotism and the ruthlessness which can inspire a prophet who believes himself entrusted with revelation.'[1] The Saryntsev couple have much in common with Tolstoy and his wife. Their conversations and arguments read like passages from the diaries and letters of Lev Nikolaevich and Sophia Andreevna. Tolstoy bluntly called the play 'his own' drama, and it is worth recalling some of the exchanges:

PETER SEMENOVICH [Saryntsev's brother-in-law]. If he denies the Church, what does he want the Gospels for?

MARY IVANOVNA [his wife]. So that we should live according to the Sermon on the Mount, and give everything away.

PETER SEMENOVICH. But how can you live, if you give everything away?

ALEXANDRA IVANOVNA [his sister-in-law]. Yes, and where did he find in the Sermon on the Mount that we have to shake hands with the servants? It says 'Blessed are the meek', but there's nothing about shaking hands.

MARY IVANOVNA. Yes of course, he gets obsessed as he always did —as he was once obsessed by music, and hunting, and schools. But that doesn't make it any easier for me.

[1] G. Steiner, *Tolstoy or Dostoevsky*, 129.

PETER SEMENOVICH. Why has he gone to town today?

MARY IVANOVNA. He didn't tell me, but I know it's about cutting down our trees. The peasants have cut down some trees in our wood...

ALEXANDRA IVANOVNA. He'll forgive them, and tomorrow they'll come and cut trees down in the park.[1]

In the following passage Saryntsev is talking to his wife:

MARY IVANOVNA. I also came to talk to you about Vanya [their son]. He behaves abominably and works so badly that he will never get through his exams. When I speak to him he is rude.

NICHOLAS IVANOVICH [SARYNTSEV]. Masha, you know I'm entirely out of sympathy with the way of life you lead and the children's education. It's a terrible problem for me, whether I have the right to watch them come to grief before my very eyes...

MARY IVANOVNA: Then suggest something else, something definite. But what?

NICHOLAS IVANOVICH. I can't say what. I can only say one thing above all: we must escape from this degrading luxury.

MARY IVANOVNA. So that the children should become peasants. I can't agree to that.

NICHOLAS IVANOVICH. Well, don't ask my advice then...[2]

Saryntsev's doctrine of non-resistance to evil proves so attractive to the young son of a princess that he refuses to serve in the army. He is imprisoned and sentenced to be flogged. Had the play been completed, the intention was for the agonised mother to shoot Saryntsev and for the unhappy 'Tolstoyan' to die protesting that it was all an accident!

Tolstoy's place in the history of European drama is a very modest one—though more distinguished, say, than Shaw's place in the history of the novel! There is a certain link between his minor occasional pieces for the stage and his popular tales to which he attributed so much importance in the last period of his life—his first play *The First Distiller* is a dramatised version of *The Imp and the Crust*—and at least a

[1] Act 1, Sc. 1.   [2] Act 3, Sc. 4.

passing reference needs to be made to the numerous tales written for the people, which are unsurpassed of their kind in Russian literature and which Tolstoy esteemed more highly than all his creative writing 'for the upper classes'.

Tolstoy's interest in popular literature grew out of his experience of teaching peasant children at his Yasnaya Polyana school before his marriage. It was a two-way process. The children had to be taught to read and write; they had something to learn from Tolstoy. But the more gifted of them had creative talents of their own. If they could not write stories down, they could make them up, and they had a rich store of inherited folk-lore to draw upon; they had something to teach Tolstoy.

After completing *War and Peace*, Tolstoy averted his gaze from the *haut monde* and the battlefield and turned to the daily life and inspiration of the common people. No doubt there were many reasons for this. His philosophy of history required him to shift his focus from the commander to those he commands. His Greek studies acquainted him with the oral epic poetry of Homer and the popular legends of Herodotus in their original form. His convalescence in the steppes of Bashkiria in 1871 brought him into daily contact with the primitive life of 'uneducated' people. When he went back to Yasnaya Polyana in August 1871 he turned with renewed interest to the task of educating children and providing them with reading matter which would be, in the broadest sense of the word, popular. The idea of writing a textbook to teach children to read is first mentioned in 1868. By way of preparation Tolstoy steeped himself in the epic poetry and folk literature of many countries and diligently studied the standard collections of Russian popular sayings and proverbs. Towards the end of 1872 he published his *Primer* in four parts, containing extracts for reading from a wide range of subjects including geography, history, literature and the natural sciences, as well as exercises in writing, spelling, pronunciation and arithmetic. The aim of his *Primer*, he wrote, was 'to serve as a manual for teaching reading, writing, grammar, the Slavonic language and arithmetic to Russian children of all ages and classes, and to provide them with a series of good articles written in good Russian'.[1] Not only should it teach children to read; it should also enable them to receive poetic impressions and experience poetic feelings at an early age. In two letters to Strakhov in 1872 Tolstoy wrote about his *Primer* and the change in his literary orientations. 'If there is any merit in my articles in the *Primer*,' he said in the first letter, 'it is in the clarity and simplicity of drawing and line—that is, the language. In a periodical this would be strange and unpleasing—as though it were not finished off—like pencil drawings without shading in a picture gallery.'[2] He goes on in the same letter to speak about the new trend in his lifetime towards the decline of upper-class art and a growing interest in the study of the art of the people, seeing in the latter the death and resurrection of the former. His second letter contains what is virtually a new literary manifesto:

I have changed my writing methods and my language, not, I repeat, because my reason told me it was necessary to do so, but because even Pushkin now seems funny to me, not to mention our own elucubrations; while the language which the people speak and which has sounds to express everything a poet may wish to say, is dear to me. This language moreover—and this is the most important thing—is the best poetic regulator. If you try to say anything superfluous, bombastic or morbid, the language will not permit it. But our literary language is spineless: so spoilt, that whatever nonsense you write looks like literature.[3]

Tolstoy concludes that he admires what is concrete, clear, beautiful and unpretentious, and that he finds it all in the poetry, language and life of the people. This is what he aimed to capture and reproduce in his *Primer*, but his experiment did not meet with the enthusiastic response he had expected. Criticisms were made of his use or abuse of the Orel and Kaluga dialects, and his provincialisms; his excessive partiality for fables, especially by Aesop; his fondness for stories with an element of fatalism and passive submission; and his neglect of

[1] J.E. LXI, 338.   [2] J.E. LXI, 274.   [3] J.E. LXI, 277.

the established Russian classics. Not much of the *Primer* has stood the test of time, but two of the stories deserve a special mention, not least because their author considered them in later life to be his only works of true art. *A Captive in the Caucasus* was described by Tolstoy as 'an example of the methods and the language in which I am now writing, and will write, for grown-ups'[1]—despite the fact that it was published in a textbook for school children. Its story of the capture, imprisonment and escape of a Russian officer in the Caucasus is pared to the bone. To quote Eykhenbaum:

It is pure graphic art. It is not an imitation of folk-lore; it is an étude, the artistic purpose of which is the purity and simplicity of the drawing, the fineness of the lines and the clarity and un-sophisticated nature of the subject. There is no psychological colouring, no digressions, no descriptive details. It is based on simple, primitive, 'natural' feelings and relationships devoid of any morbidity or refinement; the whole action is built up on the elementary struggle for life. The events of the story take place during the war between the Russians and the hillsmen, but the narrator provides no historical information, limiting himself to the one short sentence: 'There was a war on in the Caucasus at the time.' For the first time in Tolstoy the narrative is built on the events themselves, on the subject itself—on the simple interest in how it will end. Nothing is required from the reader, except sympathy for the hero threatened with destruction.[2]

Tolstoy based his story on his own experiences and perhaps also on the *Memoirs* of Baron Tornau. Its title recalls an anonymous story in the *Reading Library* for 1838, and more especially Pushkin's narrative poem. To quote Eykhenbaum once more:

Tolstoy's story seems to be a demonstration against Pushkin's poem in title and subject: the romantic prisoner is transformed into an ordinary officer, Zhilin, who dreams of returning home to his mother in Russia; the romantic Circassian aflame with passion, is

---

[1] J.E. LXI, 278.
[2] B. M. Eykhenbaum, *Lev Tolstoi, semidesyatye gody* (Leningrad 1960), p. 83.

replaced by a young Tartar girl who has no feelings for the prisoner except common pity. Instead of a verse narrative full of excitement and pathos there is the calm, concise language of an ordinary narrator.[1]

Pushkin may have seemed 'funny' to Tolstoy, but the poet's lucid, laconic, and verb-dominated prose style is very near to the style which Tolstoy himself evolved in order to write for the people.

The second story which Tolstoy particularly admired—*God Sees the Truth but Waits*—is an adaptation of the one told by Karataev in *War and Peace*, and illustrates the fallibility of the law and the virtues of meekness, humility and forgiveness. Much of the morally wholesome and edifying reading matter which Tolstoy composed for his *Primer* has little appeal outside the nursery and the classroom. The same is not true, however, of many of the popular stories which he wrote a decade or so later with *Anna Karenina* and his religious crisis behind him. Perhaps the best known of these is *What Men Live By* (1881), which he heard from a *byliny* singer from Olonets, whom he invited to Yasnaya Polyana to record his repertoire. A parable on the theme of love, it is an adaptation of the story, well known in different versions in the Talmud, the Apocrypha, the Koran and the Arabian Nights, of an angel sent by God to live on earth in human form and to learn the ways of men. What he discovers is that men live by acts of kindness, self-sacrifice and love, and that their love for one another is the true manifestation of the living God. Tolstoy's angel is perhaps the only element of the supernatural to appear in his man-centred world, where God lives in and through human beings, but not above them. The style of the parable is typical of the popular stories in its short sentences, asyndeton, omission of personal pronouns, pithy speech and proverbial saws. Typical, too, is the tendency to make verbal prefixes carry the semantic load by ringing the changes on a basic verbal root: *vyshel, poshel, voshel* ('went out', 'went up', 'went in'), the effect of which is

---

[1] *Lev Tolstoi, semidesyatye gody*, p. 84.

easily lost in English by the temptation to change the verbs to 'went out', 'walked up', and 'entered'.

How Much Land Does a Man Need? (1886) has claims to be the most successful of Tolstoy's popular tales. Its theme is the evil of acquisitiveness. A peasant believes that the ownership of land is the key to happiness. If he could only acquire all the land he wants, he would fear nobody, not even the Devil. But the Devil thinks differently.

The opening chapter, which I quote in full, is an excellent example of the style and tone of this, and many similar stories of the 1880s:

An elder sister from town came to visit her younger sister in the country. The elder was married to a tradesman in town, the younger to a peasant in the village. The sisters drank tea and talked. The elder sister began to boast and praise life in the town, saying how she lived in style there, and how she dressed the children up, and how she ate sweets and drank, and how she went for drives, and to theatres and entertainments.

The younger sister was hurt and began to disparage the life of a tradesman and to stand up for the peasant's life.

'I wouldn't change my way of life for yours,' she said. 'We may live drably, but we've nothing to fear. You live in style, but you either make a lot or you lose everything. You know the proverb: profit and loss are twin brothers. It's often the way with money—here today, gone tomorrow. Our peasant ways are safer. A peasant's life may be a lean one, but it's a long one. We shan't be rich, but we'll have enough to eat.'

But the elder sister began:

'Enough to eat, yes—and your pigs and calves too! No refinement, no manners! Your man can work as hard as he likes, but you'll die as you live—on a dung heap—and your children too.'

'Well, what if our life's like that?' said the other. 'At least it's secure. We don't lick anyone's boots, and we're not afraid of anyone. But in town you're surrounded by temptations. You're all right today, but tomorrow the Devil may tempt your husband with cards or wine or women, and you'll be ruined in no time. These things happen.'

Pakhom, the master of the house, was on the stove, listening to the women chattering.

'It's true enough', he said. 'What with tilling mother earth all our lives, we peasants haven't time for any nonsense. Trouble is we're short of land. If I'd plenty of land I wouldn't fear the Devil himself!'

The women drank their tea up, chattered a bit more about clothes, cleared the dishes away and went to bed.

But the Devil had been sitting behind the stove, listening. He was pleased that the peasant's wife had made her husband boast that if he had land, the Devil himself couldn't capture him.

'All right,' thought the Devil. 'You and I'll have a bet. I'll give you land enough, and I'll capture you with it.'

The peasant becomes a landowner. Lured on by the prospect of more gain, he moves eastwards to the Bashkir country (where Tolstoy had convalesced after a serious illness). There he is told that he can have all the land he can walk round in a day, but that he must return to his point of departure before sunset. This he succeeds in doing, but the effort proves too great for him and he dies. Six feet of earth is all he needs. Tolstoy takes for his plot the Scythian custom he had read about in Herodotus. He frames it with a dream, which first foretells the peasant's fate, and then returns to him at the moment of his death. He is the victim of the classic fateful situation when defeat comes at the very moment of apparent triumph. Profit and loss, the proverb reminds us, are twin brothers.

The virtues of Christian love and forgiveness, the folly of harbouring resentment, the evils of litigation, drink, violence and the craving for money are the most common themes of Tolstoy's popular stories. Their starting-point is nearly always a legend or parable. Their style is a model of lucidity and precision. The syntax is simple, the sentences short. Sophisticated devices of psychological analysis, character development, period detail, geographical colouring and metaphorical language are almost completely absent. The untutored and unadorned speech of the peasantry, the wisdom of the proverb, moral precept and example, the edifying coda and, occasionally, the element of the miraculous—these are the basic ingredients of the great majority of the stories for the people, which belong to the same category of literature and affect the same

area of the human consciousness as the great parables of the
religious teachers and prophets of the world.

It would not be inappropriate to end this introduction to
Tolstoy's work with a reference to Jesus Christ. Dostoevsky
complained that God had tormented him all his life. If we are
to believe Gorky, Tolstoy's relations with God were at times
like those between 'two bears in one den'. But it was really
Christ, not God, who tormented Tolstoy. He desperately
wanted to love him, and to follow his teachings as he understood them, as long as it was clear to all that his paragon was
human, not divine. When the Holy Synod excommunicated
him from the Orthodox Church he wrote: 'I believe that the
will of God is most clearly and intelligibly expressed in the
teachings of the man Jesus, whom to consider a God and pray
to, I esteem the greatest blasphemy.' And yet Gorky recalls
how Tolstoy used to speak of Christ the man without warmth
or enthusiasm. 'I think he considers Christ naïve and to be
pitied, but although—sometimes—he admires him, he scarcely
loves him. He seems to be afraid somehow that if Christ came
to a Russian village, the girls would laugh at him.'[1] Tolstoy's
uneasy alliance with Christ does not seem to have brought him
much happiness. Externally he 'changed himself', but internally the resistance proved too great to overcome. 'Why drag
yourself by the tail to the left', said one of Gorky's own
characters, 'when your nature with all her might pushes you
to the right?'[2] Tolstoy believed that his characters should be
true to their natures, but he was often untrue to his own.
Gorky (who of course only knew him in the last years of his
life) has left a widely known but somewhat unbalanced
picture of him as a proud and lonely colossus of a man, with
the *gamin*-like qualities of the Russian epic hero Buslaev, the

---

[1] A. M. Gorky, *Lev Tolstoi* in *L. N. Tolstoi v vospominaniyakh sovremennikov*
(Moscow 1960), II, 420. Subsequent references to Gorky can all be found in
the same source. There is an English translation: *Reminiscences of Tolstoy,
Chekhov and Andreev*, translated by Mansfield, Koteliansky and Woolf
(London 1934).
[2] In *Prokhodimets* (*The Rolling Stone*).

stubborn temper of the martyred priest Avvakum and the scepticism of the nineteenth-century 'Westerner' Chaadaev, iconoclastic, anti-authoritarian, overpowering—and essentially unhappy. While he abhorred the consequences of class privilege, he retained his aristocratic pride, and he found scant consolation in bast shoes and the cobbler's last. Yet in the tension between what he was and what he believed he would like to have been, lies his true greatness. It is this tension that found full and fitting expression in his art. It is not enough to admire his works because his characters are alive, his style clear and simple and his stories absorbingly interesting and well told. In the last analysis he is a great novelist because he was a great man.

TOLSTOY'S LIFE AND WORKS

N.B. The entries under Works *refer to publication in Russia. During the last thirty years of his life much of Tolstoy's writing was published abroad for censorship reasons, or else remained unpublished.*

Year	Works	Life
1828	—	Born Yasnaya Polyana, Tula province
1830	—	Death of mother
1837	—	Family moved to Moscow. Death of father
1838	—	Death of grandmother. Alexandra Osten–Saken became legal guardian
1841	—	Death of Osten–Saken. Moved from Moscow to Kazan under guardianship of Tatyana Ergolskaya
1844	—	Entered Kazan University (Faculty of Oriental Languages). Failed examinations
1845	—	Transferred to Faculty of Law. Dissolute life in Kazan.
1847	—	In hospital with venereal disease. Left university on grounds of 'ill health and domestic circumstances'. Returned to Yasnaya Polyana. Devoted himself to his estate and the welfare of his serfs
1848	—	Abandoned the country for Moscow and a new round of debauchery
1849	—	Moved to Petersburg. Heavy gambling debts. Brief period in Faculty of Law at Petersburg University. Soon withdrew to return to Yasnaya Polyana. Opened school for peasant children on his estate
1850	—	Life at Yasnaya Polyana. Much time devoted to music (piano). Aimless interludes in Tula and Moscow society
1851	*A History of Yesterday* (unpublished). Began *Childhood*. Unfinished translation of Sterne's *Sentimental Journey*	Cards, gymnastics, first serious attempts at writing. Set off for Caucasus with brother. Took part as volunteer in raid against Caucasian village
1852	*Childhood* published	Joined army as cadet. Served in the Caucasus. Nearly killed by grenade. Military duties interrupted by intensive spells of reading, writing, debauchery and medical treatment

Year	Works	Life
1853	*The Raid* published	Took part in campaign against Chechens. Narrowly escaped capture
1854	*Boyhood* published	Commissioned. Transferred to active service on the Danube after leave at Yasnaya Polyana. With the Russian army in Silistria. After the allied landing in the Crimea transferred to Sevastopol and stationed at Simferopol
1855	Published *The Memoirs of a Billiard Marker*; *Sevastopol in December*; *Sevastopol in May*; *The Wood-felling*	Served in Sevastopol. Returned to Petersburg in November after surrender of Sevastopol. Frequented Petersburg literary circles. Met Turgenev, Nekrasov, Fet, Goncharov, Ostrovsky and other writers
1856	Published *Sevastopol in August*; *The Snowstorm*; *Two Hussars*; *Meeting a Moscow Aquaintance in the Detachment*; *A Landowner's Morning*	Retired from army. Death of brother Dmitri. Active social life divided between *Contemporary* literary circle and Petersburg demi-monde. Summer months at Yasnaya Polyana. Infatuation for Arseneva. Contemplated marriage. Abortive project to free his serfs. Cooling of affection for Arseneva
1857	Published *Youth*; *Lucerne*	First trip abroad to France, Switzerland and Germany (January–July). Visited Paris theatres and Sorbonne lectures. Witnessed public execution in Paris. Worked intermittently on several stories while abroad
1858	Published *Albert*	Helped to found Moscow Musical Society. Farming on Yasnaya Polyana estate. Nearly killed by a bear while hunting. Visits to and from Turgenev
1859	Published *Three Deaths*; *Family Happiness*	Retreat from literature. Founded school for peasant children at Yasnaya Polyana
1860	—	Continued teaching (January–June). Studied educational theory and practice in Germany (July–August). Met Froebel. Revisited France. Death of brother Nicholas. Moved on to Italy
1861	—	Italy, France, England and Germany (January–April). Heard Dickens lecture on education and Palmerston speak in the House of Commons. Met Proudhon in Brussels. Returned to Russia in April. Quarrelled with Turgenev. Challenged him to duel. Resumed teaching at Yasnaya

Year	Works	Life
		Polyana school in May. Began work as an Arbiter of the Peace
1862	—	Continued teaching. Started educational magazine, *Yasnaya Polyana*, twelve issues appearing in 1862–1863, with contributions by himself and his teachers and students. Released from office of Arbiter of the Peace. Police raid on Yasnaya Polyana. Papers and correspondence searched. Married Sonya Behrs
1863	Published *The Cossacks*; *Polikushka*	Started work on *War and Peace*. First child born (d. 1947)
1864	—	Second child born (d. 1950)
1865	*1805* (first part of *War and Peace*) published	Intensive work on *War and Peace*
1866	Next part of *1805* published	Third child born (d. 1933). Defended soldier court-martialled for striking officer. Sculpturing as a hobby. Wrote short plays for domestic performance
1867	Forthcoming publication of *War and Peace* in 4 volumes announced	Visited Borodino in connection with battle scenes for his novel
1868	Fourth volume of *War and Peace* appeared. *A Few Words about 'War and Peace'* published	Continued work on novel
1869	Fifth and sixth (final) volumes of *War and Peace* published	Fourth child born (d. 1945). Completed *War and Peace*
1870	—	Studying drama and the Greek language. First thoughts about *Anna Karenina*
1871	—	Fifth child born (d. 1906). Continued Greek studies. Illness. Convalescence during summer in Bashkiria. Began work on his *Primer* for children
1872	Published *Primer*. Separate publication of *A Prisoner in the Caucasus* and *God Sees the Truth but Waits*	Worked intermittently on unfinished novel on Peter the Great and his times. Reopened Yasnaya Polyana school. Sixth child born (d. 1873). Contemplated emigrating to England after legal proceedings against him for fatal injury to herdsman on his estate during his absence
1873	—	Travelled with family to recently purchased estate in Samara (Bashkiria). Wrote to papers and raised fund during famine in Samara province. Portrait painted by Kramskoy. Began writing *Anna Karenina*

Year	Works	Life
1874	Published article *On Public Education*	Lectured on educational theories in Moscow and wrote article on subject. Seventh child born (d. 1875). Continued work on *Anna Karenina* and compiled new primer and readers
1875	First instalments of *Anna Karenina* published. *New Primer* and *Russian Reader* appeared	Summer with family at Samara estate. Eighth child born and died. Growing depression. Bored with *Anna Karenina*
1876	Further instalments of *Anna Karenina* published	Met Chaikovsky. Visited Samara and Orenburg (September)
1877	Final instalment of *Anna Karenina* published	Increasingly preoccupied with religious problems. Profoundly disturbed by Russo-Turkish war. Ninth child born (d. 1916)
1878	*Anna Karenina* published in book form	Working on previously abandoned novel about the Decembrists. Met some survivors of the Decembrist rising. Reading the Gospels and *La Vie de Jésus*. Reconciliation with Turgenev. Summer at Samara estate. Turgenev at Yasnaya Polyana
1879	—	Visited Kiev and its monasteries, and the Trinity Monastery of St Sergei, near Moscow. Continued to collect historical materials for projected novel. Numerous conversations on religion. Began to write *A Confession* and some religious articles. Tenth child born (d. 1944)
1880	—	Continued work on *A Confession* and began *A Criticism of Dogmatic Theology* and *A Translation and Harmony of the Four Gospels*. Met Garshin and Repin for first time
1881	—	Letter to new Tsar asking him to pardon the assassins of Alexander II. Visited Optyn Monastery. Continued religious writings. Eleventh child born (d. 1886)
1882	*On the Moscow Census* and *What Men Live By* published	Took part in three-day Moscow census. First-hand acquaintance with Moscow slums. Began *The Death of Ivan Il'ich* and *What Then Must We Do?*—both finished in 1886. Bought town house in Moscow (present Tolstoy museum). Moved family to Moscow. Studied Hebrew. Finished *A Confession*, banned in Russia

274

Year	Works	Life
1883	—	Met Chertkov. Writing *What I Believe*. Refused jury service
1884	Fragments of *The Decembrists* published	*What I Believe* banned. Portrait painted by Gay. Collected works published by his wife. Twelfth child born. Studying oriental religions. Took up cobbling. Family relations very strained. First attempt to leave home
1885	Several popular stories including *What Men Live By*, *Where Love is, God is* published. French translation of *What I Believe*	Became a vegetarian. Attempted to give up smoking. Renounced hunting and alcohol. Growing friction with wife. *Intermediary* founded with Chertkov's aid to publish his popular stories. Many written and published in 1885–6
1886	Publication of *The Death of Ivan Il'ich*, *How Much Land does a Man Need?* and other popular stories	Continued work on popular stories. Finished *What Then Must We Do?* Wrote *The Power of Darkness* (banned but performed in Paris in 1888) and began *The Fruits of Enlightenment*. Met Korolenko. Walked from Moscow to Yasnaya Polyana (130 miles) in five days. Worked on the land during summer
1887	—	Wrote *On Life*. Met Leskov
1888	*Strider* published	Thirteenth and last child born (d. 1895). Finally renounced meat, alcohol and tobacco. Growing friction between his wife and Chertkov. Intensive work on the land
1889	—	Finished *The Kreutzer Sonata*. Began *Resurrection*
1890	—	*Kreutzer Sonata* banned. Wife obtained Tsar's permission for its inclusion in Collected Works
1891	*Why Do Men Stupefy Themselves?* published	Publicly renounced copyright of all his works published after 1881. Helped to organise famine relief in Ryazan Province
1892	*The First Step* published	Articles on famine relief. Engaged on relief work, organising food kitchens. *The Fruits of Enlightenment* produced in Maly Theatre in Moscow
1893	*The Coffee-House of Surat* and *Walk in the Light While There is Light* published. French translation of *The Kingdom of God is Within You*	Finished *The Kingdom of God is Within You*. Sent it abroad to be translated

Year	Works	Life
1894	French and English translations of *Christianity and Patriotism*	Finished *Christianity and Patriotism*; *Reason and Religion*; *Religion and Morality*. Wrote preface to Maupassant's works
1895	Published *Master and Man*	Met Chekhov. *The Power of Darkness* produced in Maly Theatre in Moscow. Wrote appeal on behalf of Dukhobors
1896	—	Composer Taneev living at Yasnaya Polyana. Musical concerts. Wife's friendship with Taneev. Began writing *Hadji Murat*
1897	—	Prosecution of the Dukhobors. Published an appeal to the authorities. Writing *What is Art?*
1898	Censored version of *What is Art?* English translation published	Enlisted aid for Dukhobors. Resolved to publish *Father Sergei* and *Resurrection* to raise funds. Organised aid for starving peasants of Tula Province. Article *Famine or No Famine*
1899	*Resurrection* published	Serial publication of *Resurrection* during year. Article on Boer War
1900	—	Wrote *The Live Corpse* (unfinished). Met Gorky. International Tolstoy Society founded
1901	*Reply to the Synod's Edict* published	Excommunicated from the Orthodox Church by the Holy Synod. Short articles on military service. Serious illness. Moved with family to Crimea in late summer. Literary visitors included Chekhov, Gorky, Korolenko and Balmont
1902	—	Finished *What is Religion?* Wrote to Tsar on evils of autocracy and coercion and appealed to him to abolish private ownership of land. Returned to Yasnaya Polyana in summer. Continued work on *Hadji Murat* and *The Light Shineth in Darkness*
1903	—	Protested against Jewish pogroms in Kishinev. Wrote three stories (*Esarhaddon, Three Questions* and *Toil, Death and Disease*) for anthology, published in Warsaw in aid of pogrom victims. Wrote *After the Ball* (first published posthumously). Working on *Shakespeare and the Drama* (finished in 1904) and printed abroad in 1906

Year	Works	Life
1904	—	Decided to publish no more artistic works to avoid further quarrels with wife over copyright. Finished *Hadji Murat* (published posthumously). Wrote *Bethink Yourselves!* a pamphlet on Russo-Japanese War, published in England
1905	—	Publicist pamphlets included the anarchical *The One Thing Needed* (published in England). Wrote several stories, including *Alyosha Gorshok*, all published posthumously. Wrote introduction to Chekhov's *Darling*
1906	—	Wife's serious illness and operation. Death of his favourite daughter and disciple. Wrote *What For?* and *The Significance of the Russian Revolution*
1907	—	Wrote to Russian Prime Minister advocating Henry George's solutions to land problem, and abolition of private ownership
1908	—	Wrote *I Cannot Be Silent*, against capital punishment. Newspapers fined and editor arrested for printing it. Tolstoy's secretary arrested and exiled
1909	—	Relations with wife extremely strained. Frequent hysterical scenes and threats of suicide. Tolstoy drew up will relinquishing all copyright on all published works since 1881 and all unpublished works before 1881
1910	—	Left home. Illness and death at Astapovo railway station, aged 82

SELECT BIBLIOGRAPHY

IN ENGLISH

WORKS

The Centenary Edition of Tolstoy (21 vols., O.U.P., London 1929–37, tr. Louise and Aylmer Maude) contains most of Tolstoy's important works, excluding the diaries, notebooks and letters, as does the 24-volume edition, tr. L. Wiener, Boston and London, 1904–5. New translations of the major novels and stories have recently been published by Penguin Classics. The standard Russian edition of Tolstoy devotes 45 of its 90 volumes to the texts and the numerous draft versions of his original writings, and 45 to his diaries, notebooks and letters. The balance is not maintained in English. Select translations of his diaries include *The Diaries of Leo Tolstoy, 1847–52*, tr. C. J. Hogarth and A. Sirnis, London 1917, and *The Private Diary of Leo Tolstoy, 1853–57*, tr. Louise and Aylmer Maude, London 1927. Comparatively few of his letters have been translated into English and there is no adequate edition of them. Of interest, however, are *The Letters of Tolstoy and his Cousin Countess Alexandra Tolstoy 1857–1903*, tr. L. Islavin, London 1929, and *Tolstoy's Love Letters (to V. Arseneva) 1856–57*, tr. S. S. Koteliansky and V. Woolf, London 1923.

REMINISCENCES

Most of the reminiscences by members of Tolstoy's family—of uneven quality and value—are available in English. They include:

The Diary of Tolstoy's Wife, 1860–91, tr. A. Werth, London 1928.

Countess Tolstoy's Later Diary, 1891–97, tr. A. Werth, London 1929.

The Final Struggle, being Countess Tolstoy's Diary for 1910 (together with extracts from Tolstoy's diaries, letters and reminiscences), tr. A. Maude, London 1936.

I. L. Tolstoy (son), *Reminiscences of Tolstoy*, London 1914.

L. L. Tolstoy (son), *The Truth about my Father*, London 1924.

S. L. Tolstoy (son), *Tolstoy Remembered*, London 1961.

A. L. Tolstoy (daughter), *Tolstoy: A Life of my Father*, New York 1953.

T. Kuzminskaya (sister-in-law), *Tolstoy as I Knew Him; My Life at Home and at Yasnaya Polyana*, London 1948.

T. Sukhotin-Tolstoy (daughter), *The Tolstoy Home*, London 1950.

Of particular interest also are the following reminiscences by contemporaries:

A. B. Goldenveizer, *Talks with Tolstoy*, tr. S. S. Koteliansky and V. Woolf, London 1923 (an incomplete translation).

M. Gorki, *Reminiscences of Tolstoy, Chekhov and Andreyev*, tr. K. Mansfield, S. S. Koteliansky and L. Woolf, London 1934.

BIOGRAPHY

The standard works are:

A. Maude, *The Life of Tolstoy*, 2 vols., London 1930.

E. J. Simmons, *Leo Tolstoy*, 2 vols., Boston 1945–6 (Vintage paperback edition, 1960).

H. Troyat, *Tolstoy*, London 1960 (tr. from the French).

LIFE AND WORKS

R. Rolland, *Tolstoy* (tr. B. Miall), London 1911.

G. R. Noyes, *Tolstoy*, London 1919.

D. Leon, *Tolstoy, His Life and Work*, London 1944.

T. Redpath, *Tolstoy*, London 1960.

CRITICAL STUDIES

D. S. Merezhkovsky, *Tolstoy as Man and Artist*, London 1902.

D. Y. Kvitko, *A Philosophic Study of Tolstoy*, New York 1927.

T. Mann, *Goethe and Tolstoy* in *Three Essays*, tr. Lowe-Porter, New York 1929.

G. Wilson Knight, *Shakespeare and Tolstoy*, London 1934.

J. Lavrin, *Tolstoy: An Approach*, London 1944.

I. Berlin, *The Hedgehog and the Fox*, London 1953.

G. Gibian, *Tolstoy and Shakespeare*, The Hague 1957.

G. Steiner, *Tolstoy or Dostoevsky, An Essay in the Old Criticism*, New York 1959.

G. Struve, 'Tolstoy in Soviet Criticism' (one of a series of essays in *The Russian Review*, April 1960, which is entirely devoted to Tolstoy).

R. F. Christian, *Tolstoy's 'War and Peace': A study*, Oxford 1962.

W. Lednicki, *Tolstoy between War and Peace*, The Hague 1965.

D. Davie (ed,), *Russian Literature andModern English Fiction*, University of Chicago 1965.

J. Bayley, *Tolstoy and the Novel*, London 1966.

R. Matlaw (ed.), *Tolstoy: a Collection of Critical Essays*, New Jersey 1967.

G. W. Spence, *Tolstoy the Ascetic*, London 1967.

E. J. Simmons, *Introduction to Tolstoy's Writings*, University of Chicago 1968.

Other references to articles and chapters from books will be found in the footnotes to the text.

IN FRENCH AND GERMAN

Excluding books which have been translated into English
or which are themselves tranlations from Russian

M. Markovitch, *J. J. Rousseau et Tolstoi*, Paris 1928.

M. Markovitch, *Tolstoi et Gandhi*, Paris 1928.

N. Gourfinkel, *Tolstoi sans tolstoïsme*, Paris 1946.

P. Boyer, *Chez Tolstoi: Entretiens à Iasnaïa Poliana*, Paris 1950.

S. Lafitte, *Léon Tolstoi et ses contemporains*, Paris 1906.

N. Weisbein, *L'Évolution religieuse de Tolstoi*, Paris 1960.

K. Hamburger, *Leo Tolstoi — Gestalt u. Problem*, Bern 1950.

E. Wedel, *Die Enstehungsgeschichte von L. N. Tolstojs 'Krieg und Frieden'*, Wiesbaden 1961.

IN RUSSIAN

BIBLIOGRAPHY

N. G. Shelyapina et al., *Bibliografiya literatury o Tolstom, 1917–1958*, Moscow 1960. Confined to works in Russian published in the U.S.S.R. since the revolution. Contains more than 5,600 entries, some of very marginal relevance.

E. N. Zhilina, *L. N. Tolstoy, 1828–1910*, Leningrad 1960. A much shorter and very selective book, with a section on Russian secondary literature devoted to individual works by Tolstoy.

WORKS

The definitive Russian edition is *Polnoe Sobranie Sochinenii*, 90 vols., ed. V. G. Chertkov et al., Moscow 1928–58 (referred to in the text as J. E.—Jubilee Edition). More recently *Sobranie Sochinenii*, 20 vols., Moscow 1960–65, devotes 16 vols. to the works, 2 to the letters and 2 to the diaries. A useful two-volume selection of Tolstoy's writings on art and literature is *Lev Tolstoi ob iskusstve i literature*. Moscow 1958.

REMINISCENCES

Apart from the Russian originals of the books referred to above (which in some cases are fuller than the English versions—especially Goldenveizer, *Vblizi Tolstogo*, Moscow 1959) it is worth mentioning *L. N. Tolstoi v vospominaniyakh sovremennikov*, 2 vols., Moscow 1960. Note, too, *Dnevniki S. A. Tolstoi, 1897–1909*, Moscow 1932, not available in English.

BIOGRAPHY

Still of value is the first 'official' biography by P. I. Biryukov, *Lev Nilokaevich Tolstoi: Biografiya*, Moscow, Vol. I, 1911, Vol. II, 1913, Vol. III, 1922, Vol. IV, 1923. In the post-war period a major contribution has been the work of N. N. Gusev, especially:

Lev Nikolaevich Tolstoi, Materialy k biografii s 1828 po 1855 god., Moscow 1954.
Lev Nikolaevich Tolstoi, Materialy k biografii s 1855 po 1869 god., Moscow 1957.
Lev Nikolaevich Tolstoi, Materialy k biografii s 1870 po 1881 god., Moscow 1963. .
Letopis' zhizni i tvorchestva L'va Nikolaevicha Tolstogo, 1828–1890, Moscow 1958.
Letopis' zhizni i tvorchestva L'va Nikolaevicha Tolstogo, 1891–1910, Moscow 1960.

For the events of 1910 see V. F. Bulgakov, *L. N. Tolstoi v poslednii god ego zhizni*, Moscow 1960, and B. Meilakh, *Ukhod i smert' L'va Tolstogo*, Moscow–Leningrad 1960. A recent popular biography is V. Shklovsky, *Lev Tolstoi, Moscow 1963*.

CRITICAL STUDIES

Literaturnoe Nasledstvo 35/36, 37/38, Moscow 1939, includes i.a. articles by Lukács on Tolstoy and the development of realism, Popov on the style of Tolstoy's early stories, and an important contribution by V. Vinogradov on Tolstoy's language, as well as unpublished texts, letters and reminiscences. See also:

Literaturnoe Nasledstvo 69, Lev Tolstoi, 2 vols., Moscow 1961, and 75, *Tolstoi i zarubezhny mir*, 2 vols., Moscow 1965.

N. N. Ardens, *Tvorcheskii put' L. N. Tolstogo*, Moscow 1962.

Y. A. Bilinkis, *O tvorchestve L. N. Tolstogo*, Moscow 1959.

D. D. Blagoi et al. (ed.), *Lev Nikolaevich Tolstoi. Sbornik statei i materialov*, Moscow 1951.

B. I. Bursov, *Lev Tolstoi, Ideinye iskaniya i tvorcheskii metod 1847–1862*, Moscow 1960.

Lev Tolstoi i russkii roman, Moscow–Leningrad 1963.

S. P. Bychkov, *L. N. Tolstoi, Ocherk tvorchestva*, Moscow 1954.

V. V. Ermilov, *Tolstoi — romanist*, Moscow 1965.

B. M. Eykhenbaum, *Molodoi Tolstoi*, Prague–Berlin 1922.

Lev Tolstoi, kniga pervaya, 50-e gody, Leningrad 1928.

Lev Tolstoi, kniga vtoraya, 60-e gody, Moscow–Leningrad 1931.

Lev Tolstoi, semidesyatye gody, Leningrad 1960.

N. K. Gudzy, *Kak rabotal L. Tolstoi*, Moscow 1936.

Lev Tolstoi, Moscow 1960.

(ed.) *Lev Nikolaevich Tolstoi. Sbornik statei o tvorchestve*, Moscow 1955.

M. B. Khrapchenko, *Lev Tolstoi kak khudozhnik*, Moscow 1963.

(ed.) *Tvorchestvo L. N. Tolstogo. Sbornik statei*, Moscow 1954.

E. N. Kupreyanova, *Estetika L. N. Tolstogo*, Moscow–Leningrad 1966.

V. I. Lenin, *Stat'i o Tolstom*, Moscow 1960.

K. Leont'iev, *O romanakh gr. L. N. Tolstogo. Analiz, stil' i veyaniya*, Moscow 1911.

K. N. Lomunov, *Dramaturgiya L. N. Tolstogo*. Moscow 1956.

T. L. Motyleva, *O mirovom znachenii L. N. Tolstogo*, Moscow 1957.

L. M. Myshkovskaya, *Masterstvo L. N. Tolstogo*, Moscow 1958.

A. A. Saburov, *'Voina i mir' Tolstogo. Problematika i poetika*, Moscow 1959.

V. Shklovsky, *Material i stil' v romane L'va Tolstogo 'Voina i mir'*, Moscow 1928.

E. E. Zaidenshnur, *'Voina i mir' L. N. Tolstogo. Sozdanie velikoi knigi*, Moscow 1966.

V. A. Zhdanov, *Tvorcheskaya istoriya 'Anny Kareninoi'*. Moscow 1957.

Tvorcheskaya istoriya romana L. N. Tolstogo 'Voskresenie', Moscow 1960.

Ot 'Anny Kareninoi' k 'Voskreseniyu', Moscow 1968.

INDEX

285

INDEX

31